Books of Merit

Passion Lost

ALSO BY PATRICIA ANDERSON

NON-FICTION

When Passion Reigned: Sex and the Victorians
The Printed Image and the Transformation of Popular Culture

CO-EDITOR

Dictionary of Literary Biography, Volumes 106 and 112

Patricia Anderson

PASSION LOST

Public Sex, Private Desire in the Twentieth Century

Thomas Allen
Publishers

Toronto

Canadian Cataloguing in Publication Data

Anderson, Patricia, 1950–
    Passion lost: public sex, private desire in the twentieth century

Includes index.

ISBN 0-919028-41-1

1. Sex – History – 20th century.   2. Sex customs – History – 20th century.
I. Title.

HQ16.A52 2001   306.7'09'04   C00-933234-0

Text design: Gordon Robertson
Editor: Patrick Crean
Cover photograph: Edward Holub/Photonica
Author photograph: Tamara Roberts

The author gratefully acknowledges the support
of the Canada Council.

 The Canada Council
Conseil des Arts du Canada

Published by Thomas Allen Publishers,
a division of Thomas Allen & Son Limited,
145 Front Street East, Suite 107,
Toronto, Ontario M5A 1E3 Canada

Printed and bound in Canada

In memory of my parents,
Jeanne Nora Runnels, 1929–1990
David Ernest Runnels, 1926–2000

CONTENTS

Acknowledgements

By its nature, writing a book is a solitary endeavor. Writing this one has turned out to be more so than most, and my appreciation of those who have sustained me is accordingly enhanced.

A generous grant from the Canada Council for the Arts facilitated this book's completion. My editor and publisher, Patrick Crean, made invaluable suggestions for the final draft and has been unflagging in his supportiveness. As ever, I have also been constantly encouraged by my agent, Lettie Lee; my father, Dave Runnels; and my partner in life, Garry Nohr.

I am grateful to all.

I

A DIVIDED IDEAL

Love—and sex.

For most of the past century countless mothers warned their unmarried daughters that sex is not love, and cautioned them not to confuse one with the other. Meanwhile, men continued to distinguish between the women they loved—and the other kind. Over the course of the twentieth century, as women achieved greater equality, they similarly discovered that some men were for keeps—and others just for fun.

Yet just before living memory now begins, the distinction between love and sex was not so clear. Around the beginning of the twentieth century a single ideal—passion—embodied the whole of emotional, spiritual, and physical intimacy. It was much more than just another word for sex; it was a widely shared vision of ultimate fulfillment in the relationship of men and women.

As the century progressed, the purely physical dimension of passion split off from the larger ideal. People became more sophisticated not only about the techniques of sex but also about its social and political implications. Yet emotional and spiritual fulfillment frequently eluded them, and ironically, all too often even the physical side of relationships was disappointing.

In the midst of a burgeoning culture of sex, many longed for something more. Out of that longing grew nostalgic myths about the past, myths that have limited both our understanding of the present and our possibilities for the future. But if we look back at the twentieth century through the clearer lens of historical memory, we see people's confusions, as well as their pleasures. This enhanced perspective may thus enable us to understand the mistakes of the past and achieve the best from relationships in the new millennium.

As the Victorian era passed into history, the ideal of passion had already begun to fade. But its disappearance was gradual, the change at first almost imperceptible, and several years into the new century the old ideal still largely held sway. Even as the century ended, its traces remained—preserved in the memory of one legendary night in 1912.

Reimagining the Past

. . . mixing
Memory and desire.

— T. S. ELIOT, *The Waste Land*

The lights dim for a moment and brighten. The lovers come together in a quick, intense embrace before the rising water forces them, half wading, half swimming, toward the nearest staircase. The lights snap and flicker just before a wall of water sweeps over them. . . .

Against all odds, they manage to surface and climb to the temporary safety of an upper deck. These two have known each other only a matter of days, but the bond between them is already so strong that twice she has refused to board a lifeboat and leave him behind. As they cling together awaiting the inevitable, strains of poignant melody float out over the dark North Atlantic.

While the musicians played on, an elderly couple sat side by side. The man's fur-lined coat helped insulate him against the night's biting chill. His wife had given her fur coat to her maid when the younger woman climbed into one of the lifeboats. Past caring about physical comfort now, the wife leaned on the arm of her husband. They had been married nearly half a century. She was not about to leave him now.

"Where you go, I go," she said, with a dignity that would long be remembered. It was nearing 2:05 a.m., 15 April 1912, and the last lifeboat would soon pull away. Minutes later, the most memorable ocean disaster of all time would reach its tragic conclusion.

These two couples bridge almost a century in the history of men and women. The wealthy, sheltered, seventeen-year-old Rose De-Witt Bukater and her lover Jack Dawson, an itinerant young artist, are fictional characters in the 1997 movie *Titanic*. She survives to tell the story, while he lives on "only in my memory," as she says toward the movie's end. The other couple—Isidor Straus, founder of Macy's department store, and his wife, Ida—were passengers aboard the real *Titanic*, and both lost their lives when the ship went down.

The historical Ida and Isidor, like the fictional Rose and Jack, embody our highest ideal of love and devotion. The young lovers, like the husband and wife, faced the unimaginable together, and refused to be parted. When we respond to the romance of Rose and Jack, or remember the Strauses with admiration, we are touched by a real-life drama larger than either of their stories. The longing for passion—our continuing pursuit of the best that is possible between men and women—has both inspired and troubled us, from the age of the *Titanic* to our own.

Though it is at the heart of our brightest dreams, passion often eludes us in reality. Many of us have never experienced it at all. Divorce rates, transient relationships, and sexual dysfunction reached all-time highs during the twentieth century and continue to trouble us in the new millennium. Discontented or critical, we sometimes look to the past for someone or something to blame—or to idealize. Out of disillusionment, confusing memory with desire, we envision some golden age of relationships that never really existed. Either way, many of us feel trapped in the present, facing a future of little promise.

If the goal for the new millennium is greater fulfillment for everyone, then we need to take another approach. First, we must look beyond the gloss of myth to the realities of the past—and reimagine it as many people actually lived it.

The Ideal of Passion

When the twentieth century began, people understood *passion* as complete fulfillment—flesh and spirit in perfect union forever, man and woman coming together with ever-deepening feeling, perpetually greater mutual happiness, and (not least) constantly intensifying physical pleasure. Over the years we took this grand vision deep into our personal expectations and passed it down through the generations. Though it remains among the most overwhelming of private desires, passion today has little public significance. But when the old century was still new, things were very different: passion had the cultural prominence that sex alone now enjoys.

"Let us educate love to the higher comprehension of the entirety of life," one authority on sex and marriage urged in 1913. The well-known British birth control advocate Marie Stopes repeated the plea in her 1928 marital advice book, *Enduring Passion*. Above all, she believed, couples needed to "spiritualize" the emotional and sexual side of their relationships: "Love will thus be . . . more solid and more lasting because it will have its roots in the soul and not in the beauty of the body which changes even more rapidly than the appetites of our senses." Stopes and other marital experts of her day did not invoke spirituality in any particular religious sense but used the concept to encourage a deep connection between men and women. For in this lay the promise of what most people wanted—sexual pleasure and personal happiness: "Physical joys will be doubled by the communion of feelings and of thoughts, and our life, grown richer and more intense in profound feelings and unknown joys, will become more dignified and serene."

This ideal of consummate passion—dignified yet joyful, spiritually profound yet intensely physical—was not new. It was in fact a legacy from the Victorians. But in the forward-looking early 1900s, many could not believe that those stiff figures in already yellowing photographs had any aptitude for emotional expression or the myriad pleasures of sex.

The Victorians would be thought cold and prudish for many more years, until 1976 when the historical philosopher Michel Foucault challenged the supposedly established fact of Victorian repression in his influential *History of Sexuality*. And in the 1980s the historian Peter Gay showed that many of our most respectable nineteenth-century ancestors actually enjoyed intensely erotic intimate lives. This was no accident, for the Victorians created a culture of passion that neither denied sexuality nor privileged it over the intangibles of feeling and spirit. Their idea was to manage sex in public to allow it free rein in private. As Gay explained, observing social conventions of respectability and discretion of speech was "actually a way of carving out space" for personal "sensual gratification."

But this strategy held little attraction in an exuberant new century. Anxious to embrace modernity, people began to look critically at Victorian notions of duty and respectability. What the new age demanded, they increasingly believed, was greater attention to self-expression in all facets of life. And ranking high among these was sex. Reticence about sexual matters now began to look like either hypocrisy or the enemy of pleasure.

"Knowledge" became the catchword, as everyone from marriage experts to husbands, wives, and courting couples took up the new notion that public candor about sex would increase their happiness, as individuals and as couples. Initially, this was a good idea that did much to dispel sexual ignorance and misery. Over time, however, its benefits would diminish.

The Culture of Sex

As the twentieth century unfolded, people's sexual knowledge and experience grew—along with their eagerness for more. Today books, magazines, videos, tabloids, television, movies, advertising, and the Internet affirm and reaffirm the preeminence of sex in our culture. Meanwhile, with little cultural nourishment, the emotional and spiritual aspects of passion grow ever more difficult for people to attain, until for many, even sex itself loses its appeal.

In the culture of sex, as in many other spheres of life over the past century, the single sustaining goal has been satisfaction. Yet recent statistics show that many of us have experienced anything but. According to some estimates, the divorce rate hovers around 60 percent in the United States and is not far behind in Britain and Canada. In a University of North Carolina survey of 950 women, 98 percent reported experiencing sexual dysfunction at some time in their lives, and 87 percent said that they currently had no interest whatsoever in sex. Meanwhile the anti-impotence pill Viagra holds its place as the best-selling drug in history. Though some of its users suffer from impotence as a side effect of medical conditions, many others have tried the drug for its supposed aphrodisiac effect.

This widespread sexual discontent is not just a matter of individual physiology, or people's incompatibility with their partners. A study at Harvard points to a widespread yearning for something beyond sex, beyond even feelings of love. Grasping for the right words, participants haltingly expressed the wish for their sexual experience to intermingle with something larger, with their own individual conception of a higher power. In other words, they want intimacy to have profound meaning, to be closer to the old ideal of passion. They feel that sex has become separated from love, loyalty, connection, and spirituality. Without knowing how to go about it, they long to bring them together again.

"Sex for many people has become more meaningless as it is more available," wrote Rollo May, the noted psychotherapist, in *Love and Will*, his 1969 exploration of the relationships of his day. Reluctantly he concluded that something greater—passion—had become "tremendously elusive if not an outright illusion."

The link between sex and consumerism has also served us poorly. Though rooted in the Victorian period, consumerism has become in many ways the defining twentieth-century preoccupation—the outgrowth of advertising, mass communication, prosperity, and desire for status. And from the start, sex has been advertising's favorite ploy and the main commodity of the fashion, beauty, and entertainment industries. We have manufactured widespread dissatisfaction, sexual and otherwise, along with the cars, clothes, appliances, and entertainment that we consume (and which consume us). The whole idea behind consumerism is perpetually to want more and better, whether the commodity is luxury goods, status symbols, or sex. Addiction to sex—the compulsive pursuit of sensual gratification—is consumption at its most extreme. More commonly, when people fail to get what they desire, they either become discontented or, in self-defense, lose interest.

One unlooked-for and most destructive consequence of sexual openness is that along with candor we have developed cruelly standardized ideas about sexual attractiveness and "normal" sexual activity. Advertising and other commercial interests have promoted ideal and, for most, unattainable sexual body images. These have been especially rigorous for women, but men have by no means escaped from the tyranny of body image.

Early marriage manuals helped to uphold commercial standards of attractiveness by dispensing conventional advice about grooming and appearance. Many also issued directives as to what was "healthy," "average," or "normal" frequency and activity. (The recommended "average," according to one 1920 manual, was intercourse five or six times a week for couples under thirty-five, two to four times a week for the thirty-five to fifty-five age group, and once or twice a week for those over fifty-five.) But from the 1960s on, sexologists and therapists have insisted that there are no norms, all the while establishing them through case studies, surveys, and how-to-do-it books.

With such yardsticks of sexuality endemic in the culture, widespread anxiety about whether we measure up to a perceived standard has been the inevitable result. And this, more than anything, has perpetuated inhibition and reduced satisfaction. As May realized, standardization restricts our capacity "to transmute physiology and anatomy into *interpersonal* experience—into art, into passion, into eros in a million forms which have the power to shake or charm us."

We have no way of knowing which of the "million forms" once bonded couples like the Strauses. We only know with certainty that they and their forgotten contemporaries belonged to a culture that firmly linked passion, especially its sexual side, to the expectation of lifelong commitment—"Where you go, I go." Of course, troubled marriages and restrictive gender roles were also an everyday reality;

meanwhile unwed mothers, lonely bachelors, and superfluous spinsters, all living on the fringes of society, could tell their own tales of the imperfections of commitment as a universal imperative. But in preserving a measure of discretion and privacy, the Victorians could be sure of at least a small protected space where they could pursue whatever emotional and erotic gratification their individual circumstances allowed.

Created without benefit of that space, the movie *Titanic* reconstructed the Strauses anachronistically through the narrow lens of the culture of sex. Around the time that Rose and Jack reach the upper deck, the camera angles down into the first-class cabin of an elderly couple who, as the screenplay directed, "hold hands like young lovers." Though fully clothed, they lie side by side on a bed—the universally understood symbol of sexual activity. "Eros in a million forms" is thus diminished to the merely physical. For reflected in that single brief shot is an entire culture in which physical sex typically overshadows the emotional and spiritual dimensions of passion.

Jack and Rose are the ultimate creations of that culture. They are young and good-looking, their attraction overtly sensual. As the elderly Rose recalls, they waste little time and "do it" in the backseat of a luxury touring car down in one of the cargo holds. Glorying in the consummation of their desire, the rebellious young Rose vows to defy social convention and to stay with Jack after the ship docks.

Disaster, of course, intervenes. But it is not the sinking of the *Titanic* alone that cuts short the couple's happiness. They are fictional lovers caught up in a real historical tragedy, but they are more of our time than their own—reflections of our late-twentieth-century understanding of intimacy. Their brief, doomed affair is thus emblematic of the elusiveness of passion in the culture of sex.

"I'll never let go," she assures him as, hand in hand, they drift together on a fragment from the sunken ship. The words are in part a promise to survive, in part an expression of her profound feeling for him. And they are poignantly ironic, for in the end she has no choice but to let go, as Jack succumbs to the effects of exposure. Following the screenplay, she "gently unclasps their hands."

"I won't let go," she says, as he slips from her grasp and sinks into the black water.

One Culture, Many Dreams

Unlike the Strauses' conventional marital relationship, the love affair of Jack and Rose is that of two free spirits who come together despite the social barriers that divide them. Footloose and poor, pursuing his dream of being an artist, he is distinctly not the man her family would like her to marry or even be acquainted with: her duty is to marry money. And his duty is to know his place and not aspire to her love. In rejecting those constricted social roles, they embody the idea of individualism, the cultural valuing of the self and its unique needs over the conservative, often stifling, expectations of society. This high valuation placed on the individual has been a crucial influence in twentieth-century history.

The culture of sex is a product of individualism, and it has fostered increasing tolerance for a range of sexualities, pleasures, and lifestyles. At the same time, ironically, it is so pervasive that none of us can completely escape its standardizing effects. We would have to confine ourselves to our homes—speak to no one, never read a book, never turn on the radio, television, or computer—and avert our eyes from the magazine racks when forced out to buy groceries. Our many dreams of love and fulfillment may vary according to personality and other influences that shape individual identity: nationality, ethnicity, race, class, gender, and sexual orientation.

Yet for all our diversity, to live in today's world is to dream within the boundaries of the culture of sex.

The history that unfolds here is mostly American, but it draws at times on British and, to a lesser extent, Canadian experience. It is mostly about the romantic and sexual relationships of men and women, for heterosexuality, through sheer weight of numbers and social norms, dominates the culture of sex. But even so, it is a culture that encompasses at least some gay and bisexual experience. In the days when concealment was the rule, most who did not conform privately to the heterosexual norm espoused it publicly to varying degrees. With the progress of gay rights and the end of secrecy, many gay people now choose to exercise options once primarily associated with heterosexuality—for example, marriage or similarly committed relationships and (though these are ongoing struggles) the adoption of children and spousal benefits.

The American sociologist Edwin Schur rightly remarked that wide-reaching "sociocultural patternings of sexuality transcend sexual orientation." In other words, many things divide us as men and women and as human beings, but the culture of sex is woven from the common strands of our everyday experiences and expectations: popular entertainments, social conventions, concerns about personal attractiveness, and the yearning for passion in our lives. We ourselves have created this culture—all of us together over the last hundred years—and we all have a stake in the quality of our creation. If we want a culture that will better meet our diverse needs and myriad dreams, then we will have to make it ourselves.

Turning the Clock Forward

Over the years, the culture of sex has drawn plenty of critics. The conservatives among them would like to see the sexual clock turned back to some supposedly better time. Others, of more liberal persuasion, recognize this as futile and call for more freedom through greater public openness about sex. But after a century in which the strategy of openness has been pushed to unheard-of extremes but has still not achieved its goal, persisting in it would amount to stopping the clock altogether. What we need instead is an approach that intersects with the best of both outlooks, but which is itself distinctive and points to a course of practical action. In Schur's words, "we need to turn the social clock forward."

If we cannot go back, what then is the best way to go forward? Many people will still choose to pursue the permanence of marriage or comparable arrangements. Since the late 1980s, there has been a growing recognition that individual fulfillment and an "ethic of commitment" to relationships and to the children they produce are not necessarily incompatible. At the same time, there will be many who reject this ethic and seek passion through the less complicated route of gratification without commitment—and these are not by any means all socially or personally irresponsible people.

In other words, it is too late in history for the validity of individual choice among consenting adults to be denied. In one form or another over the past century, it has, above all, been the example of individuals standing up for themselves that has led to wider benefits. An expansion of work and life choices, regardless of gender; a growing acceptance of alternative sexualities; greater tolerance for differences of race, ethnicity, physical capacity, and intellectual ability—all of these have enhanced the quality of many lives. While there are those who will continue to resist or deny the fact, the age of pluralism has arrived and our agenda must be to live with it productively.

The challenge for the new millennium is to create a culture that will promote the greatest happiness for everyone, whatever their life choices might be, from old-fashioned marriage to alternatives that have yet to emerge. Collectively we need to foster the ethic commitment without devaluing pleasure. And the reverse also applies: pleasure must have its own rationale and not be pitted against commitment. In short, what would enrich us all is a culture that acknowledges the potential for meaning in a range of sexual lifestyles.

To achieve this goal we will have to redraw the boundaries between public and private life, so that our culture not only accommodates sexual acts and feelings but also protects their intimacy. Neither prudery nor a new puritanism, this is a strategy to grant each of us the leeway to experience the singular, the moving, and the profound—the passionate—in our relationships.

All cultural change, even sweeping change, grows from the small actions that we each take in our daily lives. The final chapter of this history suggests how, as thoughtful consumers and caring lovers, we can resist the invasive and the standardizing in our habits of consumption, choice of entertainment, and private experience. But rooted in the everyday though it may be, effective action has to carry the kind of conviction that can only come from true understanding. We must understand ourselves not only as individuals, but as individuals in dynamic relation to our culture and its history. As Rollo May eloquently put it, "History has formed us in the present so that we may embrace the future." Turning the clock forward—setting positive change in motion—begins with knowing where we have been. By clearly recognizing the realities of the past we can open our lives into a more satisfying future, based not on myth but on our own history, insightfully reimagined.

Myth or Memory?

In *Titanic*, as the Strauses lie together for the last time, Jack and Rose reach the deck. A lone violinist plays the first notes of "Nearer,

My God, to Thee," and one by one his fellow musicians take up the melody until "it reaches all over the ship on this still night." The real experience, however, was somewhat different.

On deck the Strauses awaited the inevitable, while the ship's musicians played ragtime and popular waltzes, an attempt to bolster the spirits of those left on board. Yet by the time survivors had landed in New York, several of them would swear that the band had played "Nearer, My God, to Thee." It was a much loved hymn whose solemnity must have seemed well suited to the sorrowful fate that all too few of them had narrowly escaped. And so, as news of the *Titanic* tragedy spread, the myth took hold.

Our unexamined ideas about the past are often based on such myths, born of sentiment and misremembering. Some, like the poignant association of the *Titanic* and "Nearer, My God, to Thee," are uplifting—true or not, they enrich our culture. Others, however, impoverish it by demonizing, glamorizing, sentimentalizing, or otherwise oversimplifying reality.

Historical memory—the reconstruction of the past through first-hand accounts and other available evidence—is also imperfect. But unlike myth, it attempts to recover the layers, complexities, and nuances of the past, which resonate in the present and beyond into the future. Ultimately the polarity between myth and memory reflects different approaches to change. Do we fear it, or welcome it? Do we want our culture as it is, or as it could be? Do we cling to myth, or boldly embrace memory?

Because it is so central to our humanity, the intimate relationship of men and women has been especially fertile soil for the growth of myth. Among the generation that came of age in the 1960s and 1970s are many who recall those decades as a time of true sexual liberation, with gratification there for the taking.

Their parents, meanwhile, hark back to the immediate postwar years, when real satisfaction arose from loyalty, stability, and good morals. The oldest among them are apt to reminisce about an earlier day still, when people were discreet and sexual matters purely private.

Woven into these impressions are some strands of truth and a tangle of myth. The remnants of history—the artifacts, customs, wisdom, and desires of other times—tell a story at odds with popular recollection. The first decades of the past century were by no means so discreet as those who lived through them like to recall. Nor were the early postwar years simply an age of sedate suburbanism—there was more going on in those new subdivisions than many of their inhabitants now care to admit. And colorful though it was, the so-called sexual revolution was less revolutionary, less sexy, even, than either its defenders or its detractors have claimed.

Yet the idea that a sudden upheaval transformed the relationship of men and women, releasing them from their inhibitions for better or for worse, is widely ingrained in popular belief. Attitudes and behaviors have undoubtedly changed in the past few decades, but this is not, as many would like to believe, the exclusive responsibility of one large and rebellious generation. What we now remember as the sexual revolution was intimately linked to earlier days; though dramatic, it was just another phase in a greater social and personal revolution, in which every generation of the past century has played a part. This was the shift from the nineteenth-century model of duty above self to a growing stress on individual needs and their fulfillment. A significant aspect of this great shift was the importance that each of the generations since 1900 has placed on sexual satisfaction as the very core of personal happiness.

But if this is our common past, why do so many of us recall it differently? The answer lies partly in the human tendency to apportion blame. Impatient for change, sexually progressive thinkers of the early 1900s popularized a distorted view of the Victorians. Today their supposed "prudery" or "hypocrisy" remains part of conventional wisdom, despite years of accumulated evidence to the contrary. A half century later, college-age baby boomers, out to change the world, pointed accusing fingers at the "uptight" mores of the fifties, thus lending credence to that decade's own myth of universal propriety.

At the other extreme are those who abhor change on principle. Most notably, from the 1960s until today, conservatives with a range of agendas have exaggerated the extent of the sexual revolution, making it a mythic catastrophe responsible for a welter of social problems from teen pregnancies to child abuse, crime, illiteracy, and binge drinking. "What did they do before they had the '60s to blame?" one newspaper commentator recently asked. "It's been such a boon to them that, secretly at least, they must be grateful."

Nostalgia, our inclination to "remember" what we wish had happened, has also played its part in turning memory into myth. A harmless pleasure in private, nostalgia as a cultural indulgence has deeper significance. When we collectively imagine the past as better than it ever could have been in reality, we are grasping ineffectually at what we lack in the present. The yearning for "something more" runs like a refrain through contemporary culture at all levels, from controlled studies at major universities to popular movies like *Titanic*. It has become part of everyday life.

Ask a selection of contemporary men and women the question "What do you want most in your relationships with one another?" Variously expressed, the answers are likely to be echoes of a single motif. "Connection," "intensity," "joy," "meaning." *Passion*, in all its forms and guises, is what we yearn for.

In the midst of present longings, we persist in imagining a past that never was. Meanwhile the statistics of unhappiness steadily accumulate. But in the morning glow of a new millennium, what better time to remember with fresh insight?

The signposts to the future are dotted along the road to the past. In the end, to turn away from our old illusions is to go forward in the search for passion—to discover not a world we have lost, but one yet to be claimed.

THE PROMISE OF PLEASURE

1900–1919

The turn of the century was a time of economic growth and individual prosperity, when modern conveniences eased daily life, and enthralling new entertainments captivated the masses. Everything, people believed, was getting better and better—there was virtually nothing that could not be modernized and improved.

The pervading spirit of optimism embraced the relationship of men and women with all its brave new vigor. People had begun to suspect that unrealized pleasure and unprecedented happiness were now within reach. For a time, it all seemed possible.

Even the Great War of 1914–1918 did not shatter these dreams with the same grim finality that it devastated so much else. In the face of death and deprivation, women and men found new ways to know and to take pleasure in one another. But the pleasures were often guilty and reckless, always short-lived, and the knowledge won at staggering costs. Among them was the untimely loss of the bright optimism that had briefly illuminated the new century.

Sex as the Key to Happiness

> I say things about sex which have not been said by
> anyone else, things which are of profound importance
> to men and women who hope to . . . find the key
> to the happiness which should be the portion of each.
>
> — MARIE STOPES, *Married Love*

On Monday, 1 January 1900, for the price of a penny, the new year's first issue of the *New York Times* reflected the mood of the nation. "Hope," "prosperity," "good times," "bright outlook"—these were the optimistic terms in which the *Times* reported on everything from religion to world trade to domestic real estate. A staid publication, it refrained from airing sensitive topics at the breakfast tables of its readers. Across the Atlantic, the elderly Queen Victoria still had another year to live, and the reticences of her era lingered with her.

Similarly, duty, sacrifice, and marital devotion—standards by which couples like Ida and Isidor Straus lived and died—did not suddenly disappear with the turn of the century, or go down with the *Titanic*. But with the exuberant confidence of the time, new ideas were quickly taking hold. To many, the restraints that had served the old century well now seemed as dreary as Victorian mourning clothes.

By the early 1900s, women and men alike were speaking less of duty, and more of happiness. They grew ever more aware of the rewards of good physical appearance and devoted themselves to improving their bodies. They sought gratification through the latest in pastimes and entertainments—the newfound diversions of dating, for instance, and that most modern of entertainments, the moving pictures. Above all, they became more and more certain that the key to both personal and marital happiness was sexual fulfillment. And this in turn, they now believed, required the frank exchange of information about intimate matters.

"Knowledge is needed," Marie Stopes declared. A self-made expert on marriage and birth control, she was convinced that "the origin of unhappiness" was ignorance about the physical "marriage-bond." Though she was little known at the turn of the century, a few years later Stopes would be an international celebrity. She and others who similarly worked to eradicate ignorance spoke directly to popular demand. People were eager to learn more about their bodies and how to enhance physical pleasure. Surely then, they trusted, happiness and all the rewards of passion would follow.

New Bodies for a New Century: Women

Long before the twentieth century a good appearance had helped both men and women attract the opposite sex. But never had the standard of attractiveness been so rigorous for both sexes as it quickly became in the early 1900s. With sex now the key to personal well-being, body image and sex appeal were crucial: the better you looked, the happier you were likely to be. Setting the pace for the rest of the century, commercial interests stirred up and capitalized on people's concern for personal attractiveness. Sex appeal, constantly used as a lure to sell products, now became a commodity itself, to be purchased along with the right fashion item or grooming aid.

As it would throughout the century, the challenge to find fulfillment through attractiveness confronted women more insistently than men. A 1912 advertisement for face cream in the *Ladies' Home Journal* captured the attitude of the day. It pictured a handsome man, his strong profile showing to advantage, kneeling low in front of a standing woman. "Bow to the Wittiest, Kneel to the Prettiest!" exclaimed the headline, and the copy continued: "Although we do not really kneel to the pretty woman in these modern days, still it is true that we favor her every time. Beauty is all-powerful. It is the most valuable asset any woman can have."

While face cream manufacturers claimed that feminine appeal depended on a good complexion, others urged women to abandon the curves of the old hour-glass silhouette, and to get thinner, thinner, thinner. In 1902, fueling women's already anxious efforts to lose weight, *Vogue* magazine declared that it now verged on "a crime to be fat." Advertisers echoed the sentiment. "Too Fat," scolded a 1905 advertisement in *Leslie's Weekly*, a popular illustrated paper. Holding out hope to the unattractively plump was the "perfectly harmless" (because perfectly ineffectual) product on offer: a patent medicine for taking off "Double Chin, Big Stomach, Fat Hips, etc."

By 1908 the stylish woman's shape was diminished to an elegant minimum. Feminine fashion and underclothing reflected the change. Shorter and tighter than ever before, skirts left less and less to the imagination, their hemlines ranging from just above the ankle to mid-calf by 1915. And a new invention, first known as the "Twentieth Century Device" and later renamed the zipper, further enhanced streamlined femininity. That staple of Victorian underwear, the corset, survived into the twentieth century, but by 1908 it was only lightly boned or made of elastic, and had already started to give way to its replacement, the rubber girdle. The idea now was to create the look of a sleek form with long slim hips, rather than the pinched-in waist and abundant curves of earlier days.

As women struggled to reduce their size in some places, they worked to enlarge it in another. A generous shapely bosom and deep cleavage were as essential to beauty as a slender body. The latest look was the "mono-bosom," and women adopted intimate wear that compressed the breasts into a single curvaceous form. Padded camisoles were available, but by 1912 it was more fashionable to wear a new-fangled undergarment, the brassiere. Designed "to save the figure from going unshapely," it soon became a standard item in most American women's wardrobe.

Advertisements of the day promoted various models as well as other kinds of bust enhancers. In a new and improved century no woman needed to bear the humiliation of physical underendowment. Happier alternatives included corrective corsets to compensate for "hollow and scrawny" busts and various creams purporting to aid development. One such product, with the slightly grisly name "Dr. Charles' Flesh Food," promised the customer a new bosom with all the "natural contour" that sex appeal demanded.

Despite the abundant flow of advertising, advice, and information, there remained limits on what could be said outright. Rather than direct reference to sex appeal, popular parlance favored the suggestive mention of "feminine charm," or "fascination," or personal "magnetism." Candor about once-private matters was now the order of the day, but not yet at the expense of all reserve.

New Bodies for a New Century: Men

The most fitting partner for the modern streamlined woman was an attractive man of youthful demeanor and dynamic physique. Though to a lesser extent than women, men also faced demands that they keep up their personal appearance. Physical fitness and good grooming, said the opinion-makers of the day, were the secrets of male sexual potency and, by implication, of attractiveness to women.

In 1900 the future president Theodore Roosevelt strongly advocated the value of the "strenuous life" for men. A body developed through action and athletics was not only a sign of achievement but also of virility. This had also been an accepted notion in the previous century, but in the early 1900s there was increased pressure on men to be youthful, athletic, and sexually attractive. The old-fashioned bearded, whiskered, possibly portly gentleman who might once have been considered personable, if not exactly irresistible, had given way to the clean-shaven sporting youth.

Among those born to social and financial advantage the Yale University ideal of attractive manhood prevailed. The Yale type was handsome of face and well-proportioned of body, his "manly limbs" perfect in their "symmetry and grace"; in addition he was distinctively tall, erect, and vigorous. In keeping with the lingering reticences of the day, no one explicitly said anything about sexual prowess, but the overtones of words like "vigorous" and "erect" would have been apparent enough.

The majority of men did not follow the Ivy League standard of the privileged few, but instead modeled themselves on its commercial version, the masculine ideal in clothing fashion. After 1900 stylish menswear became markedly vertical in its lines and, more than in previous years, incorporated geometric patterns. Such garments accentuated height and strength, and looking good in them demanded a lean, taut frame. In other words, good tailoring had its limits—it was the slimness, upright bearing, and youthful athleticism of the body beneath that now counted for more.

"Weakness is a crime" the exercise magazine *Physical Culture* sternly informed its 150,000 readers. Published by Bernarr Macfadden, an early guru of healthy eating and physical fitness, it railed against immoderate use of food and alcohol, sedentary habits, and "the most important of all evils"—prudery. In another magazine, *True Story*, Macfadden further linked physical appearance with male sexuality, titillating female as well as male readers with sensationalist stories that combined "sex confession" with the handsome, athletic ideal purveyed in *Physical Culture*. In this way a whole generation of readers, women as well as men, began to accept that appearance and virility were intimately and irrevocably bound together.

Advertising, which by now reached a mass market, underscored the idea. Images of good-looking, virile men promoted everything from soap and aftershave to cameras and the latest in refreshments, Coca-Cola. The makers of toothpaste launched a campaign to claim a gleaming smile as a masculine necessity: white teeth, they hinted with varying degrees of subtlety, were at the very core of successful manhood. In a 1919 advertisement in the *Saturday Evening Post*, the image of a bare-chested man helped to associate S. S. White toothpaste with masculine strength and sexual prowess. Health and toothpaste went irrevocably together, the advertisement implied, and "without health," it continued suggestively, "the strength of the body is sapped, vigor dwindles and is lost." It was perhaps no coincidence that toothpaste came to be marketed in tubes—a form of packaging that stayed firm until all used up.

New Sexual Standards

The insistence of advertisers and others on masculine vigor and feminine allure revealed the heart of relationships in the new century. Sexuality—it was the individual's greatest asset and the mainstay of the happy couple. At the same time, information about birth control methods was much more widely available, and products such as improved condoms were increasingly accepted—thus permitting the separation of sex and reproduction. Increasingly freed from the responsibility of procreation, people more and more sought erotic pleasure for its own sake.

One young bride, Helen Apte, spoke for men as well as women when she expressed both her joy in the physical gratifications of matrimony and a lingering allegiance to earlier ideals. In 1909, the first year of her marriage, she confided to her diary that married life and all it entailed seemed to her like a necklace of jewels. Wifely duty was a "clear stone," with fidelity set alongside it. But "the great flaming gem" of physical pleasure outshone both duty and fidelity.

The most extreme and vocal proponents of sexual gratification belonged to the avant-garde—a bohemian mix of reformers, socialists, feminists, writers, and artists who gathered in such hotbeds of radical thought as college campuses and New York's Greenwich Village. Swayed by the free-love philosophy of such notables as the anarchist Emma Goldman, this progressive group advocated people's right to sexual pleasure without reproductive pressures. They also focused attention on women's sexual needs, and questioned the merits of formalized marriage. Though mainly of middle-class origin, the avant-garde did not widely influence middle-class attitudes about sex and relationships. While both women and men increasingly desired erotic satisfaction, most, like Helen Apte, expected to attain it within the safe and decorous confines of matrimony.

The expectation had the strongest hold on women. The threat of unwanted pregnancy leading to a soiled reputation, abandonment by family, and rejection by society were harsh warnings to girls to avoid sex before marriage. In the 1800s social and moral pressures also admonished respectable young men against indulging in the sin and folly of premarital sex. But in the early years of the new century this prohibition eased. The general assumption was that a man would not marry until he was economically well established and able to provide for a wife and family. Since this might take a few years, it was a small transgression for a healthy, hard-working young man to indulge himself on occasion with the sort of girl he would not consider marrying. Boys, after all, would be boys. This newly relaxed attitude applied only to males. It was thus the beginning of what would soon become known as "the double standard."

Helping to uphold the double standard was the latest version of the oldest profession. More organized and commercialized than ever before, prostitution in the early twentieth century thrived not only in large cities like New York and Chicago but also in smaller centers, such as Lancaster, Pennsylvania, whose red-light district boasted twenty-seven brothels. Despite efforts by the Society for the Suppression of Vice and other antiprostitution groups, trade in sex flourished, generating profits for crime syndicates, corrupt politicians, police, and real estate agents. That pillar of wealthy America, William Randolph Hearst, was similarly not above extending his empire through the purchase of several notorious New York brothels.

Illicit though it was, prostitution in the new century was no secret. Potential clients could even purchase "sporting guides" or "blue books" that provided tourist-style information on the location, prices, and distinctive services of a city's houses of prostitution. Some establishments, with names like "French Studio," catered to specialized ethnic as well as erotic preferences. Brothels ranged in cost and quality from the fifty-cent houses, where customers waited their turn on wooden benches, to fancy premises offering opulent decor, music, and expensive liquor. In between were the five-and-ten-dollar establishments. These outnumbered the cheapest houses by nearly two to one, a strong indication that at least once in a while, respectable middle-class men resorted to prostitutes. For some, such occasions were rare lapses or celebratory sprees—for others they were the obsessive center of their sex lives.

Not uncommonly, physical urgency compelled young unmarried men to avail themselves of prostitutes from time to time. But if such episodes began with the anticipation of pleasure, they often ended in disappointment or misgiving. One young man despondently recalled his expensive encounter in a fancy house as "a mechanical procedure that . . . endured for perhaps a minute." A sex survey from the 1910s showed that many men who used prostitutes feared venereal disease, while others worried that such experiences would somehow hamper their adjustment to marital sex. For all that the mores of the day privileged male sexual expression over female, the masculine prerogative was not necessarily one of unconditional power. When the double standard involved prostitution, men staked pleasure against peace of mind and ultimate sexual confidence.

Dating and Dancing

Though it extended across the social and economic spectrum, the double standard applied less strictly to working-class girls than it did to their middle-class counterparts. Because circumstances forced them to leave home and earn a living, young working women enjoyed a measure of personal freedom and some leeway to bend the standard. But as old restrictions relaxed, and opportunities for associating in public increased, young men and women from all walks of life and all social classes displayed their mutual attraction with ever greater openness.

As women entered the work force in increasing numbers, it was soon a commonplace for the sexes to intermingle in new, informal ways—in offices, factories, and stores during working hours; in cafés and parks at lunchtime; on streetcars and sidewalks before and after work. Brought together daily, working men and women developed a new familiarity with one another. On the negative side, this fostered the historical beginnings of sexual harassment on the job, as many male workers of otherwise exemplary behavior considered their female colleagues to be fair game for leers, suggestive remarks, catcalls, and kissing noises. But on the happier side, workplace encounters between the sexes spiced long boring days with camaraderie, amusing banter, flirtation, and the possibility of something more after hours.

The commercial development of new kinds of leisure activities served both recreation and romance. Young men and women could now get together unchaperoned at amusement parks like Coney Island, in the movie houses that were fast becoming fixtures of towns all over North America, and at dance halls where the music and motion were irresistibly seductive. With new places for couples to go, the courtship rituals of the last century gave way to the modern practice called dating. Of recent vintage, this usage of the word originated in the idiom of 1890s working-class Chicago.

As more and more young people took up dating, there evolved a system of barter that would endure for most of the century. First known as "treating," it required the man to pay the costs of the date, including admission to amusement sites, restaurant meals, drinks, and transportation. This put a distinct strain on the modest incomes of many young working men. As a Chicago headline of 1919 dramatically put it, "Man Getting $18 a Week Dares Not Fall in Love." For a young woman, the more that her escort spent on her the greater the tribute to her powers of attraction, and the higher her standing among her female peers when she recounted her latest date. But treats came with a price tag, and men expected women to pay in sexual currency. The favors bestowed might be anything from flattery and teasing to going all the way.

It was a girl of strict principles indeed who managed to confine her behavior to mild flirting and perhaps a chaste kiss goodnight. For where dating took place, sexual stimulation was all around. Single men and women mingled at social clubs, some of whose activities included flirting, touching, and kissing games. Amusement parks featured fast rides that threw women and their escorts into close physical contact, often lifting skirts revealingly, while the new movie houses were dimly lit havens for unchaperoned lovers.

More than anywhere, sexuality let loose on the dance floor, and dance halls rose to the forefront of the new century's commercial enjoyments. Young people could frequent them in mixed or single-sex groups; a man could take a date or go on his own and find a "pick-up" for the evening. After the often dreary routine of work, the dance hall's bright lights, music, refreshments, and promise of romance beckoned enticingly. And nowhere outside the bedroom itself was sexual expression more blatantly physical. The girl's arms around her partner's neck, his hands possessively on her hips, couples swayed together in dances like the "lovers' walk," "hug me close," and the "shiver." Cheeks pressed together, they moved in what was often a simulation of sexual intercourse. "The motion of the pelvic portions of the body," as one social investigator remarked, was the distinguishing feature of the new dances.

The stimulations of dating and popular amusements—not to mention the urgings of their escorts—were clearly more than some

31

young women could resist, however much they might believe in the ideal of purity. By 1910 the rate of premarital pregnancies had risen from a low of 10 percent in the mid-nineteenth century to 23 percent. Other evidence from contemporary sex surveys indicates a low rate of premarital intercourse among middle-class girls. The increased incidence of unmarried pregnancy appears to have come mostly from working-class women, whose opportunities for transgressing the double standard exceeded those of sheltered middle-class daughters.

Because affluence allowed women of marriageable age to remain within the protection of the family circle, the home-centered courtship rituals of the previous century persisted among the middle class into the early 1900s. An interested gentleman would call upon the young lady of his choice, make polite conversation to her family, and perhaps take some refreshment. Then if luck and parental tolerance were on their side, the couple could enjoy some unchaperoned time alone. Seated side by side on the parlor settee, or "vibrating on a chord of sympathy" as they played a piano duet, the enamored couple could take pleasure in one another's physical proximity. Meanwhile parents within earshot discouraged things from getting out of hand.

But the romantic opportunities of young middle-class women were not entirely confined to home. Some girls attended the new coeducational colleges where they encountered young men in both classroom settings and the campus social scene. Lectures, dances, teas, spectator sports, and sorority and fraternity events all promoted a free and easy interchange among young men and women.

Whether or not they went to college, middle-class youth soon took up the new custom of dating—but with certain refinements. Instead of patronizing dance halls, young men took their dates to more sedate dance palaces. There couples performed subdued versions of the modern dances, their movements modified to exclude the blatantly sexual motion favored by patrons of dance halls. And while managers of working-class establishments commonly turned a blind eye to the practice of "picking up," those who ran middle-class dance palaces and cabarets actively discouraged contact between strangers. As the popularity of dating spread, entrepreneurs developed amusement parks and movie theaters whose ambience suited the taste of both the middle-class and upwardly aspiring working couples. For those who wanted their dating to be decorous, such places fulfilled two important needs: on the one hand they accommodated burgeoning sexual relationships, while on the other they preserved a pleasing measure of old-fashioned discretion in the midst of the new openness.

Seductive Entertainments

Apart from the physical gratifications of dancing and dating, there were the seductions of other popular pastimes. Reading, attending stage performances, and going to the movies might offer only vicarious romantic and sexual experience, but they were pleasurably stimulating nonetheless.

Increased public tolerance for subject matter and illustrations once thought salacious was all the encouragement that some publishers needed. Least likely of all to miss out on the lucrative trend, was the publishing magnate William Randolph Hearst. By 1914 he was producing a magazine with the catchy title *Snappy Stories* that featured girls in bathing suits on the front cover. Other magazine publishers soon followed suit, while book publishers and their authors were also growing bolder. Most notable—or notorious—for steamy creations was the British novelist Elinor Glyn, whose racy romances sold widely in both Britain and North America.

A popularizer of the concept of sex appeal, she filled her novels with liberated heroines who slink around in filmy nightdresses and revealing evening gowns as they shamelessly pursue their men. In her best-known novel, the 1907 *Three Weeks*, she set up a scenario that enthralled the reading public. At the story's center is the married queen of a Balkan country who vacations in Switzerland and has an affair with an Englishman named Paul, "a splendid young animal of the best class." In the throes of arousal "the Lady," as Glyn called her, "undulated round and all over him . . . twining about him like a serpent."

It was not so much the suggestive descriptions of sexual encounters that titillated readers of *Three Weeks* and sent pleasurable *frissons* of shock through them; rather, it was the idea that the woman, not the man, should take charge of the seduction and enjoy herself with such frank sensual relish. More provocative still was the unconventionality and illicitness of it all—not only was "the Lady" older than Paul, but she was also committing adultery. Although some reviewers professed to be disgusted, and the book was banned in British schools, it was a best-seller in both England and America, an international sensation that captivated millions of readers.

Glyn heated up the publishing world, but the offerings of stage and screen often eclipsed the medium of print. Though vaudeville had its restrained side, the draw of shows in the cheaper theaters was sex, usually in the form of leering jokes, double-entendres, and suggestive song lyrics. On the exteriors of some burlesque theaters, painted images of skimpily clothed women advertised the show inside—sometimes to the dismay of neighboring parents who were struggling to raise refined young daughters.

Perhaps most notorious of the vaudeville stars was Eve Tanguay, a provocative blond singer and dancer whose signature song on stage, "I Don't Care," echoed her apparently guilt-free attitude offstage, as she hopped from bed to bed. A huge star in her time, Tanguay soon gave way to brighter and better-remembered performers—Sophie Tucker, for one. Dressed like a madam, as one contemporary observer put it, she made headlines as the "red hot mama" whose songs "burned up" many a theater. Another star whose memory would long survive made her debut on Broadway in 1911. Racy songs were her specialty, and as she delivered them she sometimes played the part of a naive innocent with no idea of the innuendo in her words. But more often she was the woman of the world, sultry of voice, giving the audience a knowing wink as she sang tunes like "If You Don't Like My Peaches Why Do You Shake My Tree?" Even in those days, the young Mae West performed with the vocal and bodily suggestiveness that would endure as her trademark.

Seductive though its stars might be, the stage was fast losing ground to the myriad sexual thrills of motion pictures. From almost its earliest years, the movie industry offered the public a range of sexual and sex-related themes. Elopement (*When a Man Loves,* 1910), sin in the big city (*To Save Her Soul,* 1909), and adultery (*Fools of Fate,* 1909) were among the titillating subjects that stirred movie audiences in the century's first decade.

Much of the content was suggestive more than explicit, but in a time before film censorship there could always be the added spice of bare flesh. After 1915 or so, such enticement became something of a trend. In the 1916 *Daughter of the Gods,* Annette Kellerman, an Australian swimmer who became a star in American silent films, performed nude in exotic settings such as vine-draped pools and the harem of a sultan's palace. Soon after, Theda Bara made her reputation as one of the early Hollywood sex symbols known as "vamps"—women who exuded a dark, dangerous eroticism. In *Cleopatra* (1917) and *Salome* (1918), she wore breast pasties that seductively showed almost as much as they hid. Not to be outdone, her rival Gloria Swanson appeared in the 1919 film *Male and Female*, exotically and often revealingly clad in furs, feathers, and thin clinging fabric.

While the movies' sensual images undoubtedly captivated people, so too did the new experience of seeing them larger than life. This was not just an entertaining novelty, but one which forever altered human perception of physical contact between men and women. "For the first time in the history of the world," marveled one new York filmgoer, "it is possible to see what a kiss looks like . . . Everything is shown in startling directness. What the camera did not see did not exist. The real kiss is a revelation. The idea has unlimited possibilities."

By the nature of their ambience the early movie houses created another first in history. Before their appearance there was nowhere a respectable young couple could go to sit close, hold hands, cling together, touch, and kiss—all in the dark. Small wonder that the back rows of movie houses soon became known as "lovers' lanes." As the Chicago social investigator Jane Addams put it around 1909, "the space is filled with the glamor of love making." An added plus, the glamour and lovemaking were widely affordable—for the modest price of two tickets, any couple could enact their own seductive scenario in the flickering shadows of the silent screen.

Sex O'Clock

In August 1913 the magazine *Current Opinion* declared that in America "sex o'clock" had struck; the image acknowledged the twentieth century's new candor about sexual matters. But readily available, straightforward information about sex remained comparatively difficult to come by. Increasingly convinced by the stimulation around them that ignorance and bliss did not go together, people craved accurate discussion of bodily functioning, techniques for enhancing sexual pleasure, and strategies for birth control.

This desire for information coincided with the growth of sex as a field of professional study. Sexology had emerged in the previous century, principally in Richard von Krafft-Ebing's encyclopedia of pathologies, *Psychopathia Sexualis* (translated into English in 1892), and in such works as *Sexual Inversion* (1897), the first of the monumental seven-volume *Studies in the Psychology of Sex*, by the British sexologist Havelock Ellis. In the early twentieth century a number of American experts built upon the work begun abroad. Among them were the obstetrician and gynecologist Robert Latou Dickinson, best known for his research into female sexuality, and the psychologist G. Stanley Hall, whose two-volume study, *Adolescence* (1904), expounded on the dangers of sexual precociousness and advocated premarital chastity.

Another psychologist, John B. Watson, contributed more to the history of scandal than to sexology. In a laboratory study to investigate the physiology of sexual response, he and his female partner made love with various measurement and observation devices inserted into or attached to their bodies. The scandal was that the married Watson's partner was not his wife but his lab assistant, Rosalie. Johns Hopkins hastened to fire him, while his irate wife sued for divorce and confiscated the records of his stimulating if imprudent experiment.

The expert who would eventually most influence popular twentieth-century thinking on sex was little known, except to colleagues, when he visited Worcester, Massachusetts, in 1909 to lecture at Clark University. But the Viennese neurologist Sigmund Freud had arrived in America at a crucial cultural moment. In professional circles, as elsewhere, sexuality was the topic of the day, and Freudian theory soon gained prominence, if not universal agreement, among spedcialists and intellectuals. At the same time, it began to lose much of its original substance, as people overlooked the nuances and fastened on the simplified idea that sex was a pervasive and irresistible force in human life, one that demanded expression and could only be denied at great peril to one's mental health.

While many of their findings would later prove to be erroneous, Freud and other pioneering sexologists chipped away at the wall of guilt and ignorance that barred their patients from sexual enjoyment. Yet for all their diligent efforts in the cause of enlightenment, most of them failed to reach or inform the average person. As late as 1930, even Freud's influence was mainly confined to professionals and intellectuals.

With a "Go-to-Hell" Look in Their Eyes

In the early years of the century, answering the everyday questions and concerns of the majority fell primarily to two women. One was the American champion of contraception and sexual knowledge, Margaret Sanger. The other was her British counterpart, Marie Stopes.

In 1911 Sanger was working as a teacher and nurse in New York, where she discovered the grim privations that poor families suffered as a result of unwanted pregnancies and too many children. The first to coin the term "birth control," she published tracts, pamphlets, and a magazine called the *Woman Rebel*—all with the purpose of disseminating information about contraceptives such as douches, condoms, and pessaries. The tens of thousands of letters that she received asking for birth control information testified to the huge need she served.

She soon ran afoul of the notorious Anthony Comstock, spearhead of the Society for the Suppression of Vice and of the Comstock Law, which severely restricted the kind of subject matter that could be sent through the U. S. mail. Though she managed to avoid prosecution for her publications, Sanger was jailed in 1917 for establishing the first American birth-control clinic in Brooklyn. Undaunted, she went on a few years later to found the American Birth Control League and to lobby for clinics for the poor.

No defender of the status quo when it came to her work, she was equally unorthodox in her personal life. A married woman with three children, she was also a petite redhead who attracted many male admirers and lovers. Among them was the sexologist Havelock Ellis, whose own married status was no bar to his developing an obsession with Sanger and deluging her with love letters. Though fond of Ellis, she did not reciprocate his ardor, and the affair was never consummated. (Nor was it likely that it ever would have been, under any circumstances. Ironically, Ellis the sex expert was impotent for most, if not all, of his life).

More central in Sanger's life was yet another famous man, the British author and notorious womanizer H. G. Wells. Intelligent, energetic, devoted to work, sex, and pleasure, he was her masculine mirror, the virtually perfect lover for a woman of her strong spirit. Vocal in her commitment to knowledge and sexual enjoyment, Sanger was quintessentially of the new century. True to character, she defined all feminine duty in light of her own approach: "To look the world in the face with a go-to-hell look in the eyes; to have an idea; to speak and act in defiance of convention."

In 1914, while evading the law of her own country, Sanger met her British alter ego, Dr. Marie Stopes. A paleobotanist and not a physician as she liked people to suppose, Stopes was yet another outspoken "go-to-hell" advocate of birth control. But more even than Sanger, she captured popular imagination with her best-selling sex manual *Married Love*, published in 1918 in England, and distributed in the United States by 1919. A group of American academics would later name it one of the twenty-five most influential books of the half-century—alongside the work of Einstein and Freud.

Married Love quickly became a sensation, not only for its overall frankness and readability, but in particular for its forthright observations on female sexual pleasure and how to stimulate it. One item of information that Stopes shared with her male readers was "the sensitive interrelation between a woman's breasts and the rest of her sex-life." As she explained it, delicately but clearly enough, "Her husband's lips upon her breast melt a wife to tenderness and are one of a husband's surest ways to make her physically ready for complete union."

Ironically, when the book was first published, Stopes was thirty-seven years old, previously married, and still a virgin. As she explained in her preface, *Married Love* was not born of experience but of her own sexual disappointment. Her former husband, the Canadian botanist Ruggles Gates (whom she'd married in 1911), is now remembered principally for his failure to consummate their marriage. She claimed he was impotent, while he protested that she was so oversexed as to daunt any man.

The End of Conventional Reticence

Whatever the truth behind Stopes's private life, *Married Love* broke through the sexual secretiveness that had troubled so many people's intimate lives. Together, the efforts of Stopes and Sanger raised openness to a new level. But even before that, the trend had been developed enough to acquire a catchphrase. The "repeal of reticence," as the magazine *Atlantic* had called it in 1914, was now all the more unlikely to be overturned.

In the preface to *Married Love* Stopes gave the "repeal" her own characteristic interpretation. If happiness through sexual pleasure was the desired end, then it was time for plain speaking. "Instinct" could not be relied on, and must give way to knowledge:

> To the reticent, as to the conventional, it may seem a presumption or a superfluity to speak of the details of the most complex of all our functions. They ask: Is not instinct enough? The answer is No. Instinct is *not* enough.

Judging by the flood of approving commentary and questions that *Married Love* provoked, men and women alike widely agreed with Stopes that when it came to sexual satisfaction, knowledge was indeed better than instinct. Her words also expressed the wider mood of the time. It was the new day of the individual, and not only reticence but other social conventions and attitudes were fast losing ground to the pursuit of personal fulfillment.

As Stopes, Sanger, and others persevered in their campaign for pleasure, tirelessly waging their battle against ignorance, the greatest war of all shook the world. Eclipsing even the shock of the *Titanic*'s sinking, it was one of the most cataclysmic events of the century. It lent force to the repeal of reticence—and greater than ever urgency to the search for passion.

War and Revelation

> The hunger of our men for home women was
> the glorious conclusive answer to all who had
> dreamed that our people are decadent . . . It was
> one of the most beautiful revelations of the war.
>
> — KATHERINE MAYO, "That Damn Y"

Officers posing stiffly in full uniform. Soldiers sharing a cigarette in a muddy trench. Weary troops on the march. Crumpled bodies and rough crosses strewn across the fields of Europe. Such scenes of the Great War of 1914–1918 are burnt into popular memory.

Alongside these are images evoked by the remembered songs of the era. "Hinky Dinky Parlez Voo" and "How Ya Gonna Keep 'em Down on the Farm?" hint obliquely at the illicit pleasures of off-duty time. Temporarily out of the horror, some fighting men sought further escape through sex, drink, and carousing—and confirmed the worst fears of those at home, who were waging their own war to preserve the physical and moral purity of the boys "over there."

The poetry of the day yields further recollections. The war poets—among them Rupert Brooke, Siegfried Sassoon, and Wilfred

Owen—presented yet another face of war. Reflected in the anguished beauty and homoerotic yearnings of their verse are all the suffering that the Great War inflicted on every life it touched.

These differing portraits of the same war are linked by a common focus, the predominance of men. Women are either in the background or absent entirely. Yet in large numbers they, too, served in the Great War. At home they took on vital factory work that kept the war effort supplied with arms and equipment. At the front they served as nurses and nurses' aides; drove transport vehicles and ambulances; cleaned, cooked, and served food in makeshift canteens; and acted as hostesses, dance partners, and companions for off-duty soldiers.

The presence of women where the men were fighting helped to shape another aspect of those years, a side of history that is not so often told. Thrust into the unprecedented ordeal of modern warfare, men and women expanded and deepened their knowledge of each other. Not only relating as sexual beings, they grew to see their common humanity rather than the mysterious otherness of distinctly opposite sexes. This heightened understanding—this "beautiful revelation," as a first-hand observer put it—was among the scant good to come out of a war whose horror had been unimaginable only a few years before.

Fighting for Purity

Many of the older generation in Britain, the U.S., and Canada feared that the young men and women overseas would come to know each other only too well—and in all the worst ways. Naive young servicemen would fall prey to French prostitutes or to immodest girls infected with "khaki fever," as British newspapers called young women's attraction to men in uniform. Venereal disease would rage out of control and immorality run rampant.

When the first shots of August 1914 were fired in Europe, organizations to protect the physical and moral purity of the fighting men sprang up in Britain. Their initial concern was for the purity of British troops and their Commonwealth allies: the Canadians, Australians, and others who came to the aid of the mother country. They were the ones thrust into the larger fray from its outset. Britain's Social Purity and Hygiene Movement was a coalition of church groups, doctors, teachers, feminists, and politicians that focused its attention on curbing the spread of syphilis and gonorrhea amongst soldiers. The concern was not only a matter of moral principle but also of pragmatism: the war had to be won, and men debilitated by disease would not be in any shape for battle.

The purity forces bombarded the troops with leaflets, articles, books, and newspapers that spelled out the ravages of venereal infection and warned against "casual sex" with its carriers: prostitutes and "unashamed amateurs." "Entirely resist" the temptations of "wine and women," was the typical advice. "While treating all women with perfect courtesy . . . avoid any intimacy." It was the double standard flying full out, as if only men could be threatened by disease, and only women could be the source of infection. As the wealthy philanthropist and moral crusader Damer Dawson reprovingly commented, "They talk as if men were innocent angels, helpless in the hands of wicked women."

Miss Dawson disapproved of laxness and depravity in either sex. She founded the Women Police Volunteers in 1914, a group that was soon joined by the Women's Patrols, established in October 1914 and affiliated with the police. Ever on the alert for vice and promiscuity, these bands of mostly middle-class, middle-aged women policed the precincts of military camps and depots, as well as the streets, parks, cinemas, and railway stations of London, looking

45

for couples who were "in a disgraceful position" and telling them to "move on."

The Patrols and Volunteers undoubtedly succeeded more in irritating people than in permanently correcting anyone's morals. Feminists protested that women's personal rights and privacy were being violated. Other women complained that the patrols insulted them with unwarranted accusations of soliciting. And the public in general was fed up with a bunch of "interfering toads" and "busybodies" poking their noses into bushes and shining flashlights in people's faces. In the *Weekly Dispatch* of 8 July 1917, the writer Max Pemberton summed it all up with an alliterative sneer—"the prude on the prowl has ruined London."

The American Purity Front

While the British were organizing their female patrols, American purity advocates continued their already well-established endeavor to provide sexual and moral education for the nation's young people. Among their long-standing concerns was the curbing of both prostitution and venereal disease. When the United States entered the war in April 1917, they redoubled their efforts, doggedly narrowing their sights on the prevention of disease.

Not unlike its British counterpart, the American purity movement was an aggregate of religious, educational, medical, and social reform groups operating at both local and state levels from coast to coast. To combat the looming physical and moral menace that war trailed in its wake, the movement joined forces with the U.S. Army and launched an aggressive propaganda campaign aimed at keeping the boys free from venereal disease. They called for "Purity . . . continence . . . a good vigorous life . . . physical fitness and moral cleanliness." Clearly such admonitions had a moral underpinning, but like Britain's purity effort, it was morality conscripted into the service of practical necessity. A film of the day said it all. Produced to educate servicemen on the transmission, treatment, and avoidable trauma of venereal disease, *Fit to Fight* gave the troops a creed to live by—avoiding infection amounted to no less than patriotic duty. Morality had its place, of course, but the real reason a soldier had to stay healthy was to fight for Uncle Sam and the free world.

On this side of the Atlantic, as in Britain, the biggest perceived threat to hygienic patriotism was the prostitute. Not only did military and civilian purity advocates have to counteract the unAmerican activities of the home-grown version but, as they were all too aware, they also had to "arm" the boys against the wiles of her more lethal sister, the French prostitute. Stateside, the army established five-mile "pure zones" around camps. Female violators were arrested without warrant and imprisoned for ten weeks at a time, on average. Their clients, meanwhile, remained free. Overseas, by order of the American Expeditionary Force's commander, General Pershing, brothels and saloons were off-limits to soldiers. And, at home and abroad, the propaganda blared on. A warning poster read: "Women Who Solicit Soldiers for Immoral Purposes Are Usually Disease Spreaders and Friends of the Enemy."

Not only were women "disease spreaders," they were traitors to their country as well. The scapegoating of prostitutes angered contemporary feminists who regarded men as the sexual predators, not the other way round. This, they felt, was the double standard carried to an outrageous extreme. They might have reflected that in another sense the pressure on men to be continent, though it targeted one group of women, was actually an assault on the double standard. It denied the idea that sexual restraint was strictly a female imperative. Men, too, shared the obligation of self-control—as propagandists and doctors alike kept assuring them, continence was no threat to virility.

Parodoxically, some young people may have been tempted into straying by the very effort that was being made to contain their behavior. The sensationalist frankness that reformers often employed in warning men against consorting with prostitutes and risking venereal infection was the "repeal of reticence" taken to new heights. Though wartime abroad, at home it was still "sex o'clock," and the purity reformers were fanning the flames of the fires they wanted to put out:

> Does any red-blooded man feel any doubt of his ability to preserve his manhood though tempted by the alluring seductions of voluptuous and beautiful women in the whirl and excitement of the gay metropolis, or the fascinations that may come to you from delicate and devoted attentions in the solitude of remote billets?

Put like that, who could resist?

Desperate Pleasures

While the strong-minded (or, perhaps, those most fearful of disease) battled and conquered temptation, others succumbed, or didn't even bother to put up a fight. In the midst of upheaval and destruction they grasped at whatever pleasure came their way.

Some were more reckless than others, with predictable results. Amongst British women, for example, the number of premarital pregnancies held at prewar levels for a time, but by 1916 the rate began to rise, and had increased 30 percent by 1919. Meanwhile, confirming the fears of the moral watchdogs, venereal disease was spreading alarmingly. With as many as 55,000 British soldiers hospitalized at any one time, infection occasionally took a greater toll than that of enemy action.

Commonwealth troops were particularly hard hit; their infection rate was two to three times that of the British. The Canadian prime minister, Robert Borden, called it a "horrible outrage" that the British had better take steps to rectify, or he would refuse to send Canadians overseas again, should a future need arise. American fighting men, on the other hand, fared better. In the twelve months ending on 31 August 1918, for instance, only about 12 percent of soldiers were treated for venereal disease. It may be that army discipline and the streak of puritanism in the American psyche combined to make U.S. doughboys the Western Front models (relatively speaking) of sexual hygiene.

That so many servicemen knowingly risked their health for what was usually casual and hasty sex is not hard to understand. In battle, elemental instincts take charge. When faced with the possibility of killing or being killed, "it was unwise to think," as one soldier expressed it. During their all too brief respites from the front lines, the men still, naturally enough, operated on instinct. Under the terrible duress of wartime, the pleasure reflex could not be denied.

The rising star of sexual theory, Sigmund Freud, explained it as the subconscious psychological connection between the two extremes of human experience—the urge to kill and the urge to procreate. This, he said, was manifested in wartime society's tendency to discard the restraints that civilization imposes on the human sexual impulse. The war poet Siegfried Sassoon expressed a similar idea, with the searing vividness of one whose insights were not theoretical, but based on first-hand knowledge of the reality. His 1916 verse composed in a front-line trench near Morlancourt, France, spoke for many:

In my heart there's cruel war that must be waged
In darkness vile with moans and bleeding bodies maimed;
A gnawing hunger drives me, wild to be assuaged,
And bitter lust chuckles within me unashamed.

Many young British women, too, who were far from being prostitutes, indulged in what the romance novelist Marie Corelli delicately called "foolish sensualities." Female workers serving across the
Channel, had reportedly gone "war-mad and sex-mad." The WAACs
(Women's Army Auxiliary Corps) soon developed a reputation as
providers of sexual gratification for the soldiers, and there was a
good deal of insinuation about the eroticism of nurses. "They dress
the wounded and undress themselves"—so ran the risqué humor
of the day, while a wartime pop song put it more politely: "I Don't
Want to Get Well—I'm in Love with a Beautiful Nurse." Much of
it was undoubtedly exaggeration. But not all—as suggested by a
sprinkling of pregnancies among WAACs, and by the availability
near army camps of rooms for short but presumably sweet trysts.

It was rumored that French women not to be outdone, gave
themselves freely to any desirous soldier heading to the front lines.
A British staff officer serving in France, General F. P. Crozier, was
suggestively approached by the twenty-year-old daughter of the
household in which he was billeted. A man of unwavering character, the general resisted the young woman's advances. But others
were not so scrupulous. On one occasion, when he inspected the
kit of two young officers, among other "astounding" items, the
general discovered "two pairs of girls' garters . . . two pairs of silk
stockings . . . one nightdress . . . a pot of vaseline, a candle . . . and
an envelope full of astonishing picture postcards."

"Souvenirs, sir," was the explanation.

The writer Philip Gibbs remembered the shopgirls of Amiens
who pleasurably occupied the few hours' leave he and other sol-

diers were allowed after the 1916 battle of the Somme. There was no time for any "romantic episode, save of a transient kind, between them and these good-looking lads in whose eyes there were desire and hunger." Their encounters were brief, and nearly anonymous, but "to these men—boys, mostly—who had been living in lousy ditches under hell fire, Amiens was Paradise."

"Mademaselles" from All Around

Swelling the ranks of willing "amateurs" like the shopgirls of Amiens were all the women whose daily business was the pleasure of others. The parents of Commonwealth soldiers who wrote their governments asking that their sons be kept away from Paris, and its supposed hordes of prostitutes, would have been shocked to learn that London was worse—hundreds of women nightly worked the Strand alone. And with no homes to return to in London, Commonwealth soldiers on leave were especially vulnerable to the lure of prostitution.

And of course, the reports of French prostitution were by no means unfounded. Brothels abounded in centers like Calais, Le Havre, and Rouen. They did a thriving business in more out-of-the way places, too—one establishment, in the little seaside town of Cayeux-sur-Mer, served an average of 360 men a day. They lined up on the sidewalk outside, while the uncurtained windows afforded a preview of what was on offer inside.

The unleashed lust that compelled so many young men toward brothels was not just the companion of war—it was also the nagging consort of acute loneliness. The American writer Katherine Mayo was moved by the all-consuming "aching restlessness," the "homesick longings," of the servicemen she met in France. "Never dare to judge," she warned her readers sternly, "[you who have] escaped the torments that he, in his racked and quivering nerves, so long endured."

A brief encounter, however tawdry, still meant a few moments of comfort and physical warmth. For many men, it was the only available substitute for what they really wanted—home, and the one who most embodied it, a girl from home. "The doughboy who would respond to a French woman of the streets," Mayo declared, "when he knew that he could go to the Y and meet a clean, sweet, friendly American girl, was so rare as scarcely to count." By the standard of later taste the smug piety of her tone was overdone. Still, she had a point.

Give Us a Girl from Home!

"Send us an American girl . . . we *do* want some real American ladies so *awful* bad!"

"By God! . . . it's been so long since I've heard a decent woman's voice that I'm just going round and round!"

"Would you mind—would you *just turn round*, ma'am, and let us look at you?"

These were the voices of American soldiers—they revealed the "hunger" for "home women" that Katherine Mayo often observed and admired. The sentiments would have struck a reverberant chord in the hearts of all the other servicemen from Canada and Britain alike who also longed fervently for the girls they had left behind. Fortunately for the men's morale, many women were not content to remain at home and insisted on getting into the thick of the action.

Some civilians and army officers initially objected to women going to the front, arguing that they would "be in the way . . . could not stand the physical strain . . . would only embarrass the men . . . be themselves disgusted with contact with common soldiers." But in the end women proved their critics wrong. Over and over they demonstrated just how little they were in the way, and how much they could do, even under fire.

One overseas Y worker received an American Army citation for "valor on the field":

> Miss Frances Gulick . . . remained at her post . . . and with total disregard for her own personal safety, continued to operate her canteen, although the town was shelled and bombed at different times by the enemy, and her canteen itself struck.

Not only intrepid, Miss Gulick was also "glorious to behold" and versatile in her abilities. She cooked, entertained the soldiers by reading aloud and telling stories, mended their shirts, sewed on chevrons, repaired cars, and drove transport vehicles "along the shell-swept midnight roads with an unbroken steadiness and a superb, laughing dash." Katherine Mayo gave this "heroine of history" full credit but hastened to add that she was not a "particular bright light," but "a fair common example, in character and in record," of many women who served at the front.

Certainly, whether they dodged shellfire or not, women at the front all saw active duty as valued workers and companions. In contrast to the gruesomeness of war were the moments of comfort shared between the fighting men and their "home women." A French photographer captured one such moment. Seated on wooden chairs amidst the ruins of a bombed-out village are two young American women, heads bent, sewing industriously. Standing around them is a cluster of six doughboys. The picture looks posed, but only just. The relaxed smiles and grins of the boys, the studied diligence and lingering smiles of the girls suggest that they have just that moment composed themselves for the camera, and that seconds before they were absorbed in lively exchange, tossing jokes back and forth. Many decades later the laughter still hangs in the picture's faintly smoky air.

Many other such scenes of wartime camaraderie between the sexes also survive in the suspended animation of old photographs. Women, smiling from under ever-present hats, serving food from mobile canteens to queues of soldiers. A pretty nurse, dark hair escaping from its wimple-like covering, sitting companionably at the bedside of a convalescent soldier. A woman from home strumming a guitar for three doughboys, the group perching on the rubble of the front. Uniformed nurses and soldiers fishing together from a Red Cross barge in France.

Elsewhere on the same front, in pencil, ink, and charcoal, the artist and magazine illustrator C. Leroy Baldridge, an American infantry private, deftly sketched his own impressions of men and women together. The encounters he portrayed were fleeting— a smiling glance between a girl and a soldier, or an unabashed leer and a quick response: "Steady Buddy," says an attractive young woman to a doughboy in one sketch. At times, perhaps in imagination more than reality, a nice girl from "over there" stood in for a girl from home, and momentarily assuaged a soldier's aching homesickness. Baldridge's charcoal deftly stroked in a buxom French girl in peasant-like garb. She laughs as an American soldier leans against the doorway in which she stands and assures her, "I know a girl at home who looks just like you."

Baldridge's friend, a fellow private and sometime poet, Hilmar (Buck) Baukhage, used verse to record another such bittersweet encounter between a soldier and a French girl who might almost have been from home. "I stood there," recalls the soldier,

Kidding her in bon fransay
But the things that I was thinking
Were a thousand miles away.

Sewed my stripe on like a mother,
Gee! She was a pretty kid. . . .
But I left her like a brother,—
Shake her hand was all I did.

Then I says: "Vous, all right, cherry—"
And my throat stuck and it hurt. . . .
And I showed her what I carry
In the pocket of my shirt.

New Intimacies, New Ideals

Some encounters between men and women remained brotherly
and innocent, as in the poetic scenario of the American soldier and
the French girl. The informalities that wartime permitted were in
themselves new intimacies, and often in themselves sufficient to
those who shared them. But men being men, and women being
women, many of their newly relaxed exchanges were hardly as platonic as sentimental verse and discreet pictorial records liked to
suggest.

At times the sexual tension was all but unbearable. The English
autobiographer Vera Brittain, who served as a wartime nurses'
aide, recollected one such charged encounter with her fiancé
Roland:

We sat on the sofa till midnight, talking very quietly. The still-
ness heavy-laden with the dull oppression of the snowy night,
became so electric with emotion that we were frightened of
one another, and dared not let even our fingers touch for fear
that the love between us should render what we both believed
to be decent behaviour suddenly unendurable.

"Roland went to the front on March 31st 1915," Brittain remembered with sad clarity. "It was Wednesday in Passion Week . . . He died of wounds at a Casualty Clearing Station on December 23rd."

The couple never consummated their powerful attraction, and others like them also managed to honor the old code of "decent behaviour." Others did not, or could not, restrain themselves. Though contemporary commentary undoubtedly overstated the loose standards of nurses, WAACs, and "sex-mad" women, sexual liaisons between some men and women at the front were inevitable. As Vera Brittain poignantly recalled, "France was the scene of titanic, illimitable death, and for this reason it had become the heart of the fiercest living ever known to any generation."

Even advertising reflected the new freedoms and intimacies that grew in the shadow of war. A 1916 cigarette advertisement shows an off-duty soldier enjoying a romantic outing with a female companion. As they glide along a secluded waterway in a small boat he sits back relaxed, his arm in a sling, while the woman rows—an image that spoke of both war's human toll and the attendant breaking down of conventional sexual roles and restraints. He suggests that they find a "nice quiet corner," "tie up in the shade for a bit" and enjoy "a soothing and seductive" cigarette together. Full of sexual innuendo, the advertisement also reflected a changing social pattern. In the duress of war, girls not only consorted with men unchaperoned, but they also smoked.

In a few cases, couples who could not resist the "soothing seductions" of togetherness chose the conventional path to consummation, and the occasional marriage took place at the front. Katherine Mayo witnessed the wedding of a young American soldier and his girl (about whom she is maddeningly silent). Under the circumstances it had to be a makeshift event, but ingenuity and good will turned it into "a real wedding—the whole—regular—

full-blown thing." Held in a decorated hut, it included "music and ushers and a best man, and . . . a wedding breakfast and dancing for all the guests . . . All the A.E.F. that could get there took part in the entire proceedings with thrills of joy."

Yet, though love sometimes kindled, and sexuality often flared, it was war, after all. So much of what men and women endured together could not possibly have sparked lust, or romance, or sentiment. Too often there was only "broken human flesh"—the words of the American Mary Borden who ran a hospital unit at the front. When the wounded came in,

> the air was thick with steaming sweat, with the effluvia of mud, dirt, blood. The men lay in their stiff uniforms that were caked with mud and dried blood, their great boots on their feet; stained bandages showing where a trouser leg or sleeve had been cut away.

Vera Brittain saw similar horrors, recalling, too, the new intimacies that caring for weak and wounded men entailed: "Short of actually going to bed with them, there was hardly an intimate service that I did not perform for one or another in the course of four years." Yet at the end of it all, she wrote movingly that while "there was much to shock in Army hospital service, much to terrify, much, even, to disgust, this day-by-day contact with male anatomy was never part of the shame." She also recalled feeling "an almost adoring gratitude," that the men demonstrated "a simple and natural acceptance of my ministrations."

And in the mire of death and destruction she "came to understand the essential cleanliness, the innate nobility of sexual love on its physical side." The war changed her attitude to the relationship of men and women—"it became less romantic and more realistic" but also added "a new depth" to her capacity to love.

No one who was "over there" could have remained as innocent of sexual matters as they had been in those long-ago days of home and peace. But at the same time, like Vera Brittain, the men and women who served together also developed a fresh and informed mutual respect that, for a time, enriched the new sexual knowledge of the young century. As Katherine Mayo observed, what came out of the war was "a new ideal of relationship between men and women . . . it showed forth the supreme beauty of the spirit"—not the spirit of men or of women distinctively, but the human spirit of both together.

The Return of Peace and Pleasure

In the euphoric frenzy of the November 1918 armistice, people cared only that war had ended and peace had begun. They celebrated by doing what came naturally and worrying about the consequences later. Strangers danced together in the streets of London, kissed with abandon, and made love in doorways and alleys. In the hometowns of America people were more restrained, but there, too, caught up in the emotion of homecoming, doughboys kissed hometown girls with all the appetite of starving men. Shocked or thrilled, and mostly inexperienced, the young women concluded that this must be the way it was done overseas—and a new name for an old pleasure soon came into being. They called it "French kissing."

The surging tide of sexual licence soon subsided, but it set a tone for the future. Although people rejoiced in peace, they were also disillusioned. Katherine Mayo wrote that the "growth of spirit"—the new ideal realized in the war—had "returned complete to our soil" and "should most certainly continue to operate." But in fact it did not happen that way. War had stolen the new century's optimism and something else had to fill the void. The substitute of choice was sexual pleasure.

The war's "beautiful revelation" of men and women's shared need for one another, not only as sexual but as human beings, did not transplant to home soil intact. Instead, the heightened expectations of sexual freedom and pleasure that had burgeoned before 1914, and grown all the stronger over the years of conflict, would dominate the next two decades. The young men and women who had lived through the flames of war were about to join forces with the so-called flaming youth of a new era.

III

IN THE THROES
OF CHANGE

1920−1939

The decade of the 1920s was a time of new sexual liberation, of postwar relief and release. The sexes related to each other with more freedom, knowledge, and expectation of gratification than ever before.

When the Great Depression intruded, all too suddenly as it must have seemed, people thrust frivolity aside, their first priority now economic survival. In the midst of the crisis men and women sought comfort in one another. At times, their encounters grew out of a desperate need to compensate for other gratifications that were now unavailable.

In the two decades following the Great War the changes and upheavals were vast. Modern permissiveness vied with conservative morality, and everyday life in many ways became unrecognizable from what it had been. Through it all, men and women's cultivation of the pleasures of one another's company was intense. Yet for all that they gained in sexual enlightenment and experience, many found happiness elusive. Something vital still seemed to be missing.

A Clash of Moralities

> The sexual morals of the community will be
> found to consist of several layers. There are
> first the positive institutions embodied in law;
> such, for example, as monogamy in some countries
> and polygamy in others. Next there is a layer
> where law does not intervene but public opinion
> is emphatic. And lastly there is a layer which is left
> to individual discretion, in practice if not in theory.
>
> — BERTRAND RUSSELL, *Marriage and Morals*

The 1920s careened onto the scene of history with a screech and a roar. Wild young college men and their daring flapper girlfriends piled into that still new but ever more indispensable invention, the automobile—endlessly joyriding in pursuit of the latest thrills. United in their postwar lust for pleasure and release, the sexes ran fast and free with one another.

Women bobbed their hair, shortened their skirts, rolled down their hose, and boldly flaunted their cigarettes. Prohibition might be the law, but a hip flask in the pocket was every man's rule of thumb. Crazed for dancing and for sex, couples turkey-trotted, muskrat-rambled, boogie-woogied, charlestoned, and shimmied in steamy dance halls and at "petting parties" where guests wore no more than bathing suits or pyjamas.

Moral values were crumbling, especially amongst the young, who laughed defiantly in the face of convention. It was the era of hot jazz and overheated fun—as the obscure 1920s novelist Warner Fabian put it, a torrid new age of "flaming youth."

Then came the stock market crash of 1929, followed by the Great Depression of the 1930s. Suddenly faced with economic disaster, flaming youth settled down and sobered up. Morality grew more conservative as financial anxieties grew, because extravagant dating and entertainments were too expensive. Sex and fun, if they were to be had at all, were rare treats that men and women all too often experienced only vicariously, in the still rich and romantic world of Hollywood movies. "Makin' Whoopee!" had given way to "Brother, Can You Spare a Dime?"

A decade of color, noise, and excitement, followed by the dreary and subdued "dirty thirties"—this is the stereotypical recollection of the two decades following the Great War. But in fact, in the developing relationship of the sexes, the 1920s and 1930s were not as distinctly different from one another as the cliché suggests. Trends that had originated in the 1920s or even earlier played out their next act in the 1930s.

In his internationally published *Marriage and Morals* (1929), the English philosopher Bertrand Russell observed that the "morals of the community"—the postwar sexual code—"consisted of several layers." Prohibitions and permissiveness often went hand in hand, and what people adhered to in public was not always what they did in private. Many contradictory attitudes marked the 1920s and 1930s, especially when it came to family life, sexual behavior, and the present and future relationship of the sexes.

The heart of it all was a clash between old and new moral standards. For a great transition was under way—in effect, a sexual and social revolution that was to bring about new sexual freedoms and knowledge as well as growth and shifts in the ideal of equitable, companionate marriage. It was part of the larger revolution of self, the surge toward individual fulfillment that had gathered momentum at the beginning of the century. The so-called flaming youth were in reality an elite, avant-garde minority, who in their extreme fashion were merely acting out the predominant trends of their day. A few of these had originated with young people themselves and diffused into the wider populace. Most were a youthful response to the accelerating change that was the aftermath of war.

The Flaunted and the Forbidden

Between 1920 and 1933 the Volstead Act, named for its author, the Republican Congressman Andrew Volstead, banned the American manufacture, transport, importation, and sale of liquor. Born of a conservative morality, the prohibition of alcohol produced a result wildly contrary to the one intended. Crime, corruption, and the original source of concern   drink   all flourished. The new speakeasies far outnumbered the old saloons, and otherwise law-abiding citizens boasted of their exploits with such renegade brews as "Cherry Dynamite," "Old Stingo," and "Jamaica Ginger," a 90-proof (45 percent alcohol) libation familiarly known as "Jake," and notorious for causing temporary paralysis among those who survived at all. Canada's more moderate and flexible prohibition laws were no more effective. Public drinking not only persisted, it actually increased, and more than half of at least one Maritime fishing fleet was involved in rum-running.

Prohibition was one of the supreme signs of an age when some flaunted what others believed should be strictly forbidden. Such contradiction went far beyond the issue of drink, showing itself even more flagrantly where women, men, and their relationship were concerned.

Take, for instance, another icon of the age, the flapper. Now legendary, she smoked, drank, made free with her body, and generally caroused with abandon. There were also some real historical figures who approximated this caricature. The archetypal flapper, in large part her inventor, was the notorious Zelda, wife of the novelist F. Scott Fitzgerald. Half of what *The New Yorker* billed as "the best looking couple in modern literary society," Zelda partied wildly, danced on tables, and dove into fountains, all at a breakneck pace, until her extravagant way of life eventually caught up with her. From 1930 on, she suffered from acute anxiety and would spend the remaining eighteen years of her life in and out of mental institutions, until her death in a hospital fire at the age of forty-eight.

Wild young women like Zelda were in fact quite rare. The flapper was in large part the creation of a moral panic fueled by a sensationalist, fundamentally conservative press that did its best to stir up fears about youthful sexuality, the decadence of bobbed hair, and the "abomination" of jazz, whose "sensuous stimulation" had "tremendously evil potential" to "relax morality and undermine the institution of the family." Such was the opinion of the *Ladies' Home Journal* in 1921, and the danger to youth was not to be minimized—in the fervent words of one of the magazine's contributors, John McMahon, "God help your child."

Florid though its prose was, the *Journal* was right about one thing—the contest of moral outlooks was not only between new and old, but also between young people and their elders. The flapper was a focus of moral panic because she stood for youth, its sexuality, and the changing sexual values that many of the young espoused.

College students were among those who prided themselves on demonstrating the new ways. Bright, affluent, and full of defiant ideas about the prudery of their parents, they popularized petting or "sex play," which covered a range of activities from kissing to more intimate fondling. But even among the daring college youth of the 1920s and 1930s petting was a prelude to finding the right mate, an exploration whose ultimate goal was marriage. The double standard continued to operate: virginity was still prized in a wife, and while "popularity with boys" made petting "the right thing to do" for most girls, both sexes widely condemned a "fast woman." Such was the conclusion of contemporary sociological studies on American campuses. In other words, more often than not the so-called flaming youth was still traditional enough to settle for a slow burn.

Sex Appeal: Flat Versus Fat

Fashions in clothing and the ideal of sexual attractiveness continued to emphasize slim, youthful bodies for both sexes and—especially for women—showing them off. The dresses of the 1920s routinely bared more arm and leg than ever before, fabrics were thinner and clingier than in the past, undergarments fewer and lighter—the day of the boned corset was long past. Feminine fashion signaled the new sexual availability of the modern women.

To hang properly, the tubelike, lightweight "flapper" dresses of the day demanded a slim figure, and cultural pressure on women to diet intensified. The new cigarette-smoking woman did not acquire the habit merely as a sign of her modern liberation. A double enslavement, smoking for many women became their first strategy in weight control. "Reach for a Lucky instead of a Sweet" was the advice of one of the century's most successful advertising campaigns.

With boyish slenderness in vogue breasts were now a problem for the generously and even the moderately endowed. In 1922 the American beauty expert Florence Courtenay recommended as an ideal bust measurement an impossible-sounding 28.8 inches. To control what had changed from a source of womanly pride and attractiveness to unsightly fatty extrusions, some women took to wearing breast binders, a flattening type of brassiere that enclosed the body smoothly from chest to waist. At a time when restraint was going out of style, it was ironic that fashion demanded the suppression of one of the most visible signs of female sexuality. And men did not fail to notice and to respond, not necessarily with approval. In a letter to the sex expert Marie Stopes, one husband complained that his wife had taken to wearing "Corslet Brazziers" to "hide her figure" so as to "appear slim in order to be fashionable."

With or without breast binders, there's no doubt that many women were unable to meet the fashionable ideal of slimness. Early Hollywood movie musicals had featured lines of pretty but by later standards overweight chorus girls, high-kicking hefty legs that would soon become entirely unacceptable for aspiring starlets. Most of the big stars of both the 1920s and 1930s ranged from at least moderately slim to ultra-sleek—Clara Bow, Marlene Dietrich, Irene Dunne, Greta Garbo, Lillian Gish, and Norma Shearer, to name a few.

The notable exception was the plump and buxom sex symbol Mae West, who was frequently on the defensive about her weight. In the May 1933 issue of *Screen Book* magazine, she told her interviewer, Frederick James Smith, precisely what was wrong with the modern ideal of thinness:

Don't tell me you think I ought to reduce. I think that the pictures are all wrong in the way they feature starved ingenues. You know, the flat-chested girls you see on the screen. If I know men, I know . . . they don't care for scrawny girls. They want something to get their hands on when they grab a girl. Or am I wrong? Continued reducing makes those Hollywood girls look like those neediest cases you hear about. Pained faces, sharp shoulders, knobby knees, terrible spaces between their legs. So flat you can't tell which way they're going.

A few months later, in the November 1933 issue of the magazine, she added:

Now understand me, I do not mean any sudden swelling out. To the bulging bosom and hips I say no! To graceful curves, yes. There is no use kidding ourselves: We're feminine and such things as bosoms do exist and they have come back. Flat chests are as taboo and outdated as yesterday's paper.

Though her image in publicity photos needed constant paring down through retouching, the woman who was "Diamond Lil" and "Lady Lou"—the modern incarnation of the now unfashionably curvaceous "belle of the nineties"—proved to know what she was talking about. In the 1930s the lithe body remained in, now often shown off in tight, clinging, bias-cut crepe de chine. But at the same time, the bosom had come back. The bras of the 1930s reflected the change, and instead of flattening the breasts, they incorporated circular stitching to enhance roundness, with the added innovation of what would become the standard for fit—the alphabetically designated A, B, C, or D cup.

While women smoked and dieted, men too were under cultural pressure to achieve and maintain a high standard of attractiveness.

But rather than zeroing in on a particular part of the body, such as the bosom, the masculine ideal of the 1920s and 1930s addressed the whole man. As with women, the main idea was to preserve or to recapture the look of healthy attractive youth. Magazine advertising promoted an array of products for men—toothpaste for bad breath, talcum powder along with palm and olive soap for body odor, Aqua Velva for "young looking" skin, and assorted hair products to prevent baldness, a condition that advertising particularly deplored. "Bald or good-looking"—this was the stark choice with which promoters of hair tonics fueled the anxieties of potential consumers.

Worse than baldness was fat. Like his feminine counterpart, the youthful and desirable man had to be slender, an ideal already well established before the war, but all the more insistent in the next two decades. The growth of the Hollywood film industry provided role models that average men not long ago might never have encountered. Now there were few who could remain unaware of the need to cultivate what *Physical Culture* magazine extolled as Rudolph Valentino's "hunky" athleticism, the purported source of his legendary attraction for women. Another muscular paragon was Douglas Fairbanks who, at the age of thirty-eight, was "as young as ever," according to *Physical Culture* in 1921. Famed for such exotic romps as *The Thief of Bagdad* (1924), Fairbanks was not about to "settle down to become ever softer and more physically flabby." As the magazine commentator assured readers, he had "the dash that represents the spirit of American youth."

The ideal embodied in Fairbanks and Valentino implicitly warned men that if they were not to fall flat with the ladies, merely conquering fat was not enough. The man who wanted to be truly attractive to women also had to develop the muscles of an athlete. This became all the more imperative in the late 1920s and 1930s as fashion in bathing suits now uncovered the upper part of the male body, almost to the point of wearing "No Suit at All," as one ad by Spalding put it.

Scrawny was not going to cut it with the ladies at beach parties—think "what a shock to some of the poor girls when they see their heroes come out with flat chests and skinny arms," was *Physical Culture's* dire warning to the unfit. A 1928 advertisement for Murad cigarettes drove home the point. The possibly disappointing first sight of her fiancé in a bathing suit could be an "emotional moment" in a young flapper's life. The best thing for her to do was to light up a cigarette—presumably to avoid the undesirably fattening alternative of squelching her feelings in a box of soft-centered chocolates.

It was no secret that at the heart of fashionable preoccupations with body image was the desire to attract the opposite sex, perhaps even to find true passion. Men's sex appeal could be spoken of frankly. "Sex appeal is in the main a masculine commodity," declared the critic Gilbert Seldes in the *New Republic* for 21 April 1926. "He-vamp, sophisticated sinner, or great lover—it does not matter if he has sex appeal."

For women, the new sex appeal still held some of the old reticence. While a woman's attractiveness had much to do with flaunting her body, there remained an aura of the forbidden surrounding the enterprise. Girls were apt to speak euphemistically of being "popular" rather than sexually alluring, which is what they really meant. A new slang term emerged that might be applied to both sexes but seems to have carried a more particularly feminine connotation. From the late 1920s and into the 1930s the word of the day for sex appeal was "it." Such a delicately neutered term might in part have reflected the contemporary double standard, but even more clearly, it was an indication of the layered code of the time. Even the forward-looking, sexually aware young still occasionally fell back on the old ways of discretion.

Sinners and Censors

The majority of young men and women were moderates, doing their best to find their way toward one another in a world of new and changing sexual standards. A few explored the extremes of that world, the realm of what others simply deemed to be sin. And where sinners flourished, so did the censors.

Among the most daring explorers of new frontiers in the relationship of the sexes were members of the literary crowd. In the 1920s the writer and critic Edmund Wilson was a young literary man about New York, working for various magazines including *Vanity Fair*. During that time he kept a series of notebooks in which he chronicled his short-lived marriage to the actress Mary Blair, his various sexual entanglements, and those of the literary stars in whose orbit he moved. Among others, he knew the Fitzgeralds, John Dos Passos, E. E. Cummings, Eugene O'Neill, Dorothy Parker, and the poet Edna St. Vincent Millay, for whom he had an unreciprocated infatuation.

A sensualist, Wilson was deeply fascinated with the opposite sex, and he described, in great detail, the women he bedded and those he merely observed. Some of his descriptions were relatively discreet. A girl he saw on the beach—"straight slender-legged Swedish-looking blond girl in red bathing suit with . . . well-developed pretty girl's breasts which were not yet excessive for her tall slim figure." Or an encounter with a New Orleans prostitute—

> She was anxious to get through with it as quickly and with as little sentimentality as possible. Wouldn't take off her clothes, didn't want me to take off mine, didn't want to be kissed for fear of disturbing her rouge . . . simply threw herself on her back across the bed with her feet hanging down at the side and pulled her skirts up over her stomach.

Wilson was also capable of much greater candor and graphic detail. Perhaps in emulation of contemporaries such as D. H. Lawrence and James Joyce, he sprinkled many of his accounts with four-letter words. It was all in the avant-garde spirit that espoused sexual openness with increasing boldness. Wilson was only one of many who recorded their erotic exploits in the 1920s and 1930s. He was by no means the most graphic.

Anaïs Nin, the author of both critical studies and erotica such as *Little Birds* and *Delta of Venus*, was a prolific keeper of taboo-breaking journals throughout the 1930s. One of these revealed her incestuous liaison with her father. In others she recollected and savored her many affairs with now obscure artists, actors, and poets, as well as with her psychoanalysts, who included Otto Rank. Her best-known lover was Henry Miller, the author of steamy novels. More even than Zelda Fitzgerald, she lived the life of the sexually free woman. Commenting with self-centered melodrama on her taste for many lovers, she wrote: "I can only add, expand. I cannot break, dissolve, push away . . . I cannot be myself without causing a tragedy. But tragedy is living."

But while the literary set took it as a creative duty to flaunt their sexuality in their personal lives and to describe the previously unmentionable in their writings, not everyone was in sympathy with their high-minded mission. In the 1920s and 1930s several books dealing explicitly with sexuality all fell under the shadow of censorship. Among the most notorious cases were Joyce's *Ulysses*, Lawrence's *Lady Chatterley's Lover*, and Miller's *Tropic of Cancer*, all of which were prosecuted for obscenity. A New York district court judge exonerated *Ulysses* in 1933, to the unbounded delight of its defending attorney, Morris L. Ernst.

"The New Deal in the law of letters is here," he declared. "The *Ulysses* case . . . is a body blow for the censors . . . Writers need no longer seek refuge in euphemisms. They may now describe basic human functions without fear of the law." Ernst's triumphant declaration was premature. *Ulysses* was vindicated, but Lawrence's and Miller's books would not see unexpurgated publication in Britain and North America for almost another thirty years.

Hollywood, City of Sin

The legal debate over art versus obscenity was likely not a consuming preoccupation of the average woman or man as they worked out their relationship with one another. But another target of censorship was closer to their hearts. Virtually everyone, after all, went to the movies.

In the early 1930s vaudeville was in decline. Though sensual dance routines, suggestive dialogue, and racy skits, often featuring male-female teams, had drawn large audiences just before and for a few years after the war, on-stage titillation increasingly paled beside the more florid seductions of the big screen. By 1922 Hollywood movies were a major industry, and sex played no small part in its growth.

Theda Bara had made her last "vamp" movie in 1919, but in the next decade her successors captivated audiences with their own alluring performances. Some are well remembered—Clara Bow, Dietrich, Garbo, Pola Negri. Others now faded in memory were no less provocative in their time—the sensuous Mae Murray with her "famous dancing feet"; Dorothy Mackaill, in *The Dancer of Paris*, wearing nothing but stones and beadwork, stripping for the finale; or Madge Bellamy showing nearly everything, in *Black Paradise*, one of the popular desert-island pictures whose scenarios gave generous employment to bare-breasted extras.

But even in the Hollywood of the roaring twenties, the forces of censorship were in play. Various voices speaking out for conservative morality, most notably the Catholic Church, had been calling for film censorship since before the war. But the campaign stepped up in 1921 following the infamous Fatty Arbuckle scandal. A young model, Virginia Rappe, died at a drunken party given by Arbuckle who had allegedly ruptured her bladder while raping her. The once popular film comedian was tried and eventually acquitted, but his career was over, and the public cried out for official regulation of sinful Hollywood's moral standards, both on and off the screen.

To satisfy the public and to protect their box office profits, the movie companies formed a coalition whose head was Postmaster General Will Hays. Together, Hays and the industry instituted a morals clause in performers' contracts and established a set of guidelines to what was acceptable on screen. This would become the Hays Code of 1930, which proscribed nudity, "lustful embraces," "suggestive postures," "indecent" dance movements, and such themes as white slavery, perversion, and rape.

The Code notwithstanding, sex continued to flourish on the silver screen of the 1930s in obscure films with suggestive titles like *Hot Stuff, Street Girl,* and *Tarnished Lady.* Clark Gable, Jean Harlow, and Mary Astor were a lustful romantic triangle in the *Red Dust* of Indochina (1932); in *Tarzan, the Ape Man* (1932) Johnny Weissmuller and Maureen O'Sullivan frolicked semi-nakedly; and Mae West freely purred out seductive one-liners in *Night After Night* (1932), *She Done Him Wrong,* and *I'm No Angel* (both 1933).

West had already been prosecuted and briefly jailed in 1927 for writing and performing in a play deemed "obscene." Its straight-to-the-heart-of-things title—*Sex*—was pure (so to speak) Mae West. A seasoned hand with censors by the 1930s, she had her way of getting around the Hays Code. She wrote offensive scenes as decoys, to distract the censors from the suggestive material she wanted to protect. They duly cut the deliberately provocative parts, while failing to notice the rest—as she had intended. "Censorship *made* me," she would tell an interviewer many years later.

Not every movie star of the 1930s could make the same claim. In 1934 the newly formed Catholic Legion of Decency and other groups that took a similarly dim view of Hollywood morality exerted increasing pressure on the Hays office to enforce the regulatory code. The office complied and in the main the movies that followed were tamer. Roaring Hollywood had been quietened—although not entirely.

In 1939 David O. Selznick released his version of Margaret Mitchell's Civil War romantic epic *Gone with the Wind.* The movie's final form was the product of much wrangling and compromise with the censors. Though no one was convinced, Rhett Butler's paramour Belle Watling passed as a saloon owner with a heart of gold, rather than the madam she really was, and near the movie's end the spousal rape scene took on romantic hues. But one crucial point of dispute remained unchanged from the novel. In his last words to Scarlett, Rhett expressed his disillusionment with her, just as Mitchell had conceived it. Though the Code called it profanity, he got away with not giving "a damn."

While critics voiced fears that one "damn" might figuratively undam a deluge of curse words, moviegoing audiences apparently did not share the concern. *Gone with the Wind* was hugely popular, and though some might have been mildly shocked, there was no mass outrage at the affront to polite speech. This was hardly surprising. Engaged in their own pursuit of passion, men and women must have sat in darkened theaters excited and enthralled at Scarlett and Rhett's stormy love affair and its vivid backdrop. As for one swear word that everybody had already heard anyway, who, frankly, would give a damn?

Sex, Cars, and Movie Theaters

The clash of opposites—of prohibitionists against hard drinkers, of advocates of sexual and artistic freedom against book burners and moral censors—was the unmistakable sign of an era of upheaval. As early as 1918 the Austrian psychoanalyst Wilhelm Reich had proclaimed the onset of a sexual revolution. He continued to make the assertion throughout the 1920s, and by the mid-1930s had spread the idea to North America. He obsessively promoted his notion that the cure for all neuroses was orgasm—to be achieved as frequently and fully as possible. This, along with other questionable theories, got him expelled from the International Psychoanalytical Association in 1934.

Later commentators, however, would vindicate his view that a sexual revolution was under way by the 1920s. Fears of flaming youth and immoral flappers running amok were sensationalist exaggerations, but even so, the first great sexual revolution of the twentieth century was especially noticeable among the young. Parents complained that their offspring had become much too bold, and Dr. Clelia Mosher, a lecturer in personal hygiene at Stanford and author of a pioneering sex survey in the 1890s, had her "sense of decent reticence constantly shocked" as students of the 1920s openly expressed their "new thinking and new ideals." Young people were also changing their behavior, as they came together in the relative seclusion of darkened theaters and under cover of the steamed-up windows of the family Model T.

Dating was now the norm among young women and men at all social levels, and sexual experimentation was no longer confined to the petting parties of a few privileged college students, according to Robert and Helen Lynd. They were first-hand observers and authors of a sociological study of one representative small city in the American Midwest. Among other local customs in "Middletown," as they called it, the Lynds looked at the dating habits of young people during the year 1924.

If movie houses were "lovers' lanes" before the war, the study implied, they were all the more so after it, the traffic hotter and heavier. Middletown's young people regularly crowded into the local movie houses. "How life is being quickened by the movies for youngsters," the Lynds delicately mused. And indeed it was. The movies of choice offered "neckers, petters, white kisses, red kisses . . . the truth bold, naked, sensational," as one advertisement ran. Local high school teachers were convinced that the movies were "a powerful factor in bringing about the 'early sophistication' of the young and the relaxing of social taboos."

The other "powerful factor" was the automobile. By the end of 1923, two out of three Middletown families owned a car, the majority late models. As the Lynds put it, "ownership of an automobile has now reached the point of being an accepted essential of normal living." It also quickly became contested ground between parents and adolescents. "'What on earth *do* you want me to do? Just sit around home all evening!' retorted a popular high school girl," whose father had "discouraged her going out motoring for the evening with a young blade in a rakish car."

The "use of the automobile" was one of the most common "sources of disagreement" between high school students and their parents. The parental reservations were understandable, for the automobile was "blasting its way" through old assumptions about how leisure time should be spent and the amount of control and chaperonage appropriate for young people—"emotionally charged sanctions and taboos," as the Lynds observed. In some cases, parents' worst fears came true. In the year preceding 1 September 1924, thirty girls appeared in juvenile court charged with unspecified "sex crimes." Of these, "nineteen were listed as having committed the offense in an automobile."

Most young people stopped short of committing "sex crimes" (or at least didn't get caught), and continued to delay "going all the way" until marriage. Even so, in providing new places of privacy that encouraged sexual experimentation, cars and movie theaters contributed to changes in behavior that would have been unthinkable among all but the hopelessly "depraved" only a decade or so earlier. A survey by a London doctor showed that one in five women born before 1904 had engaged in premarital intercourse, while for those born between 1904 and 1914, the figure rose to one in three. In the United States the change in the sexual behavior of unmarried women was less rapid. But all the same, those who admitted to going all the way were becoming more numerous: 23 per cent born between 1900 and 1909, rising to 31 per cent among those who reached sexual maturity in the late 1930s. The shift in behavior reflected a wider change in attitude. In 1928, 56 percent of intellectual periodicals and 40 percent of mass-market magazines indicated approval of at least some relaxation of older standards in favor of greater "sex freedom"—a rise from 23 and 13 percent respectively in 1918.

Marriage and the Art of Love

While sexual activity among the unmarried had changed and the double standard was breaking down, the real revolution was occurring in a more traditional venue. Behind the closed doors of the marital bedroom, conjugal relations were not what they had been. Procreation still had its place, but at the same time couples sought ever greater sexual pleasure as an equally necessary end in itself. And to achieve it they concentrated on learning what was now being called the "art" of physical love.

Reflecting in 1929 on "the transitional condition of sexual morals at the present time," Bertrand Russell concluded, in *Marriage and*

Morals, that the change was "due in the main to two causes, the first being the invention of contraceptives, and the second the emancipation of women." His observation was to some extent true of single women but applied most of all to married women. Thanks in large part to the efforts of Margaret Sanger and Marie Stopes, constant childbearing was no longer the inevitable lot of wives, as both knowledge and the availability of birth control spread. The barrier methods advocated by Sanger and Stopes—the cervical cap and the diaphragm—increasingly caught on among middle-class women who welcomed the chance to take charge of their own fertility. The majority, however, still relied on their husbands; coitus interruptus had long been the most widely preferred, if not always the most reliable, method of birth control. But while people did not necessarily adopt the newer practices, they could now feel differently about contraception, whatever the means. With pleasure now as important as reproduction, no one needed to feel guilty about giving in to one, and avoiding the other.

Sexual pleasure was fast gaining regard, not as a luxury but as a basic right. Freud had not yet become a household name, but simplified versions of his ideas on the dangers of sexual repression and the necessity of gratification were gaining currency. Still better known than Freud were Sanger and Stopes, who lent their voices to the growing chorus in praise of pleasure, particularly women's pleasure. As Sanger explained it in her 1926 advice book, *Happiness in Marriage*,

For centuries women have been taught . . . that hers should be a passive, dutiful role—to submit but not to participate. Likewise men have been schooled by tradition to seek mere selfish gratification. This lack of constructive experience is responsible for the thousands of unhappy marriages and the tragic wasted lives of many wives, cheated by thoughtlessness and ignorance of their legitimate right to marital joy.

And women listened. Having won the vote and greater equality in the political arena, they now demanded their just due in the bedroom. This new "emancipation of women" created yet another sexual revolution, this one among men. Where once it had been women's duty to please men, the tables were now turned. It was up to the man to ensure the woman's sexual satisfaction. "*He must woo her before every separate act of coitus,*" wrote Stopes in emphatic italics in *Married Love,* and repeated herself in its follow-up, *Enduring Passion* (1928): "The *wooing* of the wife and the attainment of the orgasm for her . . . is woman's legitimate right."

If anything, Sanger was even more insistent. It was the duty of the male, she wrote in a tone that brooked no contradiction, to "prepare his beloved for their mutual flight together to the high realm of ecstasy . . . He must awaken her senses and her soul. He must arouse that indefinable something in her which makes her his best beloved." And as if all that were not enough, she concluded firmly that attaining "mutual rhythm and ecstasy" was up to the man, and only the man—"he alone can accomplish this." The era of performance pressure on men had arrived.

With the charge to be a "skillful lover," weighing heavily on each husband, making love satisfactorily had become an art for men, a right for women. For both, the object was pleasure, and at the heart of pleasure was knowledge. The experts all agreed that the road to sexual hell was paved with ignorance and misconceptions.

"People have to learn to perform the sexual act," said Russell. "Ignorance does harm." Stopes agreed that "the great majority of people . . . have no glimmering of the supreme human art, the art of love." "Only knowledge can . . . set things right," she added. Sexual ignorance caused "spoiled lives," Sanger echoed, "Enlightenment is our crying need . . . Light—more light . . . is the only enduring solution to marriage problems."

Sanger and Stopes were by no means the only ones who responded to people's pleas for greater sexual knowledge. Following their lead, many other experts published their own advice books, further disseminating information about marital psychology and sexual technique. By the end of the 1930s the "repeal of reticence," which had drawn pointed commentary before the war, was a widely accepted fact of life. Knowledge of lovemaking skills now went hand in hand with people's enhanced awareness of those other all-important "facts of life."

Elusive Passion

Frankness about sex was undoubtedly the new wisdom of the 1920s and 1930s. But, not surprisingly in a time of transition, there were those who held firmly to other ways: some who were simply old-fashioned, and some who doubted that more openness would really make people happier.

Among the more extreme representatives of repression was Mildred Spock, a middle-class Connecticut housewife, stern in teaching her children that sex was an "emotional bomb" whose expression in thought or deed was nothing short of "disgusting." Despite (or because of) the drawbacks in his upbringing, Mildred's eldest son Benjamin would grow up to become Dr. Spock, one of the century's most revered authorities on child-rearing.

Mildred was no model of either passion or compassion, but in her conviction of the inherent dangers of sex, she had inadvertently struck a chord of truth. A more thoughtful warning was sounded by others, including Bertrand Russell. "When we consider the relations of men and women," he wrote, "it is clear that some sex relations have more value than others. Most people would agree that a sex relation is better when it has a large psychical element than when it is purely physical." The trouble was, he later noted, many people, especially "the inexperienced," found it "very difficult to distinguish passionate love from mere sex hunger."

Clearly the increase in discussion and knowledge of once private matters helped assuage many people's anxieties about sex. But the general growth of sexual sophistication and experience threatened to overwhelm and obscure the less tangible emotional and spiritual desires whose fulfillment also contributed to the mutual satisfaction of the sexes. While the majority of women and men now demanded, and many discovered, sexual pleasure, there began to appear signs of confusion and discontent.

Even the sexually adventurous man of letters Edmund Wilson expressed a certain confusion, as his impulse for sex intermingled with a deeper longing for passion:

> With a woman whom we want to love us . . . even with a perverse self-centered and cruel girl . . . in the midst of however sensual and cynical a love affair, we are stirred by a deep unexpected feeling of an entirely different sort—a feeling which may lead us to marry a girl of whom, at the beginning, we have never thought seriously as a wife.

Most of Wilson's contemporaries now also equated sexual pleasure, as well as some deeper feeling, with the companionate marriage. No longer just a social and religious responsibility, marriage to most people was now ideally the shining way to both sexual fulfillment and personal happiness. But as people's expectations rose, so did their capacity for discontentment. This, along with their growing attachment to the idea of individual freedom, was reflected in a divorce rate that had been steadily increasing since the second half of the nineteenth century, and which continued on its rising curve in the 1920s and 1930s. According to one sociologist, 20 percent of those who married in 1930 "may sometime be facing the problem of reorganizing themselves after divorce."

But the more dramatic change was in attitude. The Lynds noted that even the "very middle-of-the-road" world of 1924 Middletown generally accepted the "relatively greater ease and respectability of dissolving a marriage." In a 1937 survey by *Fortune* magazine, 88 percent of the presumably conservative respondents approved of divorce, although 54 percent did not want it made easier. Progressive thinkers, not surprisingly, were the most adamant on the subject. A 1930 survey of college girls found that 92.5 per cent favored divorce as the answer to an unhappy marriage, and some went so far as to advocate it on demand by either of the spouses.

It was one of the principal architects of the new marital ideal who pinpointed the shakiness of its structure. Deploring "the modern tendency to over-emphasise physical sex in daily life," Marie Stopes argued that this often spoiled "what might have been happy marriages for some young people, for they are led to expect a continuing titillating excitement in their marriages which real life cannot sustain . . . and this may sacrifice the best mental and spiritual adventures, and the more enduring elements of marriage." Though seemingly blind to her own role, Stopes rightly recognized the cultural irony that she and other sex reformers had helped to create. The more sex gained public approval as an aspect of mental and physical health, the more passion became elusive.

Hard Times

The economic depression of the 1930s dealt North America a harsh blow. Americans and Canadians had enjoyed a higher standard of living than Europeans in the 1920s, and they felt deprivation all the more keenly for it.

For some, circumstances were particularly hard. The mostly young men who rode the rails in search of work had been driven from their homes by severe necessity, and loneliness was a problem. A *Vancouver Sun* journalist visited a British Columbia relief camp in 1934 and reported that the isolation from women was demoralizing for these men in all kinds of ways. It was not the "sex deprivation" alone that troubled them but "the fact that the men feel that they are cut off from any association with women . . . and they can see no end ahead."

There can be no minimizing the hardships that many people suffered. At the same time, the sexual behavior of the 1930s cannot be written off as simply a reaction to financial hardship or the supposed excesses of the previous decade. Though there were subtle differences in the relationship of the sexes between the "roaring twenties" and the Depression years, there were also strong continuities.

Though times were now tough, love—and sex—still found a way. The quest for sexual knowledge and pleasure continued unabated. In Britain alone, Stopes's *Married Love* was reprinted twenty-three times between 1930 and 1939. This suggests that while financial hardship may have caused tensions between some husbands and wives, the ideal of the sexualized companionate marriage not only survived the Depression intact, but was stronger than ever.

Dating and petting, the foreplay to marriage, were similarly hindered but not destroyed. The straitened times put a damper on expensive outings—movie theaters, cars, and the intimacies they fostered cost money that few could afford. But young people were not about to abandon the sexual rituals that had gained wide acceptance in the 1920s. Though they might now be enjoying them on a budget, necking and petting were no longer controversial issues. A 1938 sociological study called *Sex and Youth* found that things had "toned down from the hectic postwar decade" but that there was no "return to the prewar age of innocence." As one young woman put it, "that doesn't mean that we are better than we used to be. Only that flaming youth has lost its novelty."

Popular entertainments reflected the spirit of the time. A note of cynicism had crept into some song lyrics of the 1930s—"It's Only a Paper Moon," for example, suggested the virtual unattainability of genuine passion. Yet many other contemporary songs kept faith with the ideal—"Heart and Soul," "Love Walked In," "Out of Nowhere," and "Love Is Here to Stay" were the musical renderings of Russell's idea of the "large psychical element" that enhanced mere "sex relations." The Hays Code had curbed sexual explicitness in the movies, but love, even passion, was just fine— as long as it did not titillate too openly and offend public decency. The passionate drama of *Gone with the Wind* (1939) was the crest of a wave of other grand romances—*Forsaking All Others* (1934), *Anna Karenina* (1935), *The Devil Is a Woman* (1935), *Desire* (1936), *Jezebel* (1938), and many more.

Those who wanted more blatantly sexy fare could always turn to the pulp magazines that proliferated in the 1930s. These had been around in one form or another for decades, but in the Depression era they bothered less and less with redeeming moral messages. In the previous decade (as the Lynds had remarked) the popular "sex adventure" magazines had been full of exotic settings, sensationalist plots, and florid emotion, but according to one publisher, "a moral conclusion was necessary." The 1930s pulps often sidestepped such uplifting niceties, concentrating on sex, violence, and horror. And if a vampish-looking female could be worked in—preferably clad in black lace, stockings, and garter belt—so much the better.

Sexy escapism was not only to be found vicariously between the pages of the pulps or in diluted form at the movies. People also used the real thing as a desperate respite from their troubles, and all too often the result was a far cry from the ideal of passion. In the United States the incidence of syphilis and gonorrhea rose, and in cities such as Baltimore and Washington, D.C., whose infection rates were high, overcrowding of public clinics became a serious problem. In western Canada, where the Depression was especially severe, the rates of venereal infection also rose, as did that of premarital pregnancies. As one 1932 Royal Canadian Mounted Police Report on unemployment in Edmonton observed, these problems developed inevitably from men being on relief and therefore "not being active and able to keep their minds free of sex matters."

The Depression-induced troubles between men and women, whether strained marriages, disease, or unwanted pregnancies, only went to prove what Sanger had written a few years earlier in *Happiness in Marriage*. Placing her own interpretation on the many-layered sexual code of her day, she held fast to her belief that "enduring happiness" between the sexes in the end had to be founded on more than sexual attraction or even sexual knowledge: "Love is essential. Passion is essential."

In the 1930s as in the 1920s, people *wanted* to believe it. But in their commitment to personal happiness they had become caught up in a culture that increasingly stripped away the mystery of sex, all the while promoting unrealistic expectations of it. Passion increasingly seemed elusive to some, irrelevant to others. In its place people settled for compelling but lesser substitutes—sexual pleasure, enhanced knowledge, and sometimes, escapism through sex.

But these were minor distractions compared to what would soon follow. In 1939 the century's second great war engulfed the world, and men and women were once again caught up in an upheaval that would change their lives.

IV

HOT
PURSUITS

1940–1959

The second great conflict of the century—the one that was not supposed to happen—plunged people back into war's melee of instinctual living. For many, the conflagration of World War II once again narrowed life to an elemental matter of survival and sex. And they pursued both with a fervor beyond anything yet seen in a century no longer young.

With the return of peace, people burned with a new zeal to settle down. On the surface of things, life and the relationship of the sexes seemed almost to rival the quintessential respectability of the Victorians. The new suburbs that mushroomed around the cities of North America were undoubtedly the symbols of postwar prosperity, stability, and family values. The realities, however, were often otherwise.

In the Heat of Battle

Burn fire . . . love, buddies, love
. . . It keeps us warm.

— LINCOLN KIRSTEIN, Rhymes of a Pfc

By most people's standards we were immoral,
but we were young and could die tomorrow

— AMERICAN SOLDIER TO JOHN COSTELLO,
Virtue Under Fire

June 5, 1944. At midnight the Allies would launch their long-planned "Operation Overlord," the joint American, Canadian, and British assault on the German-held beaches of Normandy. D-Day was now only hours away.

The British civilians who had recently observed military planes taking off from their bases, and who had cheered on "lorries full of fighting men," could not know for certain what it all meant. But many suspected and everyone hoped that it might be the beginning of the end of the long war. The British and their Canadian allies had been in it since the outset in September 1939, the Americans since Pearl Harbor, now two and a half years ago. Men and women on both sides of the Atlantic, military personnel and civilians alike, were deeply war-weary, their longing for an end to it all as intense as their unflagging passion for victory.

As D-Day, 6 June, drew closer, most of the civilian population carried on as they had done throughout the war. They put in their days in factories, offices, or on the land, women now working alongside or in place of men. In the evenings they cared for their families, many of them now temporarily or permanently fatherless. And in what leisure they had, men and women grasped at any distraction that might help to keep up their morale in the face of wartime deprivation, loneliness, and fear.

Though the dance halls of Britain were emptier than usual that June evening, they had been centers of social action throughout the war, and among the most popular places for men and women to meet. Movies were another way to grab a few hours' respite from the worries of wartime—Humphrey Bogart, James Cagney, Bing Crosby, Clark Gable, Judy Garland, Greer Garson, Betty Grable, Bob Hope, and Spencer Tracy were all big at the box office between 1940 and 1945. At home and abroad people listened to Bing Crosby, Frank Sinatra, and the big-band sound of Tommy Dorsey. North Americans no less than the British were apt to grow teary-eyed to the strains of Vera Lynn's "White Cliffs of Dover."

During their long stints away from women, soldiers made do with picture collections: Vargas girls clipped from *Esquire* and *Men Only*, or pinup girls featured in the service magazines *Yank, Stars and Stripes*, and the British *Reveille*. Jeanne Crain, Betty Grable, Rita Hayworth, and Ann Sheridan were favorites, brightening the drab walls above soldiers' cots in many a barracks. The girls back home also did their part to keep up their own and their men's morale by "looking to their looks." As government propaganda, advertising, and ladies' magazines constantly reminded women, "Beauty is a duty, too!"

In the midst of rationing and going without, women did their best to comply, "making do and mending," scraping the remnants of lipstick from a well-used tube, and applying the color with a careful fingertip. Reflecting the scarcity of fabric, fashion dictated short skirts and lots of visible leg. With nylon and silk in short supply, women colored their bare legs with commercial makeup or—in a pinch—sand or gravy seasoning. An obliging girlfriend or female relative would then draw a seam line up the back with eyebrow pencil.

All of it—the dancing, movies, and music; the pinup girls and pressure on every woman to look good—was part of a larger, often desperate endeavor to hang on to some vestige of the ordinary in a time that in so many ways was extraordinary. One woman who had lived through it reflected that "war was gradually not being able to distinguish the abnormal from the normal."

But in the end, people's efforts to preserve a semblance of everyday life were overtaken by the realities of war. How could it have been otherwise? Conventional sex roles turned upside down as women were "manpowered into places and jobs they would never have dreamed of." At any moment, daily life could be disrupted by "blackouts, power cuts, rationing, and shortages." And all the while there were the mounting "casualty lists of the killed and injured"—friends, relatives, lovers, fiancés, and spouses. In unprecedented numbers men and women took solace in one another, with a no-holds-barred abandon. As one British woman recalled, "We got what we could out of life, for we never knew which day might be our last."

It was the old Freudian story of war—the fear of death intensifying the urge to procreate. It had been so in World War I and was all the more true now. Revolutionary changes in sexual morality during the interwar period made the further abandonment of restraints under the duress of war inevitable. As people fought passionately for victory, for happiness, and for one another, it could hardly have been otherwise.

Hot Times

"The most wonderful days of my life." "Exciting . . . memorable." "A great experience . . . We fell in and out of love with gay abandon as troops came and went." "There was always a lively band, and . . . I danced the nights away . . . Life was pretty exciting." "There was more excitement in life . . . The war changed everything. Until then I had led a rather sheltered life." Excitement—that was the emotion that women would later remember most of all: the tumult, the exhilaration, and the romance of wartime.

Others described those years in blunter terms. "My standards of morality went to the seven winds," one woman who had been a seventeen-year-old Jewish refugee in England confessed. But while loosened moral standards were indeed widespread, although never universal, the unrestrained behavior of both men and women is not hard to understand. "Sheer loneliness" and "sheer terror" heightened "the need to be loved," as one British woman put it. "I lived in a vacuum of loneliness and fright," she recalled. She was not alone in recognizing that people invariably found ways of balancing the intolerable "terror and heartbreak, frustration, strain" with "the unbearable joy which unexpected happiness amid war can mean."

If loneliness and fear most often ignited lust in women, for servicemen the kindling spark was their regular confrontation with death. A man at war "has to love," said an American army sergeant, "if only to re-assert that he's very much alive in the face of destruction." It's "a passionate re-affirmation of his life." Most poignant of all, perhaps, were the plain words of a British woman who surely spoke for every woman and man who ever loved rashly in the heat of battle. "We were not really immoral," she said, "there was a war on."

Many who put in their war effort in the comparative safety of the home front found themselves as caught up in the overheated mood of the times as those who served in the thick of the fray. Of necessity the widespread taboo against women doing men's work had been broken and many women heartily approved. "It's thrilling work, and exciting," a female bus driver recalled. A lot more "glamour" than the kitchen, said another woman of her job in a navy yard. Though the majority of American and Canadian women still worked in traditional female jobs, such as secretarial and clerical positions, Rosie the Riveter and Wanda the Welder had come into their own. So, too, had all the female electricians, drillers, painters, boilermakers, and heavy equipment drivers who now worked alongside men in shipyards and war plants, making everything from guns and ammunition to tanks and aircraft.

Having burst the bounds of their traditionally separate sphere, many women were just as eager to break loose from the old double standard of sexual morality. It was a "sex paradise," according to one young man who found himself working with an array of women who either were single or had absentee husbands or sweethearts. The American sociologist Katherine Archibald, author of *Wartime Shipyard* (1947), observed that "in the shipyards, rumor was continually busy with . . . reports of salacious activities . . . of a stolen kiss or an amusing infatuation; even of the ultimate sin, with or without price." Of course, as Archibald was quick to indicate, rumor and truth are not the same, but in the heat of war work, no less than battle, "where there's smoke . . ."

Contributing to the war effort and improving their economic status were the primary motivations for most women doing "men's work." But there was no doubt that for many the possibility of romantic adventure was an added perk. Advertising jumped in, fueling the popular conviction that when men and women got together in the workplace, more than mere work would inevitably go on. Advertisers of cosmetic and hygiene products, such as face creams, hand lotions, and deodorants, urged women to stay feminine and attractive, both off the job—and on. In many instances the implied message was: look good, smell good, and get a man— all in a day's work. Stay "dainty-sweet every day," advised the makers of Etiquet deodorant cream, and "you'll be a more attractive woman at all times."

The same advertisement went further still. "Is it okay to have *dinner* with the *BOSS*?" asked the bold copy beneath a picture of a pretty young woman seated at a dinner table, while her older-looking date hovers attentively behind her. Backing up the picture's innuendo, the remaining copy endorsed the idea of a dinner date with the boss but added two qualifications: "provided he's not married . . . and provided you both remain strictly businesslike in the office." The small print used for these provisos suggested their relative importance in the overall scenario.

But the romance of dating the boss was lukewarm stuff compared to the high temperatures steaming up the sexes across the Atlantic. British women endured the Blitz, bombs, and mortal danger, as well as everyday shortages and deprivations of all kinds, but as if in compensation, romance was virtually around every corner. Not only were there the homegrown British boys, looking better than ever in their uniforms, but since the early days of wartime there were Canadian troops, too, all eager for female companionship. Better paid than their British counterparts, and generally more attentive toward women, Canadian soldiers had no trouble finding the romance they craved. Many British women loyally stood by their own men romantically as well as patriotically, but others plunged into "whirlwind romances" with their Canadian allies, many in the end finding "good husbands" among them.

In January 1942, the month following Pearl Harbor, the Americans arrived. Leonora Pitt from the West Midlands was seventeen years old and "madly in love" with a local boy. But she was also a keen observer of the excited reactions of others to the United States' entry into the war. "A brass band played 'Over There,'" she recollected, "Yes, the Yanks had come."

Better paid even than the Canadians, and freer in their spending habits than the frugal British, American GIs soon developed a reputation for vulgar materialism. In 1940 U.S. currency, the average GI made $60 a month, while the Canadian soldier typically received $45, and their British counterpart had to make do with the equivalent of a niggardly $12 a month. To add insult to injury, the cocky GIs lured many women away from British men. "They wooed the British girls with nylons, candy and gum, and always had plenty of whisky," Leonora Pitt remarked.

Of course, many British women remained firmly unimpressed with Americans, and some complained of their brashness, bad table manners (eating chicken with their hands, for example), coarse language, and shameless way of accosting every pretty woman who crossed their path. But as Leonora conceded, "they had charm all right," and many British women fell hard for it. So much so that American GIs widely believed that most women "over there" had loose morals. Meanwhile, many British men were resentful of the sexual competition, not to mention the Americans' free spending habits, which they could not match even if they were so inclined. Leonora put it mildly when she said, "Our lads disliked the Yanks."

"Overpaid, oversexed, and over here!"—the well-worn sour joke about Americans was surely begun and perpetuated by disgruntled British men. The women, Leonora recalled, had their own take on the newcomers: "They had bigger lorries, bigger tanks, better uniforms, bigger mouths, and, rumour had it, bigger . . . !" She also remembered the times she walked home at night and "there would be a Yank lurking behind every bush." It must have been like many other such encounters between British girls and American GIs as they found themselves caught up in the heat of the moment and the fever pitch of wartime sexuality. "From some dark corner you'd hear a voice say, 'You will take me back to America after the war, won't you?'

"'Sure thing, honey . . . Just lift your skirt a bit higher.'"

Cold Realities

Many hot and hasty encounters between men and women swept along by wartime morality began and ended as harmless sexy fun. But not everyone was so lucky, and in the cold light of the morning after, there was often a price to be paid for pleasure.

In both wartime Britain and the United States there was a rise in the out-of-wedlock birth rate, a classic indicator of relaxed sexual morality and its consequences. In Britain at the beginning of the war, an estimated 4 percent of all births were premarital or extramarital; by war's end the figure was 9 percent. In the United States before the war, out-of-wedlock births averaged 5.5 per thousand, rising to 10.5 over the six war years, with a high of 16.1 in 1945. The greatest percentage increase was among women between twenty and thirty years of age. This suggests that wartime morality had affected teenage girls less than their older contemporaries. The fact that many births were the result of extramarital affairs further indicates the breakdown of prewar standards of fidelity, for women no less than men.

A more chilling consequence of wartime morality was the increase in venereal infection. In 1944 the combined rate of infection with syphilis and gonorrhea among the Royal Air Force was

45 per thousand. The rate was higher still among American GIs, at 60 per thousand among those stationed in Britain. A few months after the Normandy invasion there was a sixfold increase among American troops. The sufferers attributed it to leave taken in Paris.

U.S. army chaplains and other guardians of old-fashioned standards complained that the army was not doing enough to curb either infection or, in particular, the promiscuity that caused it. They were especially angered at General Patton who in both Sicily and France had encouraged the establishment of medically supervised brothels. Most military leaders, it was true, were not as concerned with purifying GI behavior for the sake of tradition as the forces of conservative morality might have wished. But as in World War I, they were by no means lackadaisical when it came to keeping their men free from venereal disease and "fighting fit" for victory. Prior to the invasion of Sicily, for example, General Eisenhower ordered the ad hoc brothels that had sprung up around military bases to be closed, as he and other military leaders attempted to enforce a strict off-limits policy.

The U.S. Army also launched a combined education and scare program in an attempt to instill self-control in the men. A barrage of films, lectures, and pamphlets used gruesome imagery to warn against chance encounters with women, either "amateurs" or professionals, but especially the latter. A 1943 illustration in *Stars and Stripes* showed a GI about to enter a woman's residence, his figure casting an ominous black shadow. A large X-ed over "V" and, in even larger type, the letters "V.D.," screamed out the message that military defeat and careless sex went hand in hand. A British "Let Knowledge Grow" poster was grimmer still: it showed a death's-head skull sporting a stylish woman's hat. "Hello, boyfriend, coming MY way?" the skull enticed, while the print below warned that "Syphilis and Gonorrhea . . . may result in blindness, insanity, paralysis, premature death."

To underscore the dishonor of risking victory for a casual fling, GIs who ignored the warnings and became infected were treated, but publicly shamed. As one army veteran recalled, first "these large and smeary letters: V D" were painted on the back of your jacket and one trouser leg. Then you lined up to enter the dispensary. Ahead "were men with either arm bared or with their buttocks offered like steak to the needle." As one of the medical orderlies pointed out, it was not much of a choice—"ya'll be hurtin' anyhow." The veteran recalled how, in that moment, all his life "telescoped down to . . . a hypodermic needle with yellow drops dribbling out of it. What was it called? Pncilin? Penissiclin? Pencillin?"

Embarrassing treatments, propaganda, and other efforts at venereal disease control were only partially effective. In the end, men at war were going to be men at war, and some women, out of inclination, professional habit, and often dire need, were going to make money from them. In the summer of 1943 the British ministry of health liaised with Canadian and American military authorities to develop anti-VD measures, but the effort soon collapsed. There were just too many prostitutes for any attempt at suppression to be effective. Available records show that 75 percent of GIs were sexually active while overseas. A sociologist attached to an American unit in Normandy observed that 60 percent of his company resorted to professional prostitutes, as did British and Canadian troops in roughly the same proportion.

Though it is understandable that hard-line moralists would have been outraged at Patton, his policy of medically monitored prostitution was realistic enough. From a military standpoint it made sense to accept that promiscuity and the possibility of infection were the reality, and to do anything and everything that would ensure the men's fighting fitness. Military doctors had argued for several years that lectures, films, and pamphlets alone had little effect on behavior, but combined with army-issue condoms (which about half the GIs used at least some of the time) and the new availability of penicillin (the first truly effective treatment for venereal disease), propaganda likely helped tip the balance of numbers toward victory for the Allies. Without such measures, D-Day might well have been a fiasco, compromised by what one historian speculatively called "a pre-invasion VD-Day."

Men's Work . . . Women's Work

While men faced the constant possibility of death and sought temporary relief in reckless sex, women had their own harsh realities to deal with. They did not have to confront death in the same way as men, but they contended with both humiliation and hardship, now that work that had once fallen exclusively to men had become women's work, too.

By 1945, 350,000 women had served in the American military; in Canada the figure was about 54,000. In Britain more than half a million women were in either the armed forces or civil defense by 1943. They took on traditional female tasks such as nursing, cooking, and secretarial duties but they also worked as mechanics, engineers, technicians, drivers, and even pilots for supply and transport missions. Male instructors in both the British and the American military somewhat grudgingly conceded that they learned faster than the men, picking up more in a day than male trainees did in a week. Though servicewomen did not go into combat, they were often close to the front. American and Canadian WACs (Women's Army Corps), for example, sometimes marched only a few miles behind male troops in Europe.

WACs at the front shared the hardships of combat, living on equal terms with the men—and typically showing greater stamina, according to General Douglas MacArthur. Yet no matter how often and how convincingly they proved their competence, they were still routinely treated with disrespect or even contempt. In the United States, Canada, and Britain, smear campaigns particularly targeted the sexual morals of servicewomen. "Officers' ground-sheets" and "pilots' cockpits" were among the derogatory terms for British women in the ATS (Auxiliary Territorial Service) and WAAFs (Women's Auxiliary Air Force). These and other sexual slurs against military women made the rounds on both sides of the Atlantic.

A study by the Canadian War Information board concluded that the allegations were largely unfounded, and that the prejudice against the female military stemmed from the many role reversals that service entailed. If women now drilled, saluted, drove heavy vehicles, and repaired machinery, went the biased reasoning, then they must be sexually unconventional, too, and therefore "loose." In fact, an American survey indicated that 40 percent were celibate, and British military research revealed an identical continence rate among their women service personnel. The evidence suggests that most of the rest were monogamous.

But military authorities were nonetheless concerned about the 60 percent of servicewomen who were sexually active. Venereal infection was not a problem on the scale that it was among servicemen, but cases did exist and measures had to be taken. For the most part these consisted of educational propaganda and regular medical inspections. Leonora Pitt, the young British woman who had observed the Americans' arrival in 1942, later joined the WAAFs. She described the rigors of the Thursday night FFI—"Free From Infection"—ritual. "About 9:30 p.m.," Leonora recalled,

> you stood by your bed, barefoot and naked, except for your knickers. Can you imagine 20 girls standing to attention in airforce-blue knickers, complete with elastic around the legs?

Then you would be examined—your hair for lice, your feet
for blisters, your teeth, and then the examination for VD. I
hated it. I used to feel so degraded. There was the male medical officer, a nursing sister and the flight sergeant, strutting
along looking at us as though they were at a cattle auction.

Nor was this the only indignity that tried the physical and
mental well-being of women in the forces. To spur recruitment
and enhance the image of the female forces, authorities on both
sides of the Atlantic emphasized the positive, noble, and even
glamorous aspects of military service. The reality usually turned
out to be less appealing. "Some join the WACS to get a bit of glamour," begins one training song. But as the lyrics unfold to the tune
of "Funiculee, Funicula," the real story emerges, with references to
aching bones, making beds, scrubbing floors—"and other chores,
and other chores."

And it could get a lot worse than that. American recruits faced
filthy recruiting stations, lack of private toilets and showers, and
harassment that ranged from derogatory remarks and wolf whistles
to out-and-out sexual molestation. At one base it masqueraded as
a psychiatric exam that supposedly tested the emotional balance of
possible enlistees. An army psychiatrist made the girls strip, then
asked probing questions about their sex lives.

Across the Atlantic, the civilized British were, if anything, even
less civilized. Mary Lee Settle was a twenty-one-year-old American
from Washington, D.C., who joined the British WAAFS in 1942.
What had begun as a huge adventure soon disintegrated into a reg-
imen of "organized martyrdom." Mary Lee described "isolation,
boredom and neglect" and "secret threats" of punishment from
those higher in the pecking order. WAAFS were subjected to verbal
abuse and forced to perform mindless tasks like "washing coal
piece by piece." On top of it all, there were unsanitary conditions

and bad food: "steaming cauldrons of swill were set on a serving table beside two open garbage bins . . . the smell of the thrown garbage mingled with the smell from the cauldrons to form a thick, scummy miasma over the mess." Morale sank so low that the women sometimes fought with one another as frustrations boiled over. Early in her service, Mary Lee herself was attacked by other airwomen and thrown down a flight of stairs because they thought she was acting too "snooty."

Many women in civilian jobs were faring little better. Despite the tales of romance with the boss or eligible co-workers, the more common experience in the workplace was sexual harassment. For the most part it took comparatively mild forms—whistles, cat-calls, racy jokes, and leers—but it added up to considerable discomfort for many women.

"I never walked a longer road in my life than to the tool room," recalled one woman of her first day at a shipyard. "The battery of men's eyes that turned on my jittery physique . . . soon had me thinking . . . 'Maybe I am from Mars.'"

"You'd think," said another female shipyard worker, "these ten thousand guys [had] never before seen or heard or touched or spoken to anything remotely resembling a female . . . Nor do they show the slightest sign of knowing that women are people too. Well, it is pretty funny."

As long as the harassment stayed at the verbal level, most women were able to take it with a dose of humor. But other circumstances of women's work were not to be laughed off. Though the policy of the National War Labor Board in America was equal pay for equal work, it was rarely implemented. Moreover, almost three-quarters of women workers were married, and on top of their forty-eight or sixty hours a week in the office or factory, they were responsible for housework and child care. It is understandable they they complained of illness, exhaustion, and the grinding boredom of the work routine. As one munitions worker put it, daily reality could quickly make all but the most robust "very poor shadows of the War Effort girls" of posters and documentaries. Working in the "man's world" of factories and shipyards may have seemed glamorous and thrilling to some women, but others knew all too well that Rosie the Riveter and Wanda the Welder, with their careful makeup and tireless smiles, were largely the figments of the propagandists' imagination.

"For Better or for Worse..."

For all the extraordinariness of wartime life, "the ordinary" was "still there," too, as one woman remembered. Many husbands went to their customary jobs in the daytime and came home at night, children went to school, neighbors chatted across their fences, people listened to the radio or went to the movies. And they still fell in love, or in lust, and did the old-fashioned, conventional thing. They got married.

Yet the once ordinary act of getting married was now tinged with urgency. It might be a couple's only chance to grasp one last night of passion before their lives collapsed back into chaos. Marriage regularized the urgency, seemingly taming its all-too-common recklessness. More than that, the traditional wedding ritual not only united a man and a woman but offered them the comfort of the past. It was among the few remaining links to those days before their world had exploded into war.

In the two years following Pearl Harbor, there was a virtual epidemic of weddings. The annual marriage rate in the United States rose by 20 percent. Draft evasion was sometimes the motive, and sometimes it was money—the brides were so-called Allotment Annies who pressured vulnerable soldiers into marriage in order to collect the $28-a-month government stipend for servicemen's wives. The greedier of these predatory types did not turn a hair at bigamy—in one notorious case the unblushing bride was about to land her seventh catch before she was finally arrested. A chance meeting of two of her "husbands" in an English pub led to her discovery.

But most couples married for love, or at least for what felt like love. Those who were already engaged often moved up the date in order to have at least a brief experience of married life before the groom was called up. Still to a large degree bound by the double standard, some women who had sexually consummated their relationships now pressed for legitimation via impetuous marriage. War also gave the men who cared to use them some great lines: "It's my last leave," "I could die tomorrow," "Give me just a few nights of happiness" . . . and so on.

Carried away by emotion, many girls married in haste. Some made a go of it, others repented almost as speedily as they had marched up the aisle. Ever sensitive to the mood of the day, advertising was full of images of white-clad war brides and their uniformed husbands. Even the rich and famous were not immune. "Marry me before I go overseas and get killed!" pleaded Sergeant John Agar to the former child star Shirley Temple, a few months before the war ended. Though she sensibly pointed out that she was not even seventeen and that, besides, he was not very likely to get killed, she ended up capitulating all the same.

The marriage bug similarly bit the British, whose wartime marriage rate had also risen by 20 percent. The influx of Canadians and Americans was in no small way responsible for the British marriage boom. Before 1940 it had not been unheard-of for soldiers serving overseas to marry local women. But the extent and duration of World War II, the many men and women involved, and the length of overseas service led to a previously unequaled number of international war marriages.

A few Canadian and American men married Australians and New Zealanders, but far more married British women. Seventy thousand British women immigrated to the United States after the war, the largest single group of women to enter the country in the 1940s. American prosperity was undoubtedly a draw for many British girls who had suffered years of wartime deprivation. But for most this remained a secondary factor—the majority of war brides married because they fell in love.

In its broad outlines, the story of one British bride and her American husband portrays experiences common to countless others. In the final months leading up to D-Day, Isabel, one of the "land girls" who had taken over Britain's wartime agricultural production, met Jack, an American GI who would shortly be shipped into the "hell" of France.

"Like so many wartime couples," Isabel recalled, "we met at a dance." She also remembered that before the first dance was over, Jack announced with typical American confidence, "I'm going to marry you." "What a line," was her first thought, but as they "danced all night," she realized, "I have met my destiny." A couple of forty-eight-hour passes and a "whirlwind romance" followed. "I can't quite remember how it happened, but one night passion just took over, and suddenly I wasn't a virgin any more."

As things turned out, Isabel never regretted "crossing the line." Despite active discouragement from her parents and the U.S. army, the couple was married by special license, literally at the eleventh hour before Jack shipped out to France. "Well, at least we had that one night," Isabel said, remembering that bittersweet occasion. "No sooner had we said our vows than he had to rush back to his unit. He left me at the church, and I went back to work." It would be two years before they were together again.

As heady as international romance could be, many women and men remained true to their compatriots. Among them was Leonora

Pitt and her long-standing English boyfriend, Tom. Though she was a fascinated observer of American troops, the Yanks and their charm failed to tempt her. In May 1943, when she was eighteen and Tom twenty-six, they "arranged to be married."

Like many weddings of the day, particularly in Britain, it had makeshift elements and missing pieces—a borrowed wedding dress, small cake covered with iced cardboard, no confetti, and no church bells (those were now reserved for sounding the invasion alarm). On the other hand, by the standards of beleaguered, strictly rationed wartime Britain, where the wedding costume was often khaki and the feast Spam sandwiches, it was a lavish affair. Cream tea roses and lily of the valley formed the bridal bouquet, the church organist played the Wedding March, the reception meal was ham salad with trifle for dessert, and the couple even managed the luxury of a honeymoon in the Lake District. "At the hotel we had sandwiches and a drink before going to bed. A night of mad passion followed," Leonora fondly recalled.

After the honeymoon, she went back to the ATS and "just prayed that I could have a baby and so get out of the Forces." Tom was doing civilian work on the home front, his draft deferred "since his medical in 1941." Before long, Leonora got her wish and became pregnant with their daughter Margaret, born April 1944. For a time all was well and then, within days of D-Day, "the blow fell. Tom . . . was drafted into the army" and "due to be sent overseas." As his train pulled away, "I stood there with the baby in my arms, the tears streaming down my face . . . I couldn't stand it."

"A Girl Who's Been Married Gets Lonely"

After recovering from the initial shock of parting, Leonora did manage to adjust to the strain of separation, caring for a child on her own, and living in cramped quarters with hostile in-laws. But others lacked her powers of endurance. Married soldiers facing death often set aside their commitment to fidelity—it was an understandable and widely accepted "fact of life." Meanwhile, the grind of work together with the uncertainties and dislocations of war proved too much for many women left behind. Under such duress they, too, conveniently forgot having vowed to be faithful "for better, for worse," as they sought their own extramarital solace.

"I'm not bad," protested one young American wife, "but a girl who's been married gets lonely." She was not alone in her sentiment. "There was a lot of sleeping around," an Englishwoman remembered, adding that there were also "many innocent attachments with no sex involved." Separated couples, both married and dating, commonly if often uneasily tolerated interim platonic attachments. An advertisement for Etiquet deodorant provides a yardstick of popular sentiment. The ad proclaimed that it was acceptable for a girl to "'date' while her sweetheart is at Camp . . . *if* your sweetheart doesn't object."

But what made good advertising copy did not necessarily hold true in real life and marriages. Whether platonic or flagrantly sexual, with or without the consent of the absent partner, extramarital relationships generally led to marital strain. One hastily married woman began seeing her husband's fraternity brother, and although their behavior remained honorable, their feelings heated up. The woman dutifully broke off the relationship, but the seeds of marital discontent had been permanently planted. In other cases, they were quick to bear bitter fruit, as some women wrote "Dear John" brush-off letters and divorced their husbands as impulsively as they had married them.

Even marriages of longer standing were vulnerable to extramarital liaisons. War pulled husbands and wives apart, dropping them into new, unexpected situations where they often shared profound, life-altering experiences with others. In such circumstances old bonds could break and new ones be formed with surprising speed. It was a common story and led to many agonizing decisions and broken hearts. Among others, it happened to C. M., a young English wife who began the war newly married and "very much in love" with her husband. But war not only separated the couple, it brought new experiences in its wake. As C. M. told it,

> Now I had to meet and mix with more people . . . Our small town was swarming with either Americans, Fleet Air Arm, or other servicemen . . . I was introduced to a Fleet Air Arm boy . . . We saw quite a lot of each other from then on and later . . . he told me that he was madly in love with me. I knew then that I felt the same about him but hadn't dared to think about it.

Pregnancy soon forced thought upon her. Now carrying her lover's child, she knew that she had to make "a very hard decision." She also realized that whatever she decided would end one phase of her life and start another. The war itself was at last drawing to a close, and for all those who lived through it, the time had come for both endings and new beginnings.

Endings, Happy and Otherwise

The war in Europe ended on 7 May 1945—Hitler was dead and the Germans had surrendered unconditionally. On both sides of the Atlantic, people listened to the announcement on their radios as tears streamed from their eyes. Japan surrendered on 14 August, and with that the second war to end all wars was finally over.

At last, people were free to come and go—brides embarking on new lives overseas, soldiers returning to the loved ones left behind. Of course, not everyone made it home at war's end. Civilians—men, women, and children alike—had gone missing, died of starvation, or fallen victim to enemy bombs. And all too many servicemen's wives had received "the dreaded telegram" that said "killed in action." "I couldn't believe it," mourned one bereaved wife, "we worshipped each other. I wanted to die."

Leonora Pitt's wartime love story had a happier ending. A medical condition had kept Tom comparatively safe in the forces in England, and the couple would go on to have six children and enjoy forty years of married life. Even so, they had endured a three-year separation and, once reunited, they experienced the inevitable adjustment problems, as well as food shortages and a thirteen-year wait to move into a home of their own. But as Leonora observed, "That's another story."

For others, the course of wartime love did not run so smoothly. "Heartbroken," C.M. gave up her lover, stayed with her husband, and never revealed that their eldest son was not his. For over forty years, she kept her secret, bearing in silence "the guilt and torture" of deception for the sake of "a happy married life." "But why," she still asked herself, "did I have to meet someone else? I don't know whether . . . he is dead or alive. It would be so nice to know."

Isabel and Jack were finally reunited in New York City in 1946, but there was little left of the overwhelming feelings of romance that had originally brought them together. Just released from a German prison camp, Jack was sixty pounds thinner than when Isabel had first met him and most of his teeth were missing. "It was like seeing the ghost of a stranger," was her shocked reaction.

Many war brides had similar reactions to the once dashing heroes they had impetuously married, and British women in North America had the added problems of adapting to a new country and culture. Some also faced anti-British and anti-war-bride sentiment, usually in the form of resentful ex-girlfriends and hostile in-laws. The predictable result for a few was divorce and a return trip to Britain. But most, about 95 percent, stayed and many, including Isabel, enjoyed long marriages.

The Embers of War

That so many successful marriages came out of the war clearly testified that the institution had survived the global upheaval. But there was equally strong evidence that its structure had been shaken. Shirley Temple's short-lived marriage to John Agar was like many other, equally rash unions that would quickly end and contribute to the rising tide of divorces in both North America and Britain. In the United States the rate doubled between 1940 and 1946, and the total number of divorces during the decade reached one million; the figure in Britain was more modest—a total of 60,000 by 1947—but unprecedented nonetheless.

While marriage was shaky, traditional sex roles were gaining new life. At war's end some military women turned to civilian work, taking up clerical or other traditional female jobs. Mary Lee Settle, the American in the British WAAFs, worked for a time in London's Office of War Information before returning to the States and beginning a career as a professional writer. But she was unusual. When the war was over, many ex-servicewomen simply traded their military insignia for a housewife's apron.

A similar fate awaited Rosie the Riveter, Wanda the Welder, and all the women they represented. In North America, some went back into the kitchen willingly, but many more (about 75 percent) would have preferred to keep their jobs after the war. Neither group had much say in the matter. Women were quickly lured or pushed out of the workplace by a combination of propaganda, social pressure, and exclusionist employment policies.

Canada cut back tax incentives for married women who worked and stopped government funding of child care. Federal legislation in the United States gave returning veterans first claim on their old jobs, while reinstated corporate requirements regarding the age and marital status of female workers ensured higher layoff and lower employment rates for women. In both countries widespread conservative opinion, the church, and the media all sternly reminded Rosie and Wanda that their place was in the home. The war was over and it was time for everyday life and sex roles to return to "normal."

In other words, World War II was no feminist revolution. What it did do was pave the way for a later feminist wave that would bring changes in women's work patterns and new strategies for child care. It also eased old taboos about sexual issues. Once and for all, the "conspiracy of silence" had been broken, as wartime anti-VD campaigns brought sex to the forefront of public discussion.

Although the focus of concern was heterosexuality, the war also raised people's consciousness about other sexualities. This was particularly so among those who had been in the forces where, despite recruitment screening procedures, same-sex liaisons inevitably occurred. Never officially tolerated, active homosexuals and lesbians were occasionally court-martialed, often discharged, and often tacitly ignored—especially in the female forces, whose incidence of lesbianism was considerably lower than that of homosexuality among servicemen. The gay rights movement was still twenty years in the future, but by bringing gay men and lesbians together in numbers larger than ever before, war laid the groundwork for what would follow.

The breakdown of restraints that marked heterosexual behavior during World War II was dramatic, but not entirely without precedent. To a certain extent the crisis atmosphere of the war merely furthered revolutionary changes that had begun in the 1920s. But the war created a rapid acceleration in the biggest twentieth-century revolution of all. Impulsive marriages, rising divorce, and the passionate pursuit of immediate sexual gratification were all expressions of a growing belief in the primacy of self and personal happiness.

Though a rebound decade of attempted moral conservatism would follow, people would never again, deep in their hearts, feel the same way about premarital sex and marital fidelity. Individual behavior might return to the circumspect, but the underlying principles had sustained a mortal blow. By war's end passion was no longer a widely understood ideal, encompassing but surpassing physical pleasure. In the hearts, minds, and vocabulary of the majority, it had dwindled to another word for sex.

With peace a reality at last, the day of the sedate suburb was dawning. On the surface of things the way to happiness was via a secure job for men, domesticity for women, a nice rancher for the growing family, a green lawn, and a new car. That was what people *talked* about—meanwhile, they thought a lot about sex.

The Flagrant Fifties

6

*The era was a much more interesting one
than it appeared on the surface.*

— DAVID HALBERSTAM, *The Fifties*

It was a decade of "isms"—consumerism, moralism, conformism, and sexual conservatism. Unprecedented prosperity made the suburban good life and its trappings—houses, cars, furniture, appliances, and gadgets—widely affordable and seemingly indispensable. But in the midst of modern abundance, people managed to hang on to old-fashioned morality. They knew decent values when they saw them and were quick to detect influences that might corrupt impressionable youth and family stability. No one used the word "sexism" in those days, but the wartime blurring of gender roles was now a thing of the past, as men and women resumed their proper places in life. Men went out to work and women stayed at home. Both sexes curbed their urge for erotic expression in an effort to live down the excesses of the war years.

But if the good life in all senses was now within reach, it was already threatened by the shadow of yet another "ism." Communism—the so-called Red Menace—loomed large as yet another war erupted, this time in Korea. On the home front the notorious Republican Senator from Wisconsin, Joseph McCarthy, waged his own war, a witch hunt for Communist infiltrators and homosexual civil servants. The headlines and anxieties that McCarthy generated fueled other, largely irrational, fears. Some people worried not only about the atomic bomb and Communist attack but also about invasion by space aliens of the sort that now proliferated in pulp science fiction and low-budget movies. Others were concerned about the homosexual overtones of action comic books, the overstimulating effects of rock and roll, or the glorification of juvenile delinquency in movies like *The Wild One* (1954), with Marlon Brando, and *Rebel without a Cause* (1955), with James Dean.

The Korean War ended in 1953 and McCarthyism died an ignominious death soon after. The Cold War and fears of nuclear destruction persisted, as did intermittent moral panics about the corruption of youth. But for the most part people managed to push these to the back of their minds and focus on what was really important—in a word, normality. No one could quite define it, but everyone knew that it had a lot to do with home, family, strong marriages, good morals, social stability, and material comfort. By the middle of the decade the "normal" had taken a firm hold on popular consciousness, and life subsided into the version of the fifties that would linger most fondly in memory.

In North America the nuclear family held sway. People married earlier than ever before and the resultant baby boom produced more children than did India in the same decade. The rise of easily prepared or ready-to-serve food reflected both the new prosperity and the supremacy of the child-centered family. Maternal convenience and juvenile taste were at the heart of the bland, starchy, or sweet foods that quickly became household staples—Kool-Aid, crinkly potato chips, sweets made from marshmallow and crispy cereal, Jell-O in molds, Twinkies, and so on. Culinary adventure took the form of Rice-a-Roni and Chef Boy-Ar-Dee Spaghetti Dinner.

Once a year, the prosperous middle-class family locked up their rancher or split-level, piled into their late-model Ford or Chevy, and perhaps ventured as far as that new amusement park on the outskirts of Los Angeles. And on the way to Disneyland they might stay at one of the up-and-coming Holiday Inns and "Give Mom a Night Off" by eating a newly franchised burger at McDonald's—of which there were 145 by 1959. Back at home the family settled cozily into a colonial sofa suite or Danish modern sectional in the "rec" room or living room, in front of what was by the end of the decade the omnipresent television set. On screen *The Adventures of Ozzie and Harriet, The Donna Reed Show, Father Knows Best, Leave It to Beaver, The Mickey Mouse Club, Queen for a Day,* and *The $64,000 Question* affirmed and reaffirmed the supreme normality of marriage, family life, and material well-being.

This portrait of a decade depicts only part of the reality. Among the absent images are the everyday experiences of the working poor, minority racial or ethnic groups, and those of alternative sexualities. Also missing from the picture is the true fragility of 1950s "normality." This was especially so in sexual matters and in the relationship of men and women.

Though people tried to eradicate the extremes of war and to carve out staid lives, ultimately their efforts were unsuccessful. Men and women were intensely caught up in the often contradictory pursuits of prosperity, moral decency, social stability, personal happiness—and sex. In city and in suburb, the flashy, the defiant, the indiscreet—the flagrant—could not help but break through the fifties' facade of complacent normality.

Tantalizing Television

Predictably, the decade's agenda of self-conscious repression did much to determine the content of the foremost new medium, television. Of all the forms of popular entertainment, it was the tamest. Its audiences, after all, were mainly families, and unlike the movies, TV was part of their everyday home life. But, circumspect though it generally was, even television had its tantalizing moments of defying narrow definitions of the permissible.

Among the milder examples were the occasional series that moved beyond the conventional marital life-style of Ozzie and Harriet Nelson and their kind. In *The Bob Cummings Show* (1955–1959), for instance, Bob was a photographer and bachelor ladies' man who exuded sex appeal on-screen for a parade of attractive female models. Offscreen, the suggestion was, he was exercising more than just his appeal. Even so, the presence of his widowed sister and her son as part of his bachelor household helped to "normalize" the situation.

More daringly, the variety show host Steve Allen booked the stand-up comedian Lenny Bruce, whose routines were notorious for their "blue" material. Allen introduced his guest as "the most shocking comedian of our time." The trouble was, unable to deploy his usual stock of graphic language and sexual detail, he had to fall back on thin social satire. The audience, apparently bemused, applauded politely when prompted but barely managed so much as a weak chuckle.

There had been little such ambivalence in audience reaction to an earlier series of daring television moments. Well-preserved in both syndication and memory, one of the most popular sitcoms ever had premiered in 1951. By the following year, *I Love Lucy* was number one in the ratings. At that point, its star Lucille Ball had—depending on the point of view—the good fortune or bad taste to become pregnant. The Philip Morris Company, the principal sponsor, was less than pleased and recommended advance shootings before Lucy "showed" or, alternatively, hiding her expanding form behind chairs and tables.

The comedienne, along with her husband and co-star Desi Arnaz, managed to convince the sponsor and the network that a visibly pregnant woman would not destroy ratings. In episodes ranging over December 1952 and January 1953, Lucy grew publicly ever larger. To help moderate her blatantly undisguised condition, on-screen language paid proper lip service to 1950s sensibilities— she was not therefore *pregnant* but "enceinte" or "expecting." A few complainers still found the subject objectionable, but on the whole the television audience was enthusiastic. It was "about time" for openness about a "natural and normal" occurrence: such was the consensus expressed in letters to various newspapers. Having followed her pregnancy, 44 million people watched the culminating episode, "Lucy Goes to the Hospital." It was a tough act to follow, and the next day the inauguration of President Dwight Eisenhower drew only half that number of viewers.

If ratings were any guide, then a few years later a rising superstar would draw even larger audiences than the birth of "Little Ricky." Elvis Presley, the up-and-coming "King of Rock and Roll" performed on *The Milton Berle Show* in June 1956 and generated a flood of complaints about his vulgar movements. His next appearance, July 1st on *The Steve Allen Show*, was a toned-down attempt to deflect further criticism. But the effort backfired, as fans took extreme exception to their rehabilitated idol. Yet for all the uncharacteristic blandness of the singer's performance for Steve Allen, it still managed to catapult the show to number one.

In the end, the television host who would allow Elvis to revert to form was, ironically, the man who had insisted that he would never permit such a degenerate act on his show. As implied by his "stone face" and stiff posture, Ed Sullivan had a puritanical streak. But the problem was, his stern moral stance was bad show business. Thanks to Elvis, Steve Allen had eclipsed him in the ratings for the first time. Sullivan didn't like to be one-upped: he set aside his principles and booked Elvis for three shows.

The first was something of a compromise. "Elvis the Pelvis" launched into his signature gyrations, while the camera primly showed him only from the waist up. But in subsequent appearances this nod to discretion gave way to full-length camera angles. From a business standpoint, it was the right move—the show's ratings soared—and Sullivan managed to hang on to his self-appointed role as the guardian of public morals. No need to worry, he assured the viewing audience at the end of the third spot, "This is a real decent, fine boy." It was an effective enough face-saver, but the truth was somewhat different. As millions looked on, the studied primness that the middle-aged Sullivan stood for had given way to the self-expressive flamboyancy of a backwoods boy. The flagrant was gaining ground.

Showy Businesses

In Hollywood in the 1950s, the Hays Code was still in force, though its grip was easing somewhat, while the Catholic Legion of Decency was as likely as ever to condemn anything "too carnal." The moviegoing public, however, was developing more and more of a taste for the blatantly sexy, and the forces of censorship were in a pitched battle with the commercial motives of the producers. The turning point was the 1953 comedy of manners *The Moon Is*

Blue. It was denied the Code Seal of Approval and earned a "condemned" rating from the Legion. As the Code's director contended, it used words like "seduce" and "virgin," and adopted an "unacceptably light attitude toward seduction, illicit sex, chastity and virginity." Taking a chance, the producers released it anyway. Popular taste prevailed, and it was a box-office smash.

The Code would survive until 1966, when it was replaced by the rating system, which classed movies as G, PG, R, and X. But the barrier had been crossed and from 1953 on, movies progressively pushed the boundaries of acceptability. For example, in *Mogambo*, a 1953 remake of the earlier *Red Dust*, Clark Gable, Ava Gardner, and Grace Kelly played a steamy love triangle in an exotic African setting. In 1954 *The French Line* featured "Jane Russell in 3 dimension—and what dimensions!" Tom Ewell and Marilyn Monroe flirted with adultery in *The Seven Year Itch* (1955); magnetic William Holden and seductive Kim Novak cheated on Cliff Robertson in *Picnic* (1955); and Brigitte Bardot was nude and seductive in *And God Created Woman* (1956). Hormonal teens Sandra Dee and Troy Donahue went on a family vacation with adulterous adults in *A Summer Place* (1959), and in the same year *Some Like It Hot* starred Jack Lemmon and Tony Curtis as oversexed transvestites hiding out in an all-girl band. And so on . . .

While the movie industry was increasingly catering to the public's taste for sex, the publishing business had long been blatantly marketing the same product. The "sex adventure" pulps of the 1920s and 1930s survived in 1950s form, their paper covers more lurid than ever. Drawn with dramatic three-dimensional effects, busty women postured suggestively in skimpy wisps of fabric to advertise the sexy crime and science fiction plots that lay between the covers. Even the innocent romance paperbacks of the day spiced up their covers with similarly endowed young women who pneumatically filled out their virginal white nurses' uniforms while an improbably handsome doctor or two hovered admiringly in the background.

Not only that, but the once gentlemanly branch of the book trade, literary publishing, adopted similarly showy artwork to sell serious fiction. On the cover of a 1950 paperback edition of George Orwell's *1984* the female characters wear form-fitting jumpsuits, open to midriff level, while the men are also tightly and minimally clad to show off bulging muscles. In the foreground the two main characters, Julia and Winston, press closely against one another. Only "Big Brother," staring ominously from a poster on the wall, remains exempt from the general mood of sexy cocktail party.

As it happened, this promising direction for literary book jackets was soon cut off. Pressured by a U.S. congressional investigation of salaciousness in reading materials, publishers of pulps and classics alike toned down their products' covers. But this did not necessarily curtail the spicy content inside—or the saleability of provocative themes. J. D. Salinger's *The Catcher in the Rye* appeared in paperback in 1953, complete with the graphic language that had shocked some people when the hardcover version had made its debut two years before. In 1956, *Peyton Place*, by Grace Metalious, chronicled the dark sexual underbelly of a seemingly respectable small town. It was an instant best-seller—so exactly did it hit the nerve of a decade struggling between repressiveness on the one hand and flagrancy on the other. Its sales quickly reached the three-million mark and soared on to six million copies by the middle of 1958.

That was the year that saw the American publication of another book that defied taboos. Vladimir Nabokov's *Lolita*, the story of the sexual affair between a middle-aged professor and a prepubescent "nymphet" opened up a Pandora's box of previously unspeakable subjects, such as pedophilia and juvenile sexuality. Prominent critics deemed the book pornographic, obscene, and repulsive—in other words, tailor-made for the taste of the time. *Lolita*, not surprisingly, was yet another fifties best-seller.

By mid-decade, public taste for the sensational had even given recognition, if not wholesale approval, to members of the so-called beat generation. "Beatniks," as they were also called, were writers, artists, and self-appointed social outcasts who advocated escape from the "square" puritanical conventions of the day, via any means at hand—artistic license, Zen, "wheels," booze, drugs, sex. Among the leaders of the movement was Allen Ginsberg, author of the antiestablishment critique "Howl." A long poem dripping with anger against society, esoteric literary allusions, and explicit sexual imagery, it gained widespread notoriety when it was prosecuted in 1956 for obscenity (unsuccessfully, as it turned out). In the following year another of the movement's leaders, Jack Kerouac, published his autobiographical novel of drifting and rebellion, *On the Road*, an achievement that won him a spot on *The Steve Allen Show* in 1959. Though Kerouac probably cared as little about the dyed-in-the wool "squares" in the TV audience as they did about him, his television appearance was a turning point—the rebellious beat generation had gone from marginal to fashionable.

While Kerouac and Ginsberg were still emerging from obscurity, another rebel with a somewhat different cause was already enjoying the rewards of his own successful venture into the world of publishing. But it was magazines, not books, and a mass audience, rather than the intellectual elite, that interested the young Hugh Hefner. In 1953 he put all his savings into the publication of a shaky endeavor that would not only become the successful magazine for men, *Playboy*, but would soon grow into a commercial empire.

With his taste for Ivy League clothes and women who looked like the girl next door, on the surface he seemed anything but rebellious. In fact, though, his new magazine was in part a rebellion against his own Midwestern Calvinist upbringing. It also challenged

123

the supremacy of the marital ideal and women's right to benefit economically from men. A feature article in *Playboy*'s inaugural issue was cynically entitled "Miss Gold-Digger of 1953."

Apparently, though, the reverse situation—a man benefiting economically from a woman—was entirely acceptable to Hefner. *Playboy*'s first issue had sold a promising 53,000 copies, and what had launched it was neither its publisher's philosophy nor the literary merits of its articles. The foundation of what would become the multimillion-dollar *Playboy* empire was the inaugural issue's nude centerfold picture of the rising young star Marilyn Monroe. Hefner had shrewdly purchased rights to the photograph, which had initially featured in a calendar. He paid the photographer five hundred dollars and Marilyn Monroe nothing.

Hefner and many of the magazine's fans claimed that *Playboy* was really about the pleasures of sophisticated living, and that nude pictures were only incidental to this central agenda. This was part of the truth, but the magazine's original title told the rest of the story. Hefner had wanted to call it *Stag Party* and no amount of discouragement from his supporters had budged him. It took a letter and the threat of legal action from the lawyers of a hunting magazine called *Stag* to persuade him that *Playboy* would be a better title. That change of heart aside, Hefner's real intent was apparent—the blatant display of one sex by, and for, the other. *Playboy* was not necessarily the worst such exploiter, but it stood out as one of the glossiest and showiest.

Conspicuous Consumption

In a decade that gave rise to *Playboy*, Elvis, and Jane Russell in 3-D, people were hardly likely to be content as mere consumers of bland food for children, household cleaners for germ-conscious housewives, and modest suburban ranchers. More often than not, what went into those ranchers and what was parked in their driveways were in the best spirit of the flagrant fifties. Yet underneath all the frivolous flashiness were some serious issues—status, appropriate sexual roles, and within limits, individual expression.

Inside the home, woman's domain, individual expression meant a combination of shine, gloss, vivid colors, and modernistic design that reflected the postwar space age. Everyday objects such as toasters and coffeemakers gleamed in bright chrome that showed off their sleek, modern lines. Plumbing fixtures came in a variety of pastel shades, and no homemaker had to settle for old-fashioned white appliances when she could have a stove with flashing multicolored lights, and choose a fridge in one of the exciting tints of the day—Bermuda Pink, Buttercup Yellow, Fern Green, or Lagoon Blue. No modern breakfast nook was complete without a dinette set of chrome offset by a plastic laminate tabletop and matching chairs upholstered in turquoise, yellow, or lime-green vinyl. Living-room sofas boasted bold plaids, colonial prints, tiger stripes, and solid expanses of hot pink, turquoise blue, or sulfuric yellow upholstery fabric. Walls might be painted in a single color—chartreuse green, aqua, or sandalwood, for example—or combine a trio of shades such as sea green, sand beige, and deep coral. No-iron fiberglass curtains printed with lines and geometrics in similar colors often completed the effect.

Television commercials, as well as magazine articles and advertising, depicted countless images of women painting walls, matching fabrics, showing off their gleaming kitchens to admiring friends, or standing proudly beside a new stove or washing machine. The model for them all was Betty Furness, television's Westinghouse lady, who sold domestic femininity along with the sponsor's products. Furness and her kind were somewhat matronly but also glamorous in a respectable wifely way. Above all, their enthusiasm and wide smiles demonstrated their unquestioning faith that their starring domestic role was as bright as the sofas and stoves they sold.

For a man, the ultimate in conspicuous 1950s consumerism was his car. The bigger, newer, and gaudier the car, therefore, the more importance it gave him. At the heart of collective memories of the 1950s are the flashy, finny extravaganzas on wheels that took Dad to work, Mom shopping, and the kids on vacation. The 1955 Buick Century, 1956 De Soto Firedome, 1957 Ford Fairlane 500, 1958 Mercury Montclair Phaeton, 1959 Chevy Impala—these were the flagrant stuff of suburban dreams.

Even the most sedate family sedan might be as colorful as the home whose carport it occupied. Candy apple red, emerald green, and canary yellow were among the popular picks of the decade. The well-heeled sporty type might go for an Oldsmobile Golden Rocket, silver Pontiac Club de Mer with red upholstery, or a three-toned Ford Atmos in patriotic red, white, and blue. Upholstery might be solid-colored leather or vinyl or, perhaps, combine plastic insets with fabric emulating the pelts of improbable big game—the black-spotted silver fiberglass leopard for one. A pair of outsize, soft-form dice hanging from the rear-view mirror often provided the perfect finishing touch.

"Status may be validated in the acquisition and exhibition of . . . cars" and other "material objects." This was the conclusion of John Seeley and a team of other social scientists who investigated "Crestwood Heights," an affluent central Canadian suburb whose like was "to be seen in and around almost any great city" in North America, "from New York to San Francisco, from Halifax to Vancouver." A half century earlier Thorstein Veblen, the author of *The Theory of the Leisure Class*, had coined the phrase "conspicuous consumption," characterizing it as the flaunting of the evidence that one had sufficient means to do nothing. By the 1950s this was completely turned around; unchecked consumerism showed, instead, how hard the head of the family worked, and how much he and his wife cared about the welfare of their children.

Consumerism was also a way of both conforming and asserting individuality. A woman's life choices, for instance, might be curtailed by the credo of female domesticity, but at least when it came to interior decor she had free rein. For men the car was both the means to get to work and the way to escape from the increasingly uneasy conformity represented in Sloan Wilson's *The Man in the Gray Flannel Suit* (1955) and William Whyte's *The Organization Man* (1956). It was the company man who donned his suit in the morning and went dutifully to the office, but it was the authentic individual who drove home that night in a fin-tailed multicolored sedan. An advertisement for a 1959 Plymouth with extravagant tail fins, a mauve-and-white paint job, and candy-cane striped upholstery assured the ostensible conformist who was secretly dying to break loose that "Good Taste Is Never Extreme."

Cars also purportedly did their bit for male sexual fantasy. One writer for a mid-fifties trade magazine likened contemporary car design to Marilyn Monroe. The combination of narrow angles and curvaceous fins was an automotive reminder of the seductive contrast between Monroe's nipped-in waistline and lavish bosom. What normal man could resist?

Consumerism not only gripped adult men and women but became an irrepressible force in the lives of North American adolescents. The concept of the teenager, as distinct from child or adult, had become historically fully developed at least a decade before in the persona of the "bobby-soxer," but never before had teens formed such a distinctive and powerful consumer group. In the mid-1950s they represented 43 percent of the record market and 53 percent of moviegoers. They bought 44 percent of all cameras sold, 39 percent of all radios, and 9 percent of new cars. By exercising their consumer choice in clothing, music, and entertainment, teens expressed their distinctiveness from their parents and, at the same time, conformed with their peer group.

As it did with adults, consumerism also helped to reinforce gender roles. For example, owning a car, however run-down, went a long way toward marking a boy's passage to manhood. On the other hand, achieving womanhood through consumerism was a more complicated undertaking, requiring constant expenditures on makeup, hair products, clothing, bras, and girdles—all to meet the rigorous contemporary standard of appropriate femininity and blatant sex appeal. In Crestwood Heights, as elsewhere, "the girls were almost unanimous that 'glamor' was an integral part of the female role." And the ideal of beauty had a relentless hold on teenage girls. Lipstick alone was costing them a staggering $40 million annually by 1959.

This was also the year that saw the introduction of a new product that could only have emerged in the flagrant decade of cars with fins, space-age design, and lime-green vinyl dinette suites. It was made of plastic. It was sexy, streamlined, and modern. It had a black-and-white zebra-striped covering and yellow top. Its twin protrusions not only defied gravity but were shaped like the nosecones of rockets. The product was Barbie.

It was also the culminating icon of a time that placed unparalleled value on consumerism and all that went with it. The doll itself was inexpensive and widely affordable. At the same time, it came with an array of brightly colored costumes and accessories that conferred status on the child who accumulated them. It encouraged individualism through imaginative play, but also helped to define gender roles—among its separately sold accessories were a beauty parlor, wedding ensemble, dream home, and boyfriend, Ken. No mere plaything, the Barbie doll stood for social stability, upward mobility, and material comfort. Best of all, it was flashy.

Woman's Lot

Barbie was mainly marketed to prepubescent girls but also carried a message to the grown woman consumer. Not only did the doll reinforce the traditional female gender role but, as noticeably busty as any movie sex symbol, it embodied the ideal woman's physical glamour and attractiveness.

While the ideal woman was undoubtedly alluring, she was also domestic. In magazine and television advertising, the housewife dispensed Kool-Aid to children, rid her houses of germs, decorated rooms, and showed off her new stove—and she did all this in high heels, a dress, and flawless makeup, the attire of the woman who means to attract her man. But she was always ladylike, and so much in command of herself and her domain that nothing ever ruffled a hair of her flattering professional coiffure.

In most advertisements for domestic products, the sex appeal of the woman was discreet. But when it came to products specifically designed to enhance attractiveness—dresses, swimwear, and lingerie, for example—the flagrant spirit of the time leapt into the limelight. A distinct air of sexual fetishism hung around high-heeled pumps with pointed toes and the tight sheath dresses that fashionably pinched in the waist and accentuated the breasts. Bathing suits often exaggerated the bust even more than dresses, sometimes constricting the waist as sternly as the corsets of two generations ago. And padded bras boasted space-age construction that endowed virtually every woman with Barbie's nosecone breasts.

While many women ostensibly accepted their status of domestic sexpot—presumably some even genuinely enjoyed it—others were not so pleased with either their role or themselves. In a decade that blatantly emphasized women's physical assets over most others, widespread feelings of unworthiness were inevitable—most women did not look like Marilyn, Jane, or Barbie. Whether they wanted to or not, the majority of women felt compelled to make some effort to avoid being the object of contemporary prejudices against homeliness, overweight, and aging. The billions of dollars they spent on cosmetics, electric hair dryers, lingerie, and visits to beauty parlors and slimming salons is a fair indicator of their endeavor. It is only possible to imagine the extent to which so many suffered emotionally in the cause of beauty.

Pretty or plain, women were also supposed to take on the burden of housework without complaint. Even among the privileged wives of Crestwood Heights there was "considerable ambivalence," sometimes out-and-out resentment, about the homemaker's role. "Honestly, I find it hard to take," said one woman speaking of her experiences with motherhood. "I'm just the poor old workhorse, and I take all the abuse."

All too often, ambivalence or resentment turned into depression. Some of it was postpartum, and the much reprinted guru of child-rearing, Dr. Spock, had some recommendations for women who suffered from "the blue feeling." "Go to a movie, or to the beauty parlor, or to get yourself a new hat or dress." To anyone reading those words several decades later, his tone might sound unbearably patronizing. But the advice was not all bad, and certainly it beat the alternatives to which some women turned. For many, smoking and alcohol were not just social practices but deeply rooted addictions that offered the illusion of coping. Doctors also conspired, prescribing addictive "uppers" to boost daytime energy and barbiturates to ensure a sound night's sleep—this, surely, was one of the darkest aspects of 1950s sexism.

Fortunately, many other women refused to remain unhappily housebound. They took off their aprons, made arrangements for the children, and went out into the workplace. One of the myths about the 1950s is that married women played virtually no part in the workforce. Though there was an immediate postwar drop in the number of women employed outside the home, the figures rose steadily throughout the 1950s. In the United States the employment rate for married and single women increased four times as fast as that of men during the decade. By 1960 close to a third of married women went out to work and represented more than half of all women in paid employment. The Canadian figures were less striking, but there was still a steady rise in the employment of both married and single women from the mid-1950s on.

Many took such traditional female jobs as office work, teaching, nursing, and social work. The more lucrative professions were still unwelcoming to women; as late as 1960 only 3.5 percent of lawyers were female. Women with limited education had to content themselves with low-wage, low-status jobs, and the concept of equal pay for equal work had not yet been heard of. In the mid-1950s, for example, women factory workers on average earned 70 percent of what their male counterparts received.

Women generally accepted the inequitable work situation with little or no protest. Their social conditioning had schooled them to unquestioning acceptance, and for many women a job—any job—offered escape from the demoralizing boredom of domesticity. In lower-income families, women worked because they needed the money—however small, their salaries made the difference between near poverty and at least getting by. Even in relatively affluent middle-class households a second income became increasingly welcome, if not absolutely necessary, as the decade wore on. After all, the latest in houses, cars, furniture, appliances, and holidays demanded constant disposable income. The good life definitely wasn't cheap.

Sex, Marriage, and the Collapsing Norm

Consumerism was by no means the only temptation to which people succumbed. Conventional morality dictated that sex took place only in the marital bedroom, and many couples strictly followed that prescription for happiness. But many others paid only lip service to convention, as their actions overstepped its bounds.

Marriage for the old-fashioned purpose of procreation was still a must in the fifties—if nothing else, it was the rationale for all those ranchers in the suburbs. But following the trend of the century's previous decades, the foremost consideration was the couple's pleasure. And if sex was for pleasure more than procreation, it followed that marital happiness and fidelity depended less on fertility than on sexual fulfillment. On this crucial point the marriage experts all agreed. When out in public with your husband, advised one sex guide for women, whisper in his ear that you are not wearing panties. But this bit of suggested titillation was the merest foreplay when it came to sexual guidance for married couples. Each expert had a characteristic way of putting it, but the message was always the same—a good sex life meant a good marriage.

Over and over, the marriage manuals of the fifties, along with earlier works still circulated, offered the same formula for marital success. "A satisfying sex life." "Harmony in the sexual sphere." "A vigorous and harmonious sex life." "Mutual enjoyment in the sex union." In keeping with a time that valued marital sex so highly, the introduction to the 1957 edition of *Ideal Marriage*, by Theodore Van de Velde, promised "all the data bearing upon the physiology and technique of sexual congress." At the same time, out-and-out flagrancy had to be kept in check and, as the introduction reassured readers, the sex advice in the book would be delivered "without a scintilla of eroticism."

The same kind of ambivalent attitude to sex also showed itself in the public's response to what was popularly known as "the Kinsey Report." This in fact was two reports, based on a sex survey conducted by Professor Alfred C. Kinsey and colleagues at the University of Indiana. The first report, *Sexual Behavior in the Human Male*, had appeared in 1948, and people were still talking about it when the second, *Sexual Behavior in the Human Female*, came out in 1953. People were shocked—many bookstores and libraries refused to stock the books, the press attacked them, and the *New York Times* declined to review them. The reports were disgusting to some, a sensation for most; sales were brisk.

What disturbed people about the Kinsey reports was not that a lot of sex was going on—everyone already knew that—but the fact that it was made so explicit, broken down precisely into percentages and specific acts. Most upsetting of all was the extent to which the statistics undermined conventional standards of morality and ideas of normality. According to Kinsey, for example, about 5 percent of the male population was exclusively homosexual, and 50 percent of men who remained single to age thirty-five had homosexual encounters. Kinsey also reported that nearly 50 percent of women were not virgins on marriage and that 26 percent of wives engaged in extramarital sex. Although this last figure lagged well behind the 50 percent of married men who had affairs, along with the erosion of the ideal of female virginity it nonetheless shook the double standard to the core. Kinsey noted, too, the handful of married women who joined their husbands in the social game of "wife-swapping," as the press called it—a practice that had begun in World War II among pilots and their wives, continued during the Korean War, and then spread to the suburbs surrounding air bases.

The uproar over the Kinsey reports was inevitable, and in his own time and subsequently, his methods and findings would be continuously debated. His survey was not geographically or socially representative, critics charged. Furthermore, because the participants were volunteers, there may have been an unrepresentative number of sexual obsessives, exhibitionists, and exaggerators, all too willing to recount and, likely, to embellish their sexual experiences. Kinsey once travelled 1,500 miles to interview a single respondent who claimed he had engaged in sexual acts with hundreds of women, men, children, and animals. But if the study was in many ways flawed, it was still suggestive of the tenuous hold that "normality" had on many people's lives.

In the course of his research, Kinsey himself had managed to stray off the norm's straight and narrow. Although he claimed to be an upholder of traditional values, he was, to say the least, sexually unorthodox: he was a bisexual masochist, and not only did he prostitute his wife to colleagues, but he also seduced his male graduate students, participated in group masturbation sessions, and engaged in sexual self-torture. With the exception of the last-mentioned practice, he diligently photographed and documented these endeavors—purely, of course, in the spirit of scientific inquiry.

Illicit Sex—Even in the Suburbs

Extremist though Kinsey was, and however dubious his research methods, his reports nonetheless reflected everyday reality. Premarital and extramarital sex *were* more common than most people would publicly admit. But here and there, a few were willing to reveal how thin the veneer of 1950s sexual morality really was.

The autobiographer and political lecturer Max Eastman, for one, recalled a premarital affair of "naked lust," as well as several infidelities during a marriage that ended in separation. Though

Eastman's politics were radical, his sexual behavior was no more outrageous than that of many others who also took a liberal view of conventional morality. Dori Schaffer, a middle-class woman in her twenties, was another sexual liberal whose premarital escapades heated up the pages of the diary she kept during the 1950s. "I writhe and moan as he loves me. We explode together in sexual celebration." This was how she described one sexual encounter in what was by no means the diary's most graphic passage.

But for all her apparent lack of inhibition, Dori was not entirely liberated from the conventional ideal that in the end sex and marriage had to go together. "I feel I must get married very quickly," she told her diary, "I'm afraid that I will either become a slut or else withdraw completely." Dori never did marry happily, a victim perhaps of the lingering popular distinction between good girls and bad. Men married the first kind and treated them well— the others simply got what they deserved.

Though marriage undoubtedly remained the ideal for many, as it did for Dori, idealism increasingly allowed for sexual activity. And when it came to susceptibility, a person's age, status, and gender mattered little. Among teenagers at all social levels, for example, heavy petting was a fact of dating life. Down at the local "submarine races" (as "lovers' lanes" were now commonly called), the steamed-up windows of the '53 Plymouth or Dad's '57 Chevy signaled the steamier goings-on in the back seat. While teenage girls still widely stopped short of "all the way," female virginity was losing its importance, as long as a girl was neither promiscuous nor unlucky enough to get pregnant. Going steady was the prelude to engagement, and the beginning of the end of many girls' virginity. As one woman remembered, most of her friends lost it to steadies about a year into the relationship.

While teenagers were taking their sexual experimentation ever further, their elders were also stretching the limits of the norm.

Grace Metalious, the creator of the ever-lusting Peyton Place, had herself strayed into an affair as her marriage faltered, just before the publication of her best-seller. In his memoir, *The Fifties*, Edmund Wilson recalled meeting Ella, a twice-widowed Toronto woman in her early fifties who confided that she had recently had an affair with a Canadian writer. "He was married and had been impotent," Wilson recounted, "but Ella had got him going again and had sent him back to his wife 'healed.'"

Even the staid occupants of Crestwood Heights had their secrets. Husbands who indulged in extramarital affairs fueled neighborhood gossip—their peers judged them to be irresponsible, deviant, and "spoiled." But the condemnations were based as much on adultery's detrimental effect on a man's professional image as they were on strictly moral considerations. For other practical reasons—among them, their "economic vulnerability"—women were less likely to engage in extramarital affairs. But according to one woman, some did take the risk and "go off," as she put it. Others, like herself, merely thought about it a lot. "This phrase 'going off' occurred over and over again," the interviewer observed.

Infidelity, whether in thought or in actual deed, was one of the signs of a time that exalted marriage beyond what reality could bear. Even in the fantasy world of television, the illusion was becoming harder to sustain. By the end of the fifties that most popular of television sitcoms about marriage, *I Love Lucy*, was declining in the ratings. To counter the trend and to enhance audience identification with the characters of Lucy and Ricky Ricardo, the script moved the couple out to where most of their viewers now lived—the suburbs. The show's new Connecticut setting looked idyllic, and the Ricardos were as zanily happy together as ever. But behind the scenes all was not well. Desi Arnaz had been having affairs for years, the marriage was otherwise troubled, and it would end in divorce in 1960.

Lucille Ball and Desi Arnaz were not unusual. Divorce had been rising on a steepening incline since the 1920s and had peaked in 1947. After leveling off in the early 1950s, the rate was climbing again by the decade's close. Marriage of course would persist, but under the already increasing strain of high expectations, individual discontents, and changing morality, the marital idyll of the 1950s was over, even before the decade itself came to an end.

"How Ya Gonna Keep 'Em . . . ?"

Critics have called the fifties a hypocritical time, but the truth was not that simple. Some people were hypocritical, and others lived by the principles they professed. But what the fifties really represented was a failed crusade, a misguided but well-meaning mission to recapture a normality that had already vanished, if in fact it ever existed. The old song "How Ya Gonna Keep 'em Down on the Farm (After They've Seen Paree?)" applied in the 1950s no less than in its own day.

After the role reversals, excitement, and sexual liberation of the war years, it was too much to ask of people that they settle with perfect contentment into a staid suburban life. For a time, consumerism offered a distraction from temptation, a reward for good behavior, and a mode of self-expression, but by mid-decade the novelty of owning things, and buying more things, was starting to wear off, and people were looking for escape routes.

Like the reckless abandon of war, the outwardly repressive materialism of the fifties was yet another phase in the century-long revolution toward ever more complete individualism. In "Crestwood Heights," as it was throughout most of 1950s North America, "the supreme value is the happiness and well-being of the individual." A stable marriage was still the perceived heart of that happiness, but if it failed to measure up, then individualism dictated anything from quiet estrangement to extramarital solace or divorce. From the mid-1950s on, the simmering pot of individualism also included a new youth subculture with a growing sense of alienation from the older generation, and a female population increasingly at odds with the role of domestic sexpot. In short, the social and moral agenda of the fifties was doomed to fail—not by reason of insincerity but because of its historical impossibility.

Though many did not realize or care to face it at the time, the sexual morality they espoused had already widely changed, both within marriage and outside it. "We suffer today a popularising of over-emphasized sex," complained the now elderly sex expert Marie Stopes in 1956. There was little "heart" left in marriages and liaisons, concluded Edmund Wilson. "What is wrong with us?" asked the editor of a Cleveland newspaper. "Something is not there that should be—something we once had."

In the next decades the search for that "something" would intensify. Unfortunately, people's desperate efforts to improve things would only take them further from the social utopia and personal fulfillment they sought.

V

MIXED
PLEASURES

1960–1989

The 1960s and 1970s were years in which social unrest mingled with enhanced sexual and self-expression for both sexes—and for women most strikingly of all. Yet even before the sixties had ended, people increasingly, uneasily, recognized an unhappy truth. For every new social and sexual liberation won, there arose a corresponding discontent or disillusionment. In the beginning it seemed as though men and women were about to grow closer than ever before, but as things turned out, disappointments and confusions soon eroded their enjoyment of one another and of their newly gained freedoms.

As the "me decade" of the seventies gave way to the image-conscious individualism of the eighties, the malaise grew. People now widely realized the high price of sexual and personal fulfillment. The costs ranged from economic, through emotional, to devastating tolls on physical health.

Passion was now truly an outmoded ideal. Great sex was what people were pursuing, many with unblushing directness. The concept was simple enough, the reality often harder to attain. Even those who achieved their desires soon found themselves strangely dissatisfied. A few even dared to articulate a question that was still unthinkable to most. Was sex itself becoming obsolete?

A Partial Revolution

> The sexual form of love . . . understandably became
> our preoccupation . . . But sex, too, has become Western
> man's test and burden more than his salvation.
>
> — ROLLO MAY, *Love and Will*

Something had to give. The discontent that surged just below the sedate surface of the 1950s was soon to swell into a breaking wave. But in light of what would follow, the first years of the 1960s were subdued.

A barometer of popular feeling, entertainment of the time offered few challenges to the social and sexual status quo. On the big screen, Doris Day and her leading men Rock Hudson and Cary Grant (their sexual proclivities still closeted) appeared in mildly titillating comedies that hinted coyly at sex, but continued to uphold the double standard of premarital virginity for women— even those of Day's uncertain age (*Lover Come Back*, 1961; *That Touch of Mink*, 1962). The once shocking Elvis Presley was now mostly appearing in tame romantic musicals, where the setting might change from Hawaii to Acapulco, but plot and characters varied little (*Blue Hawaii*, 1961; *Fun in Acapulco*, 1963). Television was blander still. Between 1961 and the first half of 1964 the top show was *The Beverly Hillbillies*—little more than a conventional family sitcom featuring newly rich bumpkins, instead of the usual suburbanites.

On the social and political scene, for a few brief moments, the legend of Camelot came to life. Youthful and dynamic (*his* sexual proclivities also still closeted) the newly elected President Kennedy embodied an energy and optimism unrivaled since the very first years of the century. Together with his glamorous wife, he stood not only for a better world but for the best that might be attained between men and women. The Camelot metaphor, by placing the Kennedys in a far-off, mythical time, allowed the aura of a half-forgotten ideal to touch them with its magic. Though no one put it this way at the time, what the couple symbolized, on some level, was passion.

Some people believe it was the Kennedy assassination that changed the mood of the times. Or it might have been the escalating war in Vietnam or perhaps the antiestablishment voice of the beat generation, which had finally gained a significant hearing. Or maybe the number of disaffected baby boomers attending college reached a critical mass. Most likely a combination of these circumstances fueled the spirit of social revolt.

By 1968 the Beatles were singing about revolution, and many young people had joined in the chorus, lacing social unrest with defiantly liberated sexual behavior. Though the change from passivity to protest—from sexual discretion to defiance—was slow off the mark, once it got going the momentum was seemingly unstoppable, and the "sexy sixties," as they came to be known, would "swing" on into the first years of the "me decade" of the 1970s. Years later, the men and women who came of age at the time, their disapproving elders, and even their yet-to-be-born children would recollect those decades as the "sexual revolution."

A colorful phrase that often swirled in psychedelic hues, it will no doubt survive in popular parlance. But the changes in sexual behavior—though sometimes dramatic, often disturbing to parents—were not so revolutionary as legend now holds. While sex was undoubtedly a preoccupation of the day, the young people of the sixties and seventies did not blast open a sealed Pandora's box of sexual ills to be let loose on an unsuspecting world. In their own way, caught in the particular stresses of the time, all but the most extreme were doing no more than carrying on down the path of increasingly open pleasure that their elders had forged.

What made the relationship of the sexes suddenly seem so revolutionary, so daringly sexy, is that one way or another, many people were once again caught up in the kind of drama and recklessness that went with war. More than just a sexual revolution, the 1960s and 1970s were a time of embattlement on several fronts. While American troops fought in Vietnam, others fought for social change at home. Student protests on university campuses and the civil rights movement in the U.S. turned the American home front into its own kind of war zone.

In the thick of it all was the fight for self, yet another episode in the twentieth century's long revolution toward ever greater individualism. And in the way of over half a century now, at its heart was sex, more than ever the presumed key to personal happiness. Yet, even before they ended, the supposedly revolutionary sixties and seventies echoed with the hollowness of incompletion. Whatever the benefits might have been—the blows for justice, the rights won, the liberation gained, the advancement of the self—all were, at most, partial victories.

A "New" Sexual World

When the decade of the "sexy sixties" finally hit its stride, the end of the old sexual world was at hand. Or so many people believed. Certainly, on the surface of things, there was much that seemed brand new in its daring.

As ever, entertainment reflected the bigger picture. The film ratings system that had replaced the Hays Code now permitted what it also warned against, in movies like *Who's Afraid of Virginia Woolf* (1966), *The Graduate* (1967), *I Am Curious Yellow* (1967), *Midnight Cowboy* (1969), *MASH* (1970), and *Last Tango in Paris* (1973), to name a few. Newly emboldened filmmakers ventured into explicit sex scenes, graphic language, and even—as moviegoers unaccustomed to such displays in public now described it—"full-frontal nudity." Meanwhile, the live theater productions *Hair* and *Oh! Calcutta!* boasted comparable sights, literally in the flesh. When men and women were not finding titillation at the movies or at stage performances, the younger among them were discovering the club scene—and dances like the bird, the surf, the swim, jerk, and monkey, whose pelvic writhings made the torso-twisting Elvis Presley seem like a quaint remnant of a gentler past.

Meanwhile, if book sales were any guide, reading material had become as liberated as movies, theater, and dancing. Helen Gurley Brown's *Sex and the Single Girl* (1962) was an international best-seller that legitimated a feminine lifestyle that was exciting, unashamedly sexy, and above all husbandless. Soon after, William H. Masters and his wife, Virginia E. Johnson, documented *Human Sexual Response* (1966), and Dr. David Reuben told his readers *Everything You Always Wanted to Know About Sex (But Were Afraid to Ask)* (1969). Not to be outdone, Alex Comfort's *Joy of Sex* (1972) offered "recipes" for everything from daily sexual fare to "gourmet" eroticism.

Striking changes in clothing fashion—ultra-short "miniskirts" for women, "love beads" and long, flowing hair for both sexes—also appeared to herald the dawning of a new sexual age. Antibiotics had greatly reduced the threat of venereal disease, and now for the first time an oral contraceptive for women, known simply as "the pill," had eliminated the fear of pregnancy and further decimated the double standard. The traditional barriers to sexual pleasure and multiple partners for both sexes had at last been surmounted. The religious right and other upholders of conventional morality fretted over unbridled premarital sex and living arrangements that did not involve legal matrimony. Among those who did marry, the institution also seemed under siege, as some husbands and wives toyed with extramarital sex, and the divorce rate skyrocketed. Among women under forty-five, for instance, it rose by two-thirds between 1955 and 1970. Overall, by the early 1970s one in every three marriages in the United States ended in divorce.

But while some condemned the new era, others hailed it. "Love-ins," "swinging," and "shacking up" were the catchwords of the liberated. Their collective mood coalesced during the days of 15 to 17 August 1969. Four hundred thousand young people (and some not quite so young), many sporting long hair, wire-rimmed "granny" glasses, and the symbolic love beads, converged on a farm in upstate New York. There they went "skinny-dipping," made love in the open air, and danced to the sound of Jimi Hendrix, Joni Mitchell, the Who, and other musicians. Their images would freeze in collective memory as the archetypes of what had come before and what would follow. It was the Woodstock Art and Music Fair, and something more than just another "happening." In the words of the activist Abbie Hoffman, it was also a state of mind—a new "nation" born of sex, rock, mood-altering substances, and the contemporary spirit of hope and rebellion.

But Was It Revolution?

"The sexual revolution"—by the late sixties the idea had a firm grip on popular consciousness. With hyperbole designed to whip the "uptight" into a moralistic frenzy, *Newsweek*, 6 February 1967, invoked sexual revolution in the same breath that it conjured the image of amoral "hippies" who "chewed upon" sex "as often and as freely as a handful of sesame seeds." But in fact it was neither "hippies" nor rebellious baby-boomer college students who had pioneered the frank pursuit of sexual experience—the credit for that belonged to their grandparents. More discreetly preoccupying their parents, the same pursuit had burst into the open once again. For virtually every new show of sexuality there was a precedent, and what to some appeared revolutionary was in fact rooted in the past.

"My eyes nearly popped out of my head," said one observer recalling the first time he saw a woman wearing a miniskirt. His reaction was genuine but hardly original. The young "flappers" of his mother's day had similarly startled more than one middle-aged male getting his first eyeful of bound breasts, knee-length skirt, and rolled-down hose. And, as perhaps he had forgotten, women had also worn short skirts during the 1940s. This had not only reflected wartime fabric shortages but also the liberated sexuality of the day.

Like the miniskirt, other icons and events of the "revolution" were not altogether new. Before the Hays Code of 1934, movies had often featured sexual themes and nudity, and even the Code itself had left room for progressively greater liberties as time went on. In the realm of theater, Mae West's *Sex*, like *Hair* and *Oh! Calcutta!*, had pushed the limits of public taste, and earlier still, vaudeville had boasted its share of innuendo and bare flesh. Similarly, the wave of sex books that seemed to be unique hallmarks of a new sexual age were part of a tradition—Masters and Johnson, Alex Comfort, and the rest were the natural heirs of Marie Stopes, Freud, Kinsey, and many others. Masters and Johnson in particular upheld the traditional ideals of marriage and family.

Even the gyrating dances of the sixties and seventies were novel but not wholly new. They not only recalled Elvis Presley but also harked back to the earliest years of the century, when many popular dances demanded energetic and suggestive pelvic movements. The difference was that the old dances involved close physical contact between men and women, while those of the alleged sexual revolution did not. Studiously avoiding touching, partners shimmied and shook in their own separate spaces, sometimes several feet distant from one another.

Among the young people who moved to the beat of the day and its dances was Walt Crowley, then a journalist for Seattle's underground newspaper *Helix*. In his memory the sixties still hum with political energy, while the so-called sexual revolution lingers as something of a nonevent. In *Rites of Passage*, his 1995 memoir of the sixties, he observed that "The period's famous 'sexual revolution' was more of a coincidence thanks to the pill and penicillin." But penicillin had been curbing venereal disease since World War II, and even the pill was actually a development of the 1950s, though it was not widely available until 1960.

In short, much of the "sexual revolution" had already happened. As Walt Crowley summarized it, "Contrary to conservative rhetoric, people were loving freely long before."

Not everybody was doing it, however. "Those were the days," declared one now middle-aged husband, "you could have great sex whenever you wanted it." Yet a woman of similar age, who lived through those same days, recollected them otherwise. "I feel like I missed the sexual revolution," she said. She spoke for the many women—and men—often overlooked in recollections of the supposedly sexy sixties and seventies. They were the ones who married in the way of their parents, made homes in family neighborhoods, raised children, and went to work. Even if they had felt the urge to "swing" or dance naked at a "love-in," most did not have the time.

In the end, the tenacious idea of a sexual revolution that fundamentally altered the history of men and women says as much about the frailty of memory, both personal and collective, as it does about anything that actually happened. Walt Crowley confronted the imperfections of recollection first hand. As he worked on his memoir, he found that his research and what he remembered often contradicted one another. "Before this book was done," he admitted, "many of my most cherished 'memories' had to be reclassified as hallucinations." Other people's recollection had been no more reliable in the sixties and seventies than Crowley's would be years later. Those who reveled in the novelty of the "sexual revolution" were too young to remember what had come before. Those who looked on in shock had managed to forget.

Vietnam and the War Against the War

If the "sexual revolution" was part forgetfulness and part hallucination, the social upheaval surrounding it—especially the protest against the war in Vietnam—was all too real. The civil unrest of the day often united men and women in common causes, recalling the two world wars when the sexes had also come together in crises and shared new kinds of mutual endeavors. But this time the goal was not victory in Europe but the creation of a less violent, more equitable society.

In Vietnam the effort dragged on relentlessly from 1961 to 1975. Fifty-eight thousand Americans died and 300,000 were wounded.

Meanwhile, the war against the war in its own way raged as fiercely, its front not foreign soil but the streets and college campuses of North America—by the end of the 1960s hundreds of thousands of people had gathered at rallies to protest American involvement in Vietnam. Apart from the dead and wounded, what has been called "the tainted war" cast its shadow over millions of lives. The North Americans most obviously affected were the 2,700,000 who served in Vietnam, but as one historian of the war observed, the 16 million who received deferments, exemptions, or disqualifications had still faced "the threat of the draft" and "the moral crisis of deciding what to do about it." And the more than half a million others who resisted variously experienced the terror and isolation of "leaving the country or going underground."

Vietnam fueled yet another conflict, the "generation gap" that had arisen between the baby boomers and their parents. Denouncing middle-class hypocrisy, condemning shallow consumerism, and exposing the "corporate rip-off" were all expressions of young people's disaffection with their elders, and they felt wholly justified in protesting a war that was not of their generation's making. In the old way of war and the new way of the times, they mixed the fight for peace with the quest for individual expression and happiness. And sex, as ever, was at the top of the agenda. "Make love, not war," urged the Students for a Democratic Society. "Make love, not war," echoed other political activists across the country. It was a rallying cry that could not help but resonate widely—perhaps most of all in the hearts of still virginal armchair protesters who had not yet left the shelter of family homes in suburbia.

Newspapers and magazines from the time have preserved the images of the protesters, young men and women united in common purpose. Many, no doubt, were ill-informed on the issues, but their idealism and earnestness shows in the frowns of concern under mops of "Afro" hairdos, and in clear eyes behind granny glasses. Group scenes still convey the closeness and camaraderie of many of these protesters. In this, and in the black and white of the photography, there is a reminder of the Great War, the first war in which men and women experienced a similar sense of mutuality.

But the resemblance ends there. The photographs of men and women together on the French front of 1914 to 1918 captured moments of peace in the midst of war. Many images from the late 1960s and early 1970s, however, were scenes turned suddenly ugly as the very violence that demonstrators protested against burst out among them. In both memory and reality the events at Kent State University would long stand for every such incident that might have started with outrageous behavior, but ended in outrage, pure and simple.

The trouble at Kent State began after President Nixon announced the latest assault on enemy strongholds in Cambodia. After days of student rioting and destruction of property, Ohio sent the National Guard to gain control of the campus. In his memoir, Walt Crowley recreates what happened next:

> They took a position on a low hill . . . with their guns aimed at the surrounding clots of chanting, jeering students . . . Suddenly, the troops began firing. Four students fell dead or mortally wounded . . . and fifteen more were injured.
>
> . . . In a decade drenched in blood nothing had quite the impact as the deaths of these . . . students, alive one second amid the sunshine of a spring day on a midwestern campus, sprawled dead or dying the next, their bodies ripped by the bullets of American soldiers no older than their victims. It had come to this: America's children were killing each other.

It was bloody scenes like this—not sex, revolutionary or otherwise—that once and for all ended our innocence.

The Women's War

In an era of upheaval, violence, and eroded trust, it seemed that the least individuals and certain groups could do in defense was to fight for their rights. Antiwar protests were part of a larger mood of combativeness that sought to remedy social injustice on various fronts. The campaigns for gay advancement and racial equality were among the causes that made dramatic strides forward during the 1960s and 1970s—though in both cases the victories were far from complete. Most significant to the relationship of the sexes was the escalating battle on yet another front. The modern feminist movement had begun when Victorian women began fighting for improved property rights, educational opportunity, and the vote. Some initial ground gained, this first wave of feminism had quietened, though never receded. In the revolutionary mood of the 1960s it gathered force and swelled once again.

It was perhaps the Miss America pageant of 1968 that brought the century's second great feminist movement—"women's lib" as it was often called—to the forefront of popular consciousness. Feminist demonstrators converged on the Atlantic City convention hall and loudly declared their contempt for the "mindless-boob girlie" show held inside. To drive home their point the protesters threw the trappings of sexual objectification—bras, girdles, high heels, and so on—into a giant "freedom trash can." They then placed ribbons and crown on a sheep that they paraded to the tune of—what else?—"There she is, Miss America."

But this second wave of feminism had been stirring earlier, in the discontent just below the surface demeanor of many supposedly happy homemakers. In 1957 a housewife who was also a journalist had set herself the task of articulating this discontent—this "problem that has no name," as she first referred to it. Her project took several years to complete, but Betty Friedan finally published

The Feminine Mystique in 1963. It gained a wide following throughout the 1960s and 1970s, and as many a woman reader repeatedly told the author, "It changed my whole life."

The nameless problem, it turned out, was the feminine mystique itself, in particular the forfeiture of self that it demanded of "truly feminine women." In response to a questionnaire that Friedan sent out, two hundred women put into words what many more had been thinking. "I begin to feel I have no personality . . . Who am I?" "I just don't feel alive." "The problem is always being . . . mommy, or . . . wife and never being myself." And so on.

What was needed, Friedan concluded, was "a new life plan for women." There was no one simple way for the individual to realize this, but in general the plan required dismissing the idea of housework as a career, seeing marriage without "the veil of overglorification imposed by the feminine mystique," getting an education, and above all using it:

> She must learn to compete then, not as a woman, but as a human being. Not until a great many women move out of the fringes into the mainstream will society itself provide the arrangements for their new life plan. But every girl who manages to stick it out through law school or medical school, who finishes her M.A. or Ph.D and goes on to use it helps others move on. Every woman who fights the remaining barriers to full equality which are masked by the feminine mystique makes it easier for the next woman.

In the end, Friedan hoped, women individually and collectively would find themselves, would share with men "the full human knowledge of who they are." "The time is at hand," she declared, "when the voices of the feminine mystique can no longer drown out the inner voice that is driving women on to become complete."

A force in itself, *The Feminine Mystique* lent its momentum to a range of women's issues. It was as if a dam had burst, as the latest wave of feminism washed widely over the political and cultural terrain. Among the breakthroughs that feminists applauded were the formation of the National Organization for Women in 1966; the University of Michigan's introduction of affirmative action in 1971; the congressional approval of the Equal Rights Amendment in 1972 (though ratification by the requisite majority of state legislatures would ultimately fail); the appearance of *Ms.* magazine, also in 1972; the legalization of abortion in 1973; the admission of women to the Rhodes Scholarship program in 1976; and the founding of the National Women's Studies Association in 1977. But if these seemed like battles won to many women, most were also conscious that the war was far from over. What Betty Friedan wrote in the early sixties would hold true for decades to come. We must, she insisted, "stop giving lip service to the idea that there are no battles left to be fought for women in America, that women's rights have already been won."

Crises of Self and Sex

The ongoing women's war was part of a larger war for self, in turn part of the century's long revolution toward ever greater individual and sexual expression. During the years known as the "sexy sixties" and the "me decade" of the seventies, it seemed to many that the pinnacle of self-fulfillment must now be within reach. But instead, more and more people were becoming less and less satisfied. Their desperation growing, they sought solace and solutions in the new fitness craze, encounter groups at the Esalen Institute in California, gestalt psychology, primal scream therapy, Zen, and yoga. When these remedies failed to yield up the wholeness of self they desired, many resorted to "mind-expanding" drugs—everything from marijuana to more dangerous short cuts to false happiness, such as LSD. Even before the 1960s had ended, it was becoming increasingly clear that individualism was not serving individuals very well.

The spokesmen for the identity crisis of the late 1960s was Rollo May, one of the central figures in the humanistic psychology movement that worked to make psychotherapy less clinical and more humane. In his best-selling book *Love and Will* (1969), May pinpointed the essential contradiction in modern individualism— it was not too few choices, but too many: "Just as the individual is feeling powerless and plagued with self-doubts about his own decisions, he is, at the same time, assured that he, modern man, can do anything." Following the contemporary linguistic convention of using male nouns and pronouns, May was speaking universally. For both sexes, the result of this "*contradiction* in will" was a feeling of "emptiness" or "apathy."

Sex, too, was equally in crisis, a reflection of what May called "the new puritanism," an uncompromising credo in which sexual dysfunction "is equated with sin. Sin used to mean giving in to one's sexual desires; it now means not having full sexual expression. Our contemporary puritan holds that it is immoral *not* to express your libido." To make matters worse, the new puritanism not only demanded quantity but placed burdensome emphasis on the quality of a person's sex life. Most well-meaning sex experts, among them Masters and Johnson, insisted that were no norms of sexual performance, yet their collective focus on response and technique implied a standard, which in turn placed an obligation on the individual to measure up to it. As May recognized, duty and joy made uneasy bedfellows: "So much sex and so little fun in it!" he remarked.

While ensuring that men and women had plenty of sex, joyful or otherwise, the new puritanism depersonalized the experience and alienated the sexes: people complained to their therapists of a "lack of feeling or passion," and contemporary language reflected the distancing that was now built into what was once the most intimate of encounters. We no longer "make love," May said. Instead "we 'have sex'; in contrast to intercourse, we 'screw'; instead of going to bed, we 'lay' someone or . . . 'are laid.'"

Ten years after May had identified them, the crises of sex and self had if anything grown more acute. By 1979, when the cultural critic Christopher Lasch published his own best-seller, *The Culture of Narcissism*, the empty individual of the sixties had become a full-blown narcissist, obsessively trying to fill the inner void by any means at hand:

> Having no hope of improving their lives in any of the ways that matter, people have convinced themselves that what matters is psychic improvement: getting in touch with their feelings, eating health food, taking lessons in ballet or belly-dancing, immersing themselves in the wisdom of the East, jogging, learning how to 'relate,' overcoming the 'fear of pleasure.'

For many people sex, too, had become a hollow affair, not only devoid of meaning, but missing even the ephemeral thrill of romance:

> Men and women now pursue sexual pleasure as an end in itself, unmediated even by the conventional trappings of romance.
>
> Sex valued purely for its own sake loses all reference to the future and brings no hope of permanent relationships. Sexual liaisons, including marriage, can be terminated at pleasure.

Lasch acknowledged that "the main features of the contemporary sexual scene had already established themselves well before the celebrated 'sexual revolution' of the sixties and seventies." Yet he also recognized a new estrangement of the sexes that went beyond the alienation that May had noted in the sixties:

> Both men and women have come to approach personal relations with a heightened appreciation of their emotional risks. Determined to manipulate the emotions of others while protecting themselves against emotional injury, both sexes cultivate a protective shallowness, a cynical detachment they do not altogether feel but which soon becomes habitual and in any case embitters personal relations merely through its repeated profession.

Self-absorbed defensiveness—it was a disheartening close to the decades of sex and self. The era that had once burned with the fires of sexual and personal expression had fizzled out.

The Disappointing Decades

Even today the sadness of lost idealism lingers in the memory of the 1960s and 1970s. But as the sociologist Edwin Schur pointed out in *The Americanization of Sex* (1988), this aspect of the sexual revolution rarely figures in the discourse of its conservative critics: "They would deny the simple and humane hope that fueled that revolution—that a freeing and affirmation of sexuality could help to enrich people's lives." Similarly, those who would reduce the era's social unrest to a matter of self-centered young people flouting authority are forgetting or disregarding the idealistic individualism that sparked the revolutionary mood in the first place.

Lasch argued in *The Culture of Narcissism* that it quickly became corrupted by "the irrational elements in American culture"—that is, individualism turned narcissistic and competitive, pitting "all against all," instead of cohesively working for change. Undoubtedly, too, the admixture of drugs and protest contributed to disorganization and weakening of purpose. In the end, however, demographics might well have been the decisive factor. The young people who called for change were great enough in number to make themselves heard, but they lacked the maturity, as well as the economic and political power, to turn their idealism into social reality.

Alongside the collective disillusionment born of social battles lost or abandoned, in their personal lives people also faced mounting disappointments and confusions, some of them the unlooked-for consequence of new freedoms gained. Many authors of the day voiced the mood of discouragement that had taken hold of people. They wrote of "failure," "decadence," "decline," and "confusion"—of living in "a moment when . . . the life they had known was crumbling apart."

Many women soon had to confront the uneasy reality that their hard-won battles for equality added up to what in 1978 the feminist writers Barbara Ehrenreich and Deirdre English called "an ambiguous liberation":

> The world opening up to women today is not exactly the halcyon vista of 'careers,' options, relationships portrayed by our more positive-thinking feminist leaders. For every sexually successful single there must be a hundred unsuccessful, unslim, 'unattractive' housewives. For every careerwoman, there are dozens of low-paid woman job-holders. For every divorce that frees a woman, there are others that throw women into poverty or loneliness.

For many women the supposed pay-off, liberated sex, was an equally ambiguous prize, causing anxiety or feelings of having been pressured or used by their partners. As Peter Carroll, a commentator on the seventies, would later express it, "a liberated sex style was still defined and dominated by men."

If feminism had changed women's lives, Vietnam had all the more irrevocably changed the men who had served. Because most had undergone their formative sexual experiences over there, they had difficulty separating sex from violence, or from the disinterested cash transactions that had been the norm. "Nudity was part of death there," one returned veteran told a counselor. "Romantic love died in Vietnam, right next to my friends," said another. Impersonal though it might have been, sex with a prostitute was among the few oases in the wasteland of death and destruction.

But men who had not served in the war by no means escaped the confusions now intimately bound up with sex and blurred gender roles. The social investigators Anne Steinmann and David Fox called the phenomenon the "male dilemma," and associated it with "the pain of transition." Men, they explained, "are confused about themselves and about the twentieth-century woman with whom they will live, or with whom they are presently living. How, they ask themselves, are they to relate to her, much less live with her, if they decide to live with her at all?"

The confusions that plagued men and women led to conflicts both in and outside of marriage. "The battle of the sexes" became commonplace in contemporary discussion. But it was a battle without clearly demarcated fronts. Many women found themselves consumed with hostility toward the very men who might in fact have been on their side. The journalist Sally Kempton spoke to a wider experience than her own when she wrote of "lying awake in the dark hating my husband, hating my father, hating all the men I had ever known."

Men for their part were fed up with constantly being cast as the villains of the piece. "Just what do women want, anyhow?" was the exasperated question they asked over and over as the seventies wore on. As Lasch observed, their frustration often showed in an irrationally negative or defensive "response to the emergence of the liberated woman." Thus the conflicts and confusions escalated, and with them, the disappointments that men and women felt with one another.

Longing for Something More

The mood of letdown that was now commonplace in romantic relationships was perhaps intensified by the sense of possibility that men and women had so recently shared. For if much of the sexual revolution was not entirely new, there had nonetheless emerged a widespread will to understanding between the sexes that was perhaps the era's most revolutionary development. The outgrowth of idealism, increased sexual freedom, and collapsing gender roles, that will persisted despite sexual disenchantment and friction between the sexes. But by 1970, many people were experiencing it as an absence, a mostly unarticulated feeling that they needed something more in their individual lives and love relationships.

This vague longing found an outlet in a burgeoning nostalgia for a mythic, gentler past. *The Waltons,* a sentimental family drama set in the Depression era and war years, was number two in viewer ratings for the 1973–1974 television season. Even the recently reviled fifties enjoyed a popular comeback, reinvented in the sitcom *Happy Days.* From 1976 to 1977 it was the top-rated show, and number two in the following season.

Feeling torn from the familiar ground of traditional roles, people also tried to figure out who they were by finding out where they had come from. "Everybody's Search for Roots" was *Newsweek's* fourth-of-July cover story in 1977. "Roots" was a kind of code word for what the relationship of the sexes really suffered from: a lack of deep meaning, permanence, and something else. *Passion*—Rollo May was among the few in recent memory who still invoked an old name for an old idea. Modern mores, he had observed, emphasized liberated sex, yet imposed other kinds of restraints on men and women: "People not only have to learn to perform sexually but have to make sure, at the same time, that they can do so without letting themselves go in passion or unseemly commitment."

There were of course many couples who did manage to commit, and whose relationships would endure well beyond the seventies. But for all that, there remained a widespread sense of profound absence in contemporary love relationships. It showed no more poignantly than in the way that a small book and its movie version touched a chord in the masses of people who experienced them.

A landmark, standing at the midpoint of the two decades of "sexual revolution," Erich Segal's *Love Story* was a best-selling book and box-office hit in 1970. It told the story of two college students, played by Ali McGraw and Ryan O'Neal. Despite their different backgrounds—he's preppy, she's from the wrong side of the tracks—they find each other and the kind of complete physical, emotional, and spiritual passion that many others could barely even imagine. But their life together has only just begun when unthinkable tragedy strikes. The wife, Jenny, is diagnosed with terminal cancer and, as the story draws to a close, she dies in her husband's arms.

In virtually any movie theater anywhere, as the movie reached the tragic climax, soundtrack swelling into the theme song—"Where do I begin to tell the story of how great a love can be . . . ?"—the sobs of the audience rose to a crescendo along with it. Sad as it was in itself, the story also touched people on a metaphorical level. Jenny's death represented the loss of fulfillment, the seemingly inevitable overwhelming elusiveness of passion. Women and men alike cried not only for her and for her grieving husband, but for their own lost selves, and for the passion they feared they might never personally know.

But people were also resilient, in themselves and in their relationships. As the seventies gave way, they faced the coming decade with renewed resolve to capture personal happiness—whatever the price.

The High Costs of Loving

Things did not fall apart, they congealed.

— HENRY SOUTHWORTH ALLEN,
"The '80s," *Going Too Far Enough*

The 1980s sashayed into being with a self-conscious air of wealth and power. For most people the days of "dropping out" and "doing your own thing" already belonged to the past. "Hippies" wearing beads had yielded the stage to "yuppies" whose designer clothes proclaimed hard-headed achievement rather than vague notions of love and peace. At work and at home the personal computer was rapidly becoming a fixture, and computer-literacy was suddenly a status symbol alongside the ownership and mastery of such other badges of achievement as VCRs and cell phones.

In the wake of the disillusionments of the previous two decades, making money had become a priority. If not the noblest of goals, at least economic stability was more attainable than social utopia. Cynics observed, with amusement, that even the activist Jerry Rubin had "sold out" for a career as a stockbroker. In the same vein, the journalist Henry S. Allen took stock of the eighties and remarked that "the idea was to be something, not do something. Be rich, be famous, be a success."

Going by appearances, light years in people's attitudes and behaviors divided the 1980s from the two decades before. To many, the murder of the former Beatle John Lennon, in 1980, put a sudden tragic period to an era that, however flawed, had stood for idealism and a better society. On the surface of things, the 1980s looked like a return trip to the conspicuous consumption of the 1950s. But if their ideals had betrayed them, people did not suddenly turn back the clock. Neither did they irrevocably shed every value and preoccupation of the "sexual revolution." Instead, hardened by disenchantment, they repackaged their ideals, and themselves, with a mix of "glitz" and conservatism.

As Christopher Lasch glumly observed, it was the updated version of the seventies' crisis of self. Without their old convictions to sustain them, many people now experienced daily life as an exercise in survival that reduced the individual to a small "defensive core"—"the minimal self." The most typical sign of this reduced individualism was also the hallmark of the eighties—a blurring, so Lasch said, of "the boundaries between the self and its surroundings," a widespread tendency to confuse public image with private being. As a result, people's devotion to self-development was if anything more determined than ever. Now widely forgoing encounter groups, primal screaming, and Zen, they directed their energies toward climbing the career ladder, dressing for success, and toning their bodies.

Meanwhile, the feminist movement gained followers and momentum. In part this came from the idealistic impulses toward equality of the sixties and seventies. At the same time, as Lasch insisted, the eighties minimal self had no gender, and thus feminism for many women meant pursuing image and careers with the same zeal as men. As a result, the personal lives of couples became ever more complicated, with conflict a frequent result.

Tension between the sexes was bound to affect their physical relations. And this was no small concern. Having great sex was not just a way of self-expression but yet another measure of power and achievement. Ensuring that every individual had a satisfying sex life became a collective preoccupation that pushed sexual issues and information into the public spotlight to a greater extent than ever. The move toward openness with which the century had begun had almost reached its climax.

Yet for all the contemporary emphasis on sexual gratification, "we the people" of the 1980s, Henry Allen observed, "worried that our sex lives weren't quite what they were supposed to be." As most now saw it, the problem was not an absence of passion. Except in romance novels, few managed to invoke such an antiquated ideal with a straight face—in the image-conscious eighties, even passion had undergone a "makeover." "Your legs . . . are a passion with us," a depilatory maker's advertising copy assured women. Career ambition, meanwhile, had become "the secret passion," and the way to gain job satisfaction was to "work with passion."

When it came to intimate personal experience, the word of the moment was now "relationship." If an individual's sex life was not all that was desirable, then the problem rested squarely with his or her relationship. Keen on self-improvement, some people worked on their relationships, but just as many others cut their losses and moved on, in search of greater fulfillment. Some even achieved their object and, for a time at least, enjoyed more and better sex. Few could have foreseen the high toll that would soon be exacted on individuals, relationships, and on sex itself.

The "Buff" and the Beautiful

In the eighties, having great sex and finding the perfect relationship began with the body. It was now no longer enough to be slim—you had to be toned, too. For men and women alike, achieving the ultimate in sexiness demanded muscles buffed to a hard smoothness that looked irresistible in designer clothes—and out of them. And if you managed to get fit enough to outrun the aging process, so much the better.

Following the established pattern of history, the greatest pressure to improve their bodies fell on women. "Cellulite," a word coined in 1970s advertising, loomed larger than ever in female consciousness. In fact it was only a made-up word for the fatty tissue that formed naturally on women's hips and thighs. But the beauty and fitness industries, aided by women's own zeal for self-improvement, convinced them that it was a problem—a big fat dimpled affliction that marked a woman as unfit and undesirable. Many women took the message to heart with a dedication not unlike the "obsessions of medieval nuns," as Henry Allen put it, attempting "to starve and vomit themselves into thinness."

With the same energy that they devoted to forging their way in the career world, they espoused exercise with something like the heat of passion. "Feel the burn," urged the actor-turned-fitness-guru Jane Fonda in her exercise tapes and videos. "No pain, no gain," echoed her dutiful adherents. The ultimate object was not fitness or even cellulite reduction, but enhanced sex appeal and sexual enjoyment. "Shape up for super sex," was the wisdom of the day. Sexiness had literally become survival of the fittest.

And it was not enough merely to work up a potentially erotic sweat in a comfortable T-shirt and pair of navy blue shorts left over from high school gym classes. Fitness and the right outfit went hand in hand. Proper attire for the weight room or aerobics class centered on a color-coordinated combination of spandex and Lycra, the skimpier the better, with matching socks and optional leg warmers and hair accessories. The outfit demonstrated that the wearer had style, the affluence to purchase it, and not least, the perfected body to do the outfit full justice.

In the end what made physical fitness so sexy was its connection to youth. A slim firm body and glowing skin meant that you were young, or at least looked young. The cult of youth that had been around for a century or more reached new heights in the eighties. Exercise was a primary way of warding off the effects of aging but it was not sufficient in itself. Any woman who was still sporting dated long hair and a natural-looking face was in urgent need of a more youthful and glamorous image. The typical "makeover" used bright makeup and bouncy haircuts to convert aging hippies to more youthful looking yuppies—like the glamorous female characters in *Dallas* and *Dynasty*, highly rated prime-time soap operas featuring the unbeatable eighties combo of money and sex.

The cosmetics industry further urged women to smooth away fine lines and stop wrinkles in their tracks with an array of cleansers and moisturizers. Often fortified with a vitamin or two, these also commonly featured such high-tech-sounding ingredients as "collagen," "liposomes," and "microsomes." A youthful toned body deserved youthful toned skin—so ran the underlying philosophy. And though it hardly needed saying, the promoters of hair dye chimed in anyway, reminding women of their duty to "wash gray away." Never before had being sexy required so many to spend so much on such an array of clothing, cosmetics, and chemicals.

But as the model and actor Cybill Shepherd maintained in an advertisement for hair dye, "I'm worth it." It was wholly in tune with the self-absorbed spirit of the times and sold a lot of hair dye. But for every woman who repeated the "I'm worth it" mantra and believed it, there were many more who secretly worried that in fact they were not worth it. And how could they think otherwise? A woman's educational, athletic, career, and domestic achievements seemed to amount to little under the barrage of what the media historian Susan Douglas would later describe as the "media's relentlessly coercive deployment of perfect faces and bodies . . . to co-opt the feminist effort to promote female self-esteem . . . Of all the disfigurements of feminism," Douglas regretfully concluded, "this, perhaps, has been the most effective."

Still enjoying the greater part of economic and political power, men were less vulnerable than women to cultural pressures to be youthful and fit. Less vulnerable, but by no means immune. Being athletic had long been central to ideals of masculinity and male sexuality. Now, in the ambition-driven eighties, the exercise imperative further combined with the yuppie credo of youth, upward mobility, and hard work. Some men step-touched, jumped, and knee-lifted alongside women in aerobics classes, but for many others (as for women, too) the exercise of choice was jogging or running, combined with a fitness club membership. While men enjoyed greater freedom than women to defy fashion, expensive running and workout gear still served a purpose, signaling a serious commitment to fitness—and by association, to career success and sexual prowess.

It was a measure of lingering gender inequities that men could get away with more crow's feet than women, without necessarily being considered old or unattractive. And fatty deposits around the middles of otherwise high fliers were tolerantly called "love handles," while in women they were simply expanding waistlines. But for all that men generally benefited from more aesthetic slack than women, much of their own passion for fitness was nonetheless about preserving youth. In the masculine world, achievement counted all the more if it happened young. Like some women, many men for their own reasons found turning forty to be a personal crisis. In some yuppie circles, friends of the sufferer might even go so far as to stage birthday parties as mock funerals, complete with black-dressed mourners commiserating the passing of the afflicted one's youth and vitality.

Meanwhile the cosmetics industry began to see dollar signs lurking in the anxieties of a male population that was graying and wrinkling at least as fast as women—not to mention all those who were enduring the added insult of hair loss. In other words, in the decade of the minimal self, men's insecurities were not entirely unlike those of women. To the commercial concerns that had created the cult of youth and its attendant anxieties, the politics of gender mattered little. From such a perspective, the distinction between men and women was a matter of degree and, above all, relative profit potential.

The Highest Cost

It was an sad irony that in a time when cellulite and aging took on the taint of pathology, some very real health issues also emerged. Well before the eighties had ended, people made the frightening discovery that the sexual freedoms they now took for granted might have come at a tragically high cost.

For many people an early sign of trouble brewing was a 1982 *Time* magazine article whose apparent purpose was to frighten them into chastity. The subject was genital herpes, a viral relative of the cold sore. As *Time* direly proclaimed, it was also "the new scarlet letter," an "incurable . . . scourge" that "has cut swiftly through the ranks of the sexually active." Apart from the physical symptoms, the stricken suffered "shock, emotional numbing, isolation and loneliness, sometimes serious depression and loneliness." Only toward the article's end did it report the reassuring but less news-worthy information that after the initial outbreak, subsequent bouts are usually of decreasing severity and the virus may lie dormant for years at a time.

People had only just gotten used to the presence of herpes among them when still other threats to health and sexual liberation—chlamydia, nongonorrheal urethritis, and venereal warts—suddenly seemed to be everywhere. But the most devastating by far of the STDs (sexually transmitted diseases) came to public knowledge with a July 1981 item in the *New York Times* that reported a "Rare Cancer Seen in 41 Homosexuals." By 1982 it had become a disease with a name—AIDS (acquired immunodeficiency syndrome)—and an average projected death toll of 50,000 per year. The underlying cause of the disease became known by yet another acronym, HIV (human immunodeficiency virus). Initially reported as an exclusively gay health issue, HIV and subsequently AIDS, it soon emerged, could also be contracted through heterosexual sex, transfusions of tainted blood, and the sharing of contaminated needles by drug users.

The fact that homosexual men were among those at greatest risk from the deadly disease was a setback to the gay rights movement, which had begun to gain momentum in the preceding decade. The homophobic moral right enjoyed a field day as they held forth with biblical fervor about sin, plague, and punishment. But devastating though AIDS was to the homosexual community, their image, and number, it lent force to gay activism, as many homosexual men formed a vanguard in raising AIDS awareness and educating the public about safe sex. And while AIDS continued to fuel the hatred of the unregenerately intolerant, it also had a countervailing effect on the more liberal-minded, providing a focus for developing greater humaneness in people's attitudes to sexual and cultural plurality.

170

When it eventually sank in among heterosexuals that they had no special immunity to AIDS, the initial reaction varied from mild paranoia to what the feminist Naomi Wolf would characterize as an "aura of terror" on many college campuses. Although even terror was not enough to stop some people from indulging in reckless sex, the principal beneficiaries of the simmering hysteria appear to have been the makers of condoms.

But as men and women took in the magnitude and potential devastation of AIDS, they also developed a renewed awareness of the onus that sex placed on each of them, whether they were together for a brief hour or an entire lifetime. "We can save each other by behaving responsibly toward each other," Naomi Wolf would conclude, "and damn each other by yielding to our own psychodramas at the expense of basic carefulness."

In the end STDs, especially AIDS, ended whatever lingering sexual innocence had survived the disillusionments of the 1970s. The ideal of liberated sex, men and women now knew, was a fantasy never to be realized. Free love was anything but, and the price to be paid might be the ultimate one.

Risky Business

People now began to see sex in a new, uneasy light. In a 1983 comic movie, Tom Cruise played a teenager who turns his high-class home into a bordello while his parents are out of town. The title, *Risky Business*, not only encapsulated the character's involvement with prostitution, it also unwittingly foreshadowed the new reality: that sex was now a dangerous undertaking.

Perhaps only celibates and those who had been monogamously married for twenty or more years enjoyed complete peace of mind. Prudence dictated the use of condoms, but this precaution did not entirely allay people's fears. Alarmist stories flew back and forth about condoms being misused, tearing, or missing the crucial lubricant ingredient, nonoxynol-9, which was believed to kill the AIDS-causing HIV. The media egged on the hysterics and the worriers with reports that condoms alone were not enough and that safety also required the use of rubber dental dams and surgical gloves.

It was reported that some people, mostly women, even went so far as to hire private investigators to check out prospective lovers' records to screen out those who might have STDs. When it was too late to avoid trouble, there remained at least the consolation of litigation. Or so a few people decided. Among them was a twenty-nine-year-old woman who sued the married man who had not only taken her virginity, but in return had given her a case of genital warts. (The outcome of the case went unreported.)

The widespread anxiety about the dangers of sex, and a new ambivalence toward what many people had only recently learned to regard as a guilt-free pleasure, found a mirror in several contemporary movies. For instance, in the Cannes Film Festival winner *sex, lies, and videotape* (1989), one of the male protagonists is impotent, except when watching videos of women talking about sex. It was the symbolism of paranoia—voyeurism and autoeroticism might not be as satisfying as the real thing with a real person, but they were definitely safer.

Other movies that emphasized the physical dangers of eroticism included *9 1/2 Weeks* (1986), in which Kim Basinger and Mickey Rourke portrayed a couple caught up in an emotionally and physically hazardous sadomasochistic relationship. Another erotic film that appeared the same year soon reached cult proportions: David Lynch's *Blue Velvet*, which juxtaposed an innocent boy-meets-girl plot with such dark sexual themes as sadomasochism and violent fetishism. Self-consciously blurring the line between danger and desire, it had recorded the sexually ambivalent pulse of the times.

A 1987 thriller was perhaps the ultimate cinematic expression of the eighties' divided feelings about sex. It begins with a torrid one-night stand between a single woman (Glenn Close) and a married yuppie (Michael Douglas). Unfortunately for this normally faithful husband, the woman turns out to be a dangerous psychotic who stalks him and his family in a cycle of escalating and horrific violence. *Fatal Attraction*—the movie's title summed up an entire decade's attitude to sex in a mere two words.

Overcompensation

If, as people were unhappily learning, sex could make you sick or even kill you, then at least it had better be good. So went the reasoning of the anxious, overachieving eighties. The result was a widespread preoccupation with enhancing sexual knowledge and expanding sexual experience, in real life as well as vicariously through entertainment. All in all, it was collective overcompensation for the dangers now attached to sex. As the psychotherapist Lillian B. Rubin explained, there was a "wide gap . . . between what people *say* they're frightened of and what they *do* about their fear. We see women and men, young and old, *speak* their fears . . . but act as if they had nothing to be afraid of."

Sex experts had been around since the late Victorian age, but in the eighties they came into their own as never before. In a flood of how-to books they explained seemingly everything any man would ever want to know about making love to a woman, and vice versa. They reassured "nice girls" that postcoital niceness was not a contradiction in terms, and they discovered the miraculous female G-spot, the newest and trendiest site of orgasmic ecstasy. Shere

Hite surveyed America's sexuality, allotting a volume to each of the sexes, and Sandra Kahn took stock of people's sexual preferences. And if reading about sex was not enough, it was now possible to call up a radio show and talk about it, too. In the early 1980s, the host of one such program would soon become a household name in sex education. The show was *Sexually Speaking*, its host Ruth Westheimer—or "Dr. Ruth," the name by which she would soon be well known.

In the overcompensating eighties, not only radio but also that traditionally family-fare medium, television, was loosening up. By the end of the decade, sexual talk or behavior featured on television approximately every four minutes. Increasingly the focus was on casual rather than committed sex. Movies, meanwhile, not only portrayed the dangers of sex, but also the pleasures. *The Big Easy* (1987), *Body Heat* (1981), *Bull Durham* (1988), and *No Way Out* (1987) were a few among many with sex scenes leaving little to the imagination.

The new lengths to which media now went were all part of the century-long process of demystifying sex. The consummation (so to speak) came (as it were) in the 1989 movie *When Harry Met Sally*, the story of two friends who eventually become lovers. Harry (played by Billy Crystal) and Sally (Meg Ryan) are having lunch in Katz's delicatessen. Harry is boasting of his never-failing ability to satisfy any woman he has ever been with. Unimpressed, Sally coolly informs him that most women have faked an orgasm. To illustrate the point, she puts down her fork and starts to moan.

"Oh God, oh God, oh, ah . . . Yeah, right there . . . Yes, yes, yes . . . !" she exclaims, as her performance escalates. Thrashing in her chair, pounding the table, she finishes with a final chorus of "Yes, yes, yes . . . Oh, oh—oh!" Then, with complete calm, she picks up her fork and resumes eating her salad. With that, the last bastion of sexual secrecy came tumbling down. No climax in the history of passion, it was a high point in sexual humor.

With sex now a staple of popular entertainment and public discussion, many people now enjoyed greater knowledge of the subject, along with reduced guilt and heightened pleasure. At the same time they now expected more than ever before from sex and were all the more likely to become dissatisfied. The "benchmark for the decade," according to *Playboy*, was the author Gay Talese's 1980 antidote to sexual boredom, *Thy Neighbor's Wife*, a celebration of group sex and that fifties survival, spouse-swapping. Not everybody was willing to go that far, but 1980s surveys showed a growing tendency for both men and women to refuse to accept infrequent or unsatisfactory sexual activity as a trade-off for marital security.

The occasional sex expert swam against the current and issued dire warnings about a new pathology, "sex addiction." In the forefront was Dr. Patrick Carnes, founder of SAA, Sex Addicts Anonymous. Carnes's definition of sex addiction covered a wide range of behaviors, from rape through habitual promiscuity to sexual thoughts and a subscription to *Playboy*. Most other sexologists rejected the idea of sex addiction, arguing that it was impossible to define, because sexual behavior varied widely, according to culture and the needs of particular individuals and couples. More than anyone, the sex educator Mary Calderone captured the contemporary spirit of overcompensation when she pronounced with finality, "There is no such thing as too much sex."

The Battle Intensifies

Knowing more about sex, even doing it more, were not enough to eradicate the tensions between men and women that had now been building for two decades. The battle lines extended through the public arenas of education, work, and sexual politics to private life, where conflict between the sexes ran the spectrum from discontent to out-and-out violence.

"We may well be angry," declared the Autumn 1982 editorial of *Signs*, a scholarly journal about "women in culture and society." After "years of effort," feminist scholars were still engaged in a "struggle" against "many of those who wield great power in the academic world" and who "continue to . . . think feminist questions to be of marginal scholarly interest." Meanwhile in other workplaces, women were fighting, but not yet winning, their own battles against sexual harassment and the inequities born of sexism. A cartoon in the September 1989 issue of *Cosmopolitan* magazine offered a humorous take on what were the central concerns of working women from all walks of life. The scene is a corporate executive office, the speaker a man in suit and tie seated behind a large desk. Clearly the "boss," he speaks with blustering disapproval to a slump-shouldered, weary-looking female employee: "What's this I hear about you leaving us for a firm that's giving you more money, better benefits, and actually treats you like a human being?"

Some men felt that women's battle against sexism was not a matter of correcting inequities, but simply a plot to defeat men. In reaction to feminism there grew a loosely organized, divergent men's movement. As *Quest*, a magazine for men published in Canada, reported, some of the movement's participants simply wanted "equal rights in matters of custody and access" to their children in cases of marital separation and divorce. Others, meanwhile, were looking for group validation of their ingrained belief in male superiority. The Men's Rights Association, a 1,400-member American organization, aimed to provide "a much-needed counterpoint to the largely nonsensical propaganda of women's 'lib,' and its fuzzy-headed housemales."

Ideological differences between men and women found more primitive expression in a growing number of violent images and themes in the mass media. "Brutality chic," as it was known in the advertising world, was sometimes aimed at men. For example, a photographic advertisement for Bocci shoes shows a lethal-looking stiletto-heeled lady's pump perched atop a bare masculine chest. At the point where the heel contacts flesh, it draws blood that trickles down the man's rib cage in three lurid red streams.

But more often than not, the imagery of violence found its traditional target—women. Throughout most of the eighties, television relentlessly exploited the theme of rape in everything from police dramas to made-for-TV movies. The illustration accompanying the *Quest* report on the men's movement belied the article's mostly moderate tone with disturbing symbolism. Set against a solid, angry red background, a man, his face contorted with rage, slams his fist through the biological symbol of womanhood (♀). This and many other brutal contemporary images reflected the widespread tolerance people now had for media portrayals of gratuitous sexual violence, especially against women.

The underlying reality was, if anything, worse. Physical abuse in intimate situations was as old as history itself, but "Private Violence," as a 1983 *Time* magazine cover story called it, was now increasingly in the public eye. Date rape, spousal rape, and wife battery were not necessarily on the rise, but born of insecurity, a desire for control, and rage, they were sometimes exacerbated by the widening disagreements between the sexes. In the climate of dissension, many people could not even agree on what rape actually was. At one end of the spectrum of hostility was the radical feminist Andrea Dworkin who charged that in enacting the subjugation of women by men, all heterosexual intercourse was rape. At the other end were all those, women as well as men, who blamed the victim. If a woman was asking for it (by wearing revealing clothing, acting provocatively, or drinking), went the reasoning, then she got what she deserved and it was not truly rape.

Most men and women of good will did not espouse either of these two extremes. But with the personal now politicized and widely debated, the conflict was bound to spill over into private lives. In most cases, not violence but discontent and confusion were the result. "I feel more oppressed than ever," complained all the perennially tired women, both married and single, who now worked full time, upgraded their education, ran households, and raised children. "I'm not the enemy," protested many an irritated husband and lover. Bewildered men, married and single, at home and in the workplace, complained that they just didn't know how women wanted them to behave.

In the pervasive atmosphere of gender politics, love and aggression often went hand in hand in personal relationships. Rather than a pleasurable mix of physical release and emotional bonding, eroticism itself had become a potentially divisive issue. Dissatisfaction and anxiety were now a way of intimate life, and the rate of marital breakdown in the United States had levelled off at a seemingly permanent holding pattern of one divorce for every two marriages. With no happy ending in sight, the battle of the sexes was now a war of attrition.

Combat Fatigue

Conflict, whether ideological or interpersonal, was bound to take its toll on individual well-being. "We, the people," Henry Allen observed, "had a tired feeling that wouldn't go away." New illnesses like chronic fatigue syndrome were among the costs of constantly striving for achievement. Battle-weary from competing with one another in the workplace, at fitness clubs, and at home, women and men alike sought the escapist stimulation of sex. But that, too, added to the fatigue. The increasing sexualization of society and popular culture was producing a contradictory effect, a growing sexual malaise. And this collective disenchantment with the erotic also affected individuals—so-called desire disorder now took its place on the list of overtired yuppie ills.

The disappointments of the sexual revolution, the ongoing battle of the sexes, and the now relentless presence of sex in public life had a deep cultural impact that did not go unobserved. Sex had become "an idea whose time has passed," as George Leonard, author of *The End of Sex* put it in 1983. Two years later, in *Sexuality and Its Discontents,* the historian Jeffrey Weeks referred to a "general crisis of sexuality." And toward the decade's close, the sociologist Edwin Schur characterized the sexual malaise of the times as a peculiarly American phenomenon. "Modern American society," he wrote in *The Americanization of Sex,* "has put its distinctive stamp on sexual attitudes and behaviors. Sex in our society today has, indeed, been naturalized and demystified."

As he hastened to add, this did not necessarily promote satisfaction: "Our culture and social system may be pushing sexuality very far in the direction of an emotional emptiness . . . We seem to have managed, paradoxically, to trivialize sex and at the same time invest it with too much importance." Americanized sex, he continued, was often coercive, made into a commodity, and above all, depersonalized.

As Schur explained it, the link between this cultural state of affairs and individual sex lives could be summed up in the idea of "recreational sex"—a contradictory "notion," he argued, that "ought to be questioned":

Dictionary definitions of recreation emphasize relaxation and enjoyment. Can we really say that most sex in America today is relaxing and greatly enjoyed? There are many signs that such is not the case. To the extent (however limited) that sex is being pursued compulsively, it is, by definition, not relaxing. Nor can it be very relaxing and enjoyable when technique, performance, and results become constant preoccupations. The frequency with which sex is accompanied by coercion and violence dramatically belies the 'recreation' label, or at least its application to the overall sexual scene. And the enormous demand for both prostitution and pornography strongly suggests that Americans are not freely enjoying their sexuality very much. Finally, it is noteworthy how many of us continue to experience sexual problems, and to seek help for them from a wide array of sources and through a variety of 'sexual aids.' Sex therapists, general psychotherapists, various other kinds of sex experts, and the publishers and distributors of mass-marketed sexual advice books all cater (along with the marketers of pornography) to this persisting need and are thriving by it.

In other words, in the midst of a purportedly liberated society, freed from most inhibitions about sex, people may well have been doing it more—but they were enjoying it less.

Uneasy Truce

The sexual malaise that gripped the eighties undoubtedly helped to fuel cynicism about relationships between men and women. As Henry Allen noted, *Newsweek* reported that "single career women in their thirties had about as much chance of getting married as being killed by a terrorist." Men, for their part, he continued, were "edgy—a marriage had only a 50 percent chance of lasting. 'Why get married?' they said. 'Why not just find a woman you hate and give her your house?'" But even with the odds and statistics against them, most men and women still wanted sexually and personally fulfilling relationships with one another, and that required finding some common ground. The old longing for love fostered an undeclared, intermittent, and uneasy truce in the battle of the sexes. Beyond that, a lot of men and women were simply tired of fighting with each other.

Along with other social and cultural observers, Edwin Schur noted a developing "ethic of commitment." As Schur observed, "most people questioned in opinion surveys or interviewed in more depth at least express the wish for commitment and stability." But what they wanted (or claimed to want) and what they were capable of were by no means the same. The heirs to eighty years of an ever-intensifying search for individual fulfillment, many people were now ill-equipped for commitment to others. Furthermore, they were up against a range of opposing social and cultural forces—the minimal self's confusion of physical appearance and personal worth, the objectification of women in popular media as well as pornography, the use of sex as a commodity in everything from advertising to the sex industries, and the "playboy mentality" that viewed sex as a site of acquisition and power, more than an expression of authentic feeling for another.

But while few could escape these influences entirely, not everyone was affected in the same way or to the same degree. Many people continued to seek—and many to find—satisfying sex and stable relationships. On the brink of the century's final decade, the end of the erotic world was not yet at hand. Neither was it time to sound a death knell over the relationship of the sexes. Yet as many would soon discover, some things were about to worsen before they would even begin to improve. Both publicly and privately, people's need for fulfillment would at times take them beyond the edge of desperation.

VI

DESPERATELY
SEEKING DESIRE

THE 1990s

For all the disillusionments of the previous three decades, few people in the 1990s truly wanted to believe that sex had lost its power to provide pleasure and personal fulfillment. As if we had set out to prove the viability of the old belief that "a good sex life is the key to happiness," everything from entertainment and advertising to popular psychology explored, exploited, and explained virtually all there was to know about sex in our culture and in our private lives. It was the climax of the almost century-long transformation of erotic life. The repeal of reticence at the beginning of the century had become full-frontal candor by its end.

The eighties standoff between the sexes continued, but was beginning to be tempered by a distinctively nineties spirit of self-help, which at its public extreme manifested itself in such phenomena as talk-show sensationalism masquerading as therapy. In private, it showed in the efforts both sexes made to grow as individuals and to understand one another better. As they had done in the previous decade, people also continued to strive for better and better bodies and ever more fabulous sex. But despite these sometimes desperate efforts to do things right, they frequently went wrong—and happiness slipped further than ever beyond reach.

Meanwhile, here and there, a certain wistfulness crept into the culture of sex, and occasionally the longing for something more, a trace of the old ideal of passion, also showed itself. A reflection of discontent more than a true revival, it nonetheless hinted at our readiness for change. As the century neared its end, the time had come to discover a new approach to the future.

The Barely
Splendored Media

9

Sex in Entertainment: How Far Can It Go?

— *Us*, August 1992

Sex on TV: How Far Can It Go?

— *TV Guide*, October 1993

The century's last decade had a style all its own. More than ever before, self-help was the prevailing spirit as people tried to expand their minimal selves. "Recovery" became widespread as men and women worked on their "self-esteem" and either "healed" their relationships or "let go" of them. Together, the sexes tried to "move beyond" the sexual malaise of the recent past. The ultimate goal was happiness, as it had been throughout the century, and people put their faith in ever greater sexual openness as the way to achieve it.

The nineties agenda to celebrate sex and to conquer inhibition forever was nowhere more conspicuous than in the mass media.

On large and small screens, on newsstands, and at video stores, baring all—bodily or verbally—was an everyday affair. There were now so few restraints on the discussion and representation of sex in the media that even those within the industry could not help wondering where it all would end. As in the eighties, passion was rarely mentioned outside of romance novels and advertisements. Though a new car or pair of designer jeans might well be a consumer's passion (or so the advertisers hoped), in entertainment the main idea was sex, and few hesitated to say so.

But in the midst of all the explicit splendor, there were intermittent signs that many people were tired of the constant barrage of sexual images and messages. They'd had enough and were becoming desensitized—in short, bored.

Sensational Sex

The media of the 1990s courted the sensational as never before. If they suspected that audiences were becoming jaded, producers, entertainers, and advertisers were clearly not ready to give up their bedrock belief that nothing captures mass attention like sex.

While the credo "sex sells" was older than the century, new extremes of explicitness in advertising, particular in glossy magazines and on gigantic big-city billboards, still had the power to raise eyebrows. Calvin Klein advertisements provoked the most commentary, with their chic black-and-white images of semi-nude couples modeling underwear, and naked nymphets promoting fragrance. But plenty of other advertisers were using the same strategy. Pouting lips, smoldering gazes, suggestive hand positions, and bare flesh were everywhere. "Advertising has gotten more explicit," observed one commentator for *Newsweek*. Fashions ads especially "show more skin than clothing."

With the shadow of AIDS still casting a pall over sex, contemporary filmmakers continued to explore the theme of sex and danger, mixing eroticism, nudity, bloodshed, and the darker aspects of human relationships. One of the most talked-about films of the decade's early years was *Basic Instinct* (1992), a steamy blend of explicit acts, rough sex, bisexuality, general misanthropy, and an ice-pick-wielding serial killer. Commenting on this and other similar movies, the writer Dan Zevin said it all in *Us* magazine's 1992 special issue on sex in entertainment: "Mix up some sex and violence, throw in a psycho killer and you've got yourself a hit."

The bottom line was market competition. The entertainment business was hugely profitable, and stars, producers, and advertisers all vied for consumer attention in a sex-saturated culture. The challenge was to provide more and more titillation, while leaving the audience wanting still more. Even television, traditionally the most restrained of the media, had little choice but to follow the trend, omitting some of the violence, but leaving less of everything else to the imagination than ever before. Just one viewing day might offer sex on a pool table in *Days of Our Lives*, the lighter side of sadomasochism in *One Life to Live*, spicy scandal aired on tabloid shows like *Hard Copy*, and male and female officers in—and out—of uniform on *NYPD Blue*.

But nothing captured the 1990s' mood more thoroughly than daytime television talk shows. Apart from the distinctive styles of their hosts—among others, Maury Povich, Sally Jessy Raphael, Jerry Springer, and Oprah Winfrey—the talk shows were like routine sex. They allowed little room for variation. Unashamed, they often covered the same subjects, sometimes in the same day or week as another show. In all of them the mainstay was talk—a flow of confession, confrontation, and comment among host, guests, and studio audience. An expert or two, usually a psychologist, often appeared briefly to set guests and audience straight in the closing minutes. To maintain viewer involvement, shows might also call for guests to wear suggestive costumes—bikinis, G-strings, black leather, drag, whatever the occasion dictated—and the talk might be peppered with film or video clips, satellite hook-ups, phone-ins, and surprise guests.

Sex was not the exclusive theme but it was certainly the favorite. On a single day, January 13, 1992—noteworthy for a modicum of restraint, if anything—talk show topics included the art of seduction, incestuous child abuse, and sexual harassment among teens. Between 1991 and 1995 a viewer of only moderate dedication would have encountered shows about sex and practically anything—politics, race, religion, aging, disease, drugs, nutrition, obesity, and sport. Or about sex and practically anyone—teenagers, seniors, divorce lawyers, doctors, Hell's Angels, Satanists, bisexuals, transsexuals, bisexual transsexuals, and even married heterosexuals.

It's a "turn-on to feel that other people are watching us," explained a typical guest on a typical talk show in 1993. Maury Povich was the host, the speaker and his wife proponents of do-it-yourself sex videos. Taping themselves having sex in various scenarios—wife as nurse, husband as libidinous patient, for instance—had spiced up their marriage, they claimed. It had also led them to set up a small business for distributing the videos, presumably to other couples of similar taste.

Trade in homemade erotica was growing, Maury informed his viewers, and to prove it he introduced yet another couple with a testimonial to the joys of video sex—and they too had their own distribution business. It was not really a matter of selling something, they assured the audience, but "more of a sharing"; their enterprise was "a celebration of their sexuality," and they simply wanted to include others in the festivities. No one, host or audience, bothered to challenge their dubious sincerity. The host's role was to provide multiple thrills, the audience's to relax and enjoy them, and everyone played along.

Unhappy Talking, Talking . . .

Canny talk show hosts and producers recognized that sensationalized sex alone would not sustain audience interest and high ratings: an emotional hook was needed. They discovered that sex gone wrong, and the unhappiness that resulted, was more compelling even than sex itself. Victimization, traumas, problems, and dissatisfaction were the stuff of which talk shows were made.

Guests of Maury, Oprah, Sally, and the rest testified to the miseries and dangers they had suffered: they had been assaulted by strangers, raped by acquaintances, physically and psychologically abused, infected with sexually transmitted diseases, betrayed by their spouses, or seduced by teenage baby-sitters. They were tormented by negative body images, irrational inhibitions, uncontrollable urges, and their partners' kinky tastes—plagued by too little sex in their lives, or too much.

Some of them were driven by unhappiness to confess their most intimate secrets on national television, hoping for information, alleviation, or sympathy. Others claimed—possibly sincerely—that they wanted to share the lessons they had learned through their troubles, and to help others avoid the same pitfalls. Still others sought revenge against a cheating spouse or absconding lover. And a number simply wanted to be on television, or get a free trip to New York—a comment, perhaps, on the debilitating sameness of many people's lives.

Whatever brought them to the show, once there, the idea—the only idea—was to bare their private lives. The host would prompt them, asking questions along the lines of: "I know this is painful, but tell us what he or she did to you." If a guest was not forthcoming enough, the host prompted further, often with the rationale of informing the public. "I ask this question not to pry in your business but to educate parents in our audience," said Oprah, probing for details from a young female incest victim.

Voluntary or forced, televised revelations often had a purpose even higher than educating the audience. Therapy. It gripped people in the 1990s even more than in the previous three decades, and jargon rolled so readily off so many previously inarticulate tongues that a new word was coined to describe the phenomenon. "Psychobabble"—it included glib utterances about "low self-esteem," "connecting with your authentic self," "treatment," "sharing," "communication," "recovery," "closure," "healing" . . . No longer did people simply date, live together, or marry. They entered into relationships that sometimes became "codependent," "abusive," or otherwise "dysfunctional." Anyone who protested was probably "in denial" and unquestionably needed "counseling."

Lending authority to talk-show therapy were the guest experts. Counselors, therapists, psychiatrists, psychologists, sociologists, and authors of advice books populated the talk-show sets, dispensing their knowledge in easy-to-digest dollops. Advice might be boiled down to something like "ten stupid things" to avoid, or the A to Zs of sex, or for more extreme tastes, served up as "sizzlin' secrets" (like sandpaper your way to better sex).

When it came to intimate matters, talk-show therapy was the historical culmination of a century of increasing professional and popular knowledge about sex, as well as openness in discussing it. In the early days it had been Marie Stopes and Margaret Sanger trying to alleviate ignorance. Then Freud and other pioneering sexologists had shared their work with colleagues and learned amateurs. Still later their ideas gained popularity, and therapy groups and workshops eventually proliferated. But never before the rise of talk shows had sexual information received such a mass hearing, or people's sex lives such relentless public scrutiny.

Naked Truth

The revelations of talk shows were part of an even larger collective urge to confess intimate personal information to strangers. "Opening up" was the catchphrase, as the confessional compulsion took hold of virtually all areas of life in the 1990s. Not only did it drive people onto talk shows and into group therapy and workshops, but it was the impulse behind everything from responding to consumer surveys to sporting vanity licence plates—the driver who boldly proclaimed himself to be a "STUD," in metallic capitals, was saying a lot about his aspirations and inadequacies.

Contributors to American, Canadian, and British newspapers and magazines held back little, if anything, about their own private lives and those of others. Sparing readers few of the sticky, sweaty details, they got right down to the bare facts about juvenile sexual experimentation, loss of virginity, adulterous affairs, and one-night stands. Not to be outdone, authors of memoirs churned out exhaustively explicit accounts of their "erotic journeys" and "philosophies of sex."

Celebrities, meanwhile, had increasingly little hesitation about granting candid interviews. Pamela Anderson Lee, Demi Moore, and Julia Roberts—to name just three among many Hollywood stars who felt obliged to tell all—shared anecdotes about their bodies, childhood crushes, love lives, and pregnancies. Camille Paglia, the author of *Sexual Personae* (1990) and *Sex, Art, and American Culture* (1992), was so forthcoming about her own sexual persona that one interviewer dubbed her "the mouth that roars." The experts whose stock in trade was advice to the "dysfunctional" also "opened up" about their own sex woes as a way of establishing empathy with those they tried to help. By his own admission, John Gray, the author of *Men Are from Mars, Women Are from Venus* (1992) and *Mars and Venus in the Bedroom* (1995), was a recovered sexual klutz who once had to "practically wrestle with the fasteners" of his partner's bra, making sex "very clumsy and awkward."

Public self-exposure was not just for celebrities. Even the totally obscure, if they chose, could enjoy their moment in the confessional limelight—without ever having to appear on a talk show. Thousands responded to voluminous studies of sexual behavior, submitted anecdotes to more informal compilations of sexual experience, or replied to magazine-sponsored sex surveys. "What's the best sex you've ever had?" was among the questions that one popular magazine asked its readers in 1994. The title of the magazine—*Details*—neatly summed up their graphic replies.

For sheer exhibitionism, there was little to rival the author Nancy Friday's latest collection of women's sexual fantasies. Adding a new twist to her two earlier books on the subject, both written in the 1970s, *Women on Top* (1991) focused on sex and power fantasies by "women today." Now, finally, they were "dealing with the full lexicon of human emotion." More comprehensive still was their vocabulary—culled from both clinic and street, it omitted no act or anatomical part. Yet according to Friday, the lurking enemy that "never sleeps" was still, of all things, "repression." And she said it with a straight face.

To anyone not trying to rationalize delving into people's most intimate thoughts, it was clear that the nineties habit of confessing sexual secrets had nothing to do with combating the nonexistent problem of repression. Confession had become the therapy of choice for so many because it helped to fill the voids in contemporary life. Where once people might have testified at a revival meeting or lent their voices to civic debate, they now called talk shows or shared confidences with strangers at "recovery" workshops. Where once there had been a widely shared sense of community with others, there was now "sham community," as a critic of the self-help craze, the author Wendy Kaminer, put it. Where, at the beginning of the century, openness had been a boon to intimacy, in the nineties it was intimacy's substitute. "Never have so many known so much," Kaminer wryly observed, "about people for whom they cared so little."

Bor-ing!

The trouble was, everything from talk show therapy to sex in movies and advertising depended on the same vicarious thrill. Voyeurism—snooping into the sex problems of strangers, scrutinizing their bodies, watching them in the act—it was second-hand sex, passion at its most threadbare.

"Monotonous, repetitive, unoriginal, and boring, boring, boring," complained one commentator. She was referring to sex scenes in contemporary fiction but her words captured what many must have felt, if not expressed, as the constant presence of sex in popular culture eroded its power to arouse people or even attract their attention.

One cultural icon who did get noticed was the rock superstar, sometime movie actor, and book author, Madonna. Wholeheartedly dedicated to the voyeurism of others, she was an ever-changing spectacle. From videos like *Erotica* (1992) to the sexy thriller *Body of Evidence* (1992), her "over-exposed corpus," to use the words of one film guide, was the star of the show. More than any other celebrity or sex symbol, she stood for sex in the public life of the nineties. Too much—and too little.

A much talked-about case in point was her 1992 book *Sex*, a pictorial compendium of a well-buffed Madonna in the buff, which "celebrated sadomasochism, homosexuality, exhibitionism and other pansexual delights," as one writer summed it up for readers of *Newsweek*. "I see myself as a revolutionary at this point," Madonna proclaimed, conveniently forgetting (if she ever knew) that another blond sex symbol, the sometime playwright Mae West, had used the same title, *Sex*, to sensational effect over sixty years earlier. But "what if . . . the public merely yawned?" asked *Newsweek*'s interviewer, just before the book's release. "If everybody yawned," Madonna replied, "I'd say hooray. That means something happened." It was a nice try, if not especially convincing.

As things turned out, a lot of people *did* yawn. "Dry," the critics said, "banal" and "de-eroticized." But Madonna had still managed to storm one of the last bastions of secrecy. In an age of public sex, voyeurism had remained more or less private. People sat cloaked in the darkness of movie theaters or watched their own television screens. But then, with its expensive binding and stylish photography, Madonna's *Sex* put voyeurism on the coffee table. It was a sign of the times that so many found coffee more stimulating.

By the mid-1990s the more astute entertainers were beginning to realize that it was possible to take sexual subject matter too far. Most notably, Oprah Winfrey responded to criticism from sociologists that shows like hers were possibly doing active social harm. Changing her approach, she began focusing on celebrity interviews and upbeat coverage of a wide range of lifestyle issues. Meanwhile, other talk show hosts continued to favor sensationalism, the more outrageous the better. To stay on the air, their shows must have held the interest of a large number of viewers. But others with lower boredom thresholds must quietly have tuned out to seek more stimulating pastimes.

Ultimate Exposure

Ultimately it was not the extremes of talk shows that most tested people's tolerance for the public airing of intimate subjects but a series of events that the news media had little choice but to report. "The scandal of the decade," as *Newsweek* called it, the story of President Clinton's involvement with the White House intern Monica Lewinsky broke in the *Washington Post* on 20 January 1998. The resultant furor soon extended far beyond debate over what did or did not legally constitute a sexual relationship, to minute examinaton of the question of whether the president had been guilty of perjury and obstruction of justice. Months of investigation by the independent prosecutor Kenneth Starr, continuous media analysis, and widespread speculation eventually culminated in the impeachment trial at the end of the year and eventual acquittal of the president early in 1999. The scandal's complex brew of political, legal, and moral issues raised a larger philosophical question: Which takes precedence—an individual's right to privacy or the public's right to information?

Initially, for reasons that were understandable to some, outrageous to others, the president refused to join in the confessional impulse that dominated 1990s popular culture. "I did not have sexual relations with that woman," he told the nation on 26 January 1998. In August, fresh from testifying before the grand jury, with the imminent release of Starr's report hanging over him, he admitted to having had an inappropriate relationship with Lewinsky. But as he also insisted, even presidents have a right to private lives.

Standing outside of American partisanship, international opinion, as reported on the news network CNN, leaned the same way and condemned the Starr investigation as "puritanism," a "witch hunt," "electronic lynching," and "sexual McCarthyism."

In a similar vein, but without the inflammatory language, Thomas Nagel, an American professor of philosophy and law, reflected on the situation in Washington for the *Times Literary Supplement*. While he was referring specifically to the investigation and media coverage of the Clinton/Lewinsky relationship, his words might just as well have applied to the lurid revelations of contemporary talk shows and tabloids:

> Civilization is a delicate structure that allows wildly different and complex individuals to co-operate peacefully and effectively only if not too much strain is put upon it by the introduction of disruptive private material, to which no collective response is necessary or possible.

The average American would not likely have put it that way, but the presidential scandal nonetheless sparked a dawning mass awareness of the crucial importance of privacy—even for those in the public spotlight. Though people were divided on legal and political issues, and virtually unanimous in condemning Clinton's behavior, there was also wide agreement that it was a private matter. Opinion polls varied from 63 to 81 percent of respondents indicating that the independent prosecutor, the media, and the nation should mind their own business.

People were beginning to understand that openness, if taken too far, could destroy not only individual but public well-being. But the insight was still fragile, and made little immediate impact on the larger culture of exposure. As the 1990s neared their end, it remained to be seen whether the idea would take lasting hold of popular consciousness. Or would it quickly be forgotten in the uproar of the next public sensation?

Art Meets Life

Years before there appeared to be even the possibility of a return to the ideal of privacy, the exposures of public life in the 1990s—everywhere from entertainment to news reporting—had made themselves felt in people's personal lives. On the one hand there were the high expectations that sexy television, movies, and advertising fostered. On the other was the desensitization that resulted from being bombarded by too much of what was once titillating. But it was more even than that. The media were so powerful, so dominant in everyday life that the boundary between reality and its representation became increasingly blurred.

"Life has become art, so the two are now indistinguishable from each other," argued Neal Gabler, the commentator on American popular culture, in *Life, the Movie: How Entertainment Conquered Reality* (1997). Put another way, the repeal of reticence with which the century began had over the years become a culture of relentless openness and explicitness. And progressively, that culture had encroached upon large areas of private life, imposing its ever more rigorous standard of sexual gratification and behavior—thus leaving less and less imaginative space for individual eroticism to flourish.

But most people did not see their own intimate lives in this light. How could they? From the therapeutic perspective of talk shows, recovery workshops, and everyday life, the problem was not with culture but with themselves. In order to correct and perfect their relationships it was individuals and couples, therefore, who had to change their own particular habits of intimacy. Men and women of the 1990s took this contemporary wisdom to heart—and, sometimes, to great lengths. If there were few limits on how far the media could delve into sexual matters in public, then no measure was too extreme to improve them in private.

Doing It Right—
and Getting It Wrong

Better Sex, Better love!
— Advertisement for *Secrets of Making Love*,
Playboy Home Video Series

Pleasure turns into a chore, and a bore.
— SYLVERE LOTRINGER, *Overexposed*

In the indifferent spaces of your heart,
you may even find . . . room to dance again.
— ROBERT JAMES WALLER,
The Bridges of Madison County

Passion. In the 1990s the word made a modest comeback in sexual self-help circles. Authors of advice books told couples how to achieve "passionate marriage" and "lasting passion," while sex instruction videos assured them "there's nothing more thrilling than passion." The updated version of the old key to happiness, "passion" in the self-improving 1990s meant more than just sex, or even great sex—it now stood for better and better sex. Which in turn was supposed to guarantee better love, better relationships, and greater personal fulfillment.

With a zeal that the Victorians once directed toward social and moral duty, men and women now poured their efforts into the cause of better sex. While this was not new, it had a particularly nineties style. People not only worked on their bodies but paid often obsessive attention to the sexiest parts. No longer content merely to master basic sexual techniques, they now widely experimented with new experiences. On top of it all, they tried doggedly to appreciate every complex nuance of contemporary sexuality and gender. Since the eighties, people had come to know only too well that sex was not merely personal but social and political. Demanding a firm grip on the issues of the day, better sex was also correct sex.

But rather than enhancing many people's satisfaction, the new enlightenment increasingly built to a climax of confusion. How necessary was all that technique anyway? And could anyone actually remember it when the time came? How could you be sure of enjoying yourself and not offending someone else? Was sex even worth all the effort it now seemed to require?

Amid the babel of advice, opinions, and agendas, addressing what was starting to look like the decade of dysfunction, the clearest message was "try harder." Everyone ought to try harder to respect one another, to understand sex—to do it right. Some people's efforts paid off, if only for a time, but many others felt perennially dissatisfied. By the end of the decade, increasing numbers were struggling to grow beyond their former minimal selves and to channel that growth into their relationships. The sense that something was missing—something they could not name—was becoming more compelling. How could they put so much effort into finding themselves, and still feel so lost? They resolved, yet again, to try harder.

Body Parts—Hers

A decade ago, great sex had begun with the body. Now better sex began more precisely still, with the body's sexiest parts. And often, unhappily, these were the ones that needed the most work.

The fitness craze of the previous decade stretched its muscles into the 1990s. People worked out with weights, watched their weight, and weighed the merits of one food over another (lurking fat grams especially were to be avoided). A few voices of dissent, mostly heard on talk shows, insisted that fat was sexy, even when it oozed out of minuscule bikinis or swimming trunks. But the brutal fact was, thin had been in for the entire century, a trend not likely to reverse itself in a hurry. Even the decade's showiest celebrant of Freud's "polymorphous perversity" (anything goes with practically anyone) had one strict standard: no sex with a fatty for Madonna. As they had been in the 1980s, the sexiest bodies were the slimmest bodies, the hottest sex for those who still "felt the burn."

This was the popular ideal for both sexes, but women typically were under greater pressure to attain bodily perfection. Throughout the twentieth century their character, status, and sexuality had been intimately bound up with how they looked. This showed in all areas of life, but advertising in particular enjoyed a long history of both creating and reflecting ideals of attractive femininity. Now, more blatantly than ever, television commercials and magazine advertisements focused not just on good-looking bodies, but on parts of bodies—the firmest and the sexiest that barely pubescent models and airbrushing could offer. Through extreme close-ups, computer enhancement, and strategic cropping, the parts took on a life of their own—pouting out in full-page invitation from lipstick advertisements, kicking up their heels in barely-there panty hose, or thrusting themselves perkily over the lace trim of push-up bras. And, swaying sensuously, shapely denim bottoms filled up entire television screens. In the advertising of the 1990s the sexy female body was literally the sum of its parts.

It had become virtually a moral obligation that all body parts be perfect, even in the midst of increasing tolerance for many other things—careless manners, swearing in public, and doing fifty in a thirty zone. As the baby boomers grew older, even being middle-aged was acceptable, as long as it did not show too offensively. Yet in an age of purported acceptance, harsh judgment was reserved for fat thighs, round tummies, and bulging bottoms. The most common atonement was exercise. Without doubt it helped, but as even the most devout adherents well knew, it seldom created what nature had failed to bestow. While many women simply accepted this, many others could not. Just how did some women manage to be thin and, at the same time, look so sexy? It was a question that any woman serious about perfection, who had ever seen a recent movie or advertisement, could hardly have failed to ask.

Thanks to magazine articles, talk shows, and Hollywood gossip, the answer was near to hand: nature might be stingy but cosmetic surgery was generous. It had been the fastest-growing medical specialty of the 1980s and showed no signs of decline, as women subjected their various parts to the surgical knife. For better bodies—and better sex—they had their lips implanted with sexy pouts, their bottoms lifted, tummies tucked, and thighs suctioned to reduce them to the leanness of the low-fat food they consumed. Most of all—by implantation of a bag filled with silicone gel or saline solution—women acquired the full, firm, high breasts that they had always longed for. The breasts that models and movie stars had, the ones that men desired (or so many women believed).

The women who had undergone surgery, concerned feminists, and members of the medical profession hotly debated the effects of breast implants, for good or for ill, on their recipients. While many women reported no severe symptoms, an increasing number, 400,000 by 1994, suffered health problems—everything from shoulder and arm pains, skin rashes and fatigue to malignant tumors and lupus (a chronic inflammatory disease affecting connective tissue, skin, and major internal organs). Often inadequately informed about potential risks, two principal groups of women had sought breast improvement. The first were women who had lost one or more breasts to cancer and required reconstructive surgery. The second consisted of those who, with every good intention, tried to make themselves sexier and happier by improving their bodies. Some of them sacrificed their health in the process.

Looking back, it might seem that the widespread adverse side effects of breast implants would have brought an end to such surgery for purely cosmetic reasons, as women awakened to the dangers of too much pursuit of perfection. But in fact, the equation of beautiful body parts and sexual attractiveness had too powerful a hold. In 1994 nearly 40,000 American women—up from 32,600 in 1992—still submitted to breast implantation for aesthetic, not corrective reasons.

Those who escaped the worst of the possible side effects still suffered an ironic aftermath. What they had done for beauty and better sex defeated both, as many of the implants migrated to lodge unsexily in armpits or the clavicle area, or grew rock-hard, lumpy, and insensitive to touch. Even women who experienced no negative symptoms whatsoever, and who found both their self-esteem and sexual satisfaction enhanced by implants, still paid a price. Whether they knew it or not, in trying to achieve better sex and greater personal happiness, they gave up something of themselves— their own unique, original bodies and special eroticism.

Body Parts—His

Long enjoying the greater political and economic advantage, men had historically been less pressured than women to achieve physical perfection. But they were never entirely off the hook, and with inequities between the sexes leveling, men, too, felt compelled to strive for better bodies.

The fitness craze that had gripped them a decade earlier showed few signs of abating. Advertising and other media continued to promote pumping iron, building muscle, working out, getting lean and mean. Though their bodies were not as commercially exploited as women's, men nonetheless faced a barrage of images of the perfect manly parts they could—and should—develop. The well-sculpted biceps, washboard stomachs, and granite-hard buttocks of half- or entirely naked actors constantly reproached the average guy's under-muscled arms, incipient paunch, and nondescript rear. Meanwhile male models, even more perfect than the actors, showed men what they could be with the help of the right pair of jeans, sport shoes, cologne, or underwear—and with many, many, virtuous trips to the neighborhood gym.

Of course, a lot of men stayed firmly flabby, stomachs obstructing their view of their own feet. But others, made of sterner stuff, mustered the will to do something about their failing muscle. For most, moderate working out was the happy solution. But some took a good thing too far and—endlessly jogging, ceaselessly pumping—devoted themselves slavishly to the cult of excessive exercise. When even this failed to satisfy their desire for perfection, some men followed the risky route that women had charted. According to Michael Lafavore, editor of *Men's Health*, by the end of 1995 men "accounted for a big chunk of the plastic surgery business, and calf and bicep implants and silicone pecs were in vogue."

More determined still were all those courageous he-men who took what was undoubtedly the most drastic measure of all. They dropped their cotton boxer shorts and stepped out of their old-fashioned briefs, right into a new phase of history. The age of Lycra spandex underwear for men had arrived. When the rituals of the gym were not enough, alternative support was to be found in uplifting "Butt Boosters," "Man Bands" for waistline control, "Slenderizing Manshape Undergarments"—once known as girdles—and "Super Shaper Briefs."

There was no doubt about it—once so securely above vanity, men were growing uneasy, their confidence slipping along with the sagging pectorals of advancing age. The ideal of masculine attractiveness embodied in sexy-looking actors and models was flexing its own muscle. "Our eyes have been opened," said Michael Lafavore, speaking for many men of the 1990s, "maybe women don't really mean it when they say 'Honey, I love your love handles.' Maybe women really like beefcake."

He had a point. In 1995 one of the newer talk shows, *Leeza*, featured "international hunks . . . looking for love," and "beefcake" was clearly what the all-female audience wanted. In their enthusiasm for it, these attractive, well-dressed women, in their twenties and thirties by the look of them, showed just how far they had come in the struggle for equality. Casting any over-stimulated construction crew into the shadows, they whistled, clapped, leered, and cat-called at the "merchandise," as Leeza delicately described the hunks. It was all in fun—the women's way of getting some of their own back by turning the tables on the male gaze—and the men on stage played along. But for the average less-than-hunky man, women's growing insistence on better built bodies was hardly a morale-booster.

In the end men's bodily anxieties, whether fueled by women or not, came down to one part in particular. In the locker room of a gym, Don Gillmor, writing for the Toronto *Globe and Mail*, took note of the endowments on display—"homely, lolling . . . mottled, lumpy, belittled, mean-spirited, cashew-like, oddly coloured." Some things, clearly, exercise did not enhance. But as contemporary surveys suggested, the average man accepted, and made the most of, what he had. Even so, a few big thinkers hankered after what the psychologist Bernie Zilbergeld called "the fantasyland model . . . two feet long, as hard as steel and can go all night."

In real life, the closest thing to the fantasy was a size-enhancing implant (which could also correct impotence). Compared to all the women who had received breast implants, the men who resorted to such measures for the sake of measurement were still a small group. But their number was enough to attract the attention of a talk show. "Men Who Pump Up Their Sex Lives" was a 1993 *Maury Povich* show featuring a surgeon or two and some recipients of cosmetic largesse. In the revival meeting spirit of the show a few men testified to their newly redeemed sex lives. But as one of the doctors verified, the operations were not free of complications such as misshapenness. "Just imagine a hammerhead shark," one sufferer complained.

The audience's laughter was understandable. But it was not funny that however statistically insignificant they might still be, some men were prepared to exchange health for a bodily ideal. Part of an emerging trend of the decade, it was the downside of equal opportunity. In the progressive, self-improving nineties you could feel bad about yourself regardless of gender.

By the Book, or Buy a Sex Aid

If attaining physical perfection was itself an imperfect, sometimes risky endeavor, at least its larger purpose was unquestionably desirable. Better sex for both sexes—men and women alike were more than ready for it, even if it took more effort than going to the gym.

It turned out to be easier than that, though. You just walked into the nearest bookstore, video shop, or sex boutique and made a few purchases. There was practically nothing to better sex after all. It was a matter of acquiring the latest sexy techniques and accessories or, perhaps, playing one of the simple numbers games in advice books: "16 ways to love your lover," "make love six nights a week," "the 101 best places for a quickie," "fifty fabulous ideas for driving her wild" . . .

As a rule the books were slim volumes, but they held enough recipes for sizzling sex to satisfy most appetites. Boiled down to skimpy paragraphs, short sentences, and staccato phrases, they were as spicy as anything in *The Joy of Cooking* and a lot simpler to follow. If you overlooked an ingredient, there was no cause for concern. It would be repeated a page or two later, then again and again, with bold type in little boxes, or between rows of asterisks or arrows. And all of it was dished up in a tone as relentlessly encouraging as that of a Little League mom cheering on her less than talented offspring from the sideline.

Apart from their upbeat tone, the sex advice authors had in common a knack for packaging sex as a matter of basic techniques, hints, and ideas that anyone could master. Some, like John Gray, the best-selling author of *Men Are from Mars, Women Are from Venus* (1992) and *Mars and Venus in the Bedroom* (1995), offered common sense wrapped up in new jargon. Others relied on point-form "steps" and "tips," questions and answers, and lists of sexy words and things. The title of a 1995 reference book by the decade's favorite sex therapist, Dr. Ruth Westheimer, captured the anyone-can-do-it-better spirit of contemporary sexual self-help. Part of a well-known how-to series, the book was called *Sex for Dummies.*

In a time of sound bites and images, not everyone had the time or inclination to read a sex advice book—even one for dummies. Instead, you could buy an audio cassette or videotape and do it the 1990s multimedia way. *Real Moments for Lovers* (1995), an audio cassette by the advice book author Barbara De Angelis, repeated "certain simple ideas" about "the importance of emotional connection through physical connection," according to one reviewer. The goals of such repetition were "unending joy" and "boundless, timeless, endless bliss." Though it was hard to imagine anyone wanting more, the promises of some videotape series were nonetheless tempting: "*Discover the Secrets of Sexual Satisfaction!* . . . Achieve the Ultimate in Sexual Fulfillment . . . DRAMATICALLY IMPROVE YOUR SEX LIFE . . . to derive more excitement, enjoyment and sexual satisfaction than you ever dreamed possible!" This and other advertisements for similar videos not only appeared on television but in a variety of high-profile publications—everything from *Cosmopolitan* and *Psychology Today* to the *New York Times Book Review*. Such wide placement reflected the universality of the potential market for sexual self-improvement in the century's last decade.

If books and tapes were not enough to revive a humdrum love life, mail-order catalogues and sex shops offered an assortment of additional sex aids, toys, and accessories. Sundry creams, oils, vibrators and novelty underwear were the standard offerings. Meanwhile, as *Details* magazine reported in 1994, several inventors were "feverishly at work to improve the nation's sex life" all the more. "Quick-draw" men's briefs with pull-down flaps for "playing fast and loose," and a vibrating bar of soap for better showering were among the products patented by the "device squad" of erotically committed patriots who served the cause of better sex for America.

With the threat of sexually transmitted diseases prominent in people's minds, inventors took up the challenge of making latex sexy or, failing that, at least amusing. One of their number patented a mini-pump for enhancing the size of even the most ordinary condom, and someone else invented one that played music. But the inventor Marc Snyder of Oakland, California, outdid them all. Activated by running a fingernail along a strip on its underside, his "Amazing Talking Condom" spoke English, as well as several other languages, and offered a selection of messages: "I love you," "You turn me on," or "Thank you for your business." It was the ultimate invention in a century of sexual openness, and for the one most closely involved, this called for a celebration. "Let's party!" said the condom.

Sex in the Real World

"Mindblowing sex in the real world"—that was the promise of one advice book. But in fact the erotic world of advice books, videos, and sex toys often bore little resemblance to real life. In the midst of a culture that insisted that sex should be "mindblowing," many people experienced it as mundane. Others hardly experienced it at all.

At first the findings of the 1990s' most acclaimed sex survey sounded like good news. The social scientist Robert T. Michael and the other authors of the survey's abridged version, *Sex in America* (1994), found that "although America may not be as sexy a place as it is often portrayed, most people are satisfied with the sexual lives they have chosen or that were imposed upon them." This might have been good news, were it not for that troublesome word "satisfied." It worked well on a survey form because it covered a range of subjective experiences and responses. But what it meant in real human terms was not altogether clear. Bland and slippery, "satisfied" was not necessarily sexy. The *Sex in America* team added a further qualification to their findings: people were satisfied, "or at least not highly dissatisfied, with the sexual lots they have drawn." The real world was slipping further and further from the pinnacle of ecstasy promised by the advice books.

Indications were that, despite all the pressures to do it right, many people were getting sex wrong in all kinds of ways. Often they treated it as they would any chore that took effort and, with time and exposure, grew tedious. In other words, they managed to do it infrequently, or not at all. The authors of *Sex in America* reported that close to one third of those surveyed "have sex with a partner a few times a year or have no sexual partners at all." At the opposite end of the spectrum only 8 percent of men and 7 percent of women had it four or more times a week. Overall, the authors found rates "so modest, at best, that they confound our expectations."

This was not just a national trend, nor was it short-lived. A few years later, another report indicated that overall global sexual activity was down from 112 times per year in 1997 to 106 in 1998. In Canada a 1995 survey by *Maclean's Magazine* found that only 10 percent of those surveyed described themselves as sexually active. A later Angus Reid Poll reported a modest average national frequency rate of 6.2 times per month in 1998.

South of the border, meanwhile, the low rate of activity reported in *Sex in America* was possibly declining further. In 1996 the *Ladies' Home Journal* noted decreasing desire among double-income couples, for whom no sex or infrequent sex was becoming the norm. In January 1998 Oprah Winfrey reported that 40 million American women, the majority between the ages of twenty-four and thirty-six, complained of loss of desire. A 1999 study published in the *American Journal of Medicine* found that sexual dysfunction affected 31 percent of men between ages eighteen and fifty-nine, and 43 percent of women in the same age group, with the problem greater among the younger half of the women.

The modest rates of sexual frequency that characterized the 1990s were a source of anxiety to some. From time to time, the worrisome subject came up in women's magazines, while a 1994 survey for *Details* found that of the respondents, whose ages ranged from eighteen to thirty-four, 60 percent of single people and 55 percent of those married felt they did not have enough sex. But often, the reverse was true. Some people actively chose celibacy as a way of avoiding anxiety and disappointment.

For some, the concerns were the same ones that had been hanging around throughout the century—men worried about their performance, women about their attractiveness and the adequacy of their response. Meanwhile all the sex advice that proliferated to allay anxiety may well have contributed to it instead. Fabulous, wild, mindblowing sex was a daunting standard to achieve at the best of times, and it was all the more so for a couple who had already put in a long day of work outside the home, then attended to the necessary chores inside it—lurching from one task to the next in the stressed-out exhausted way of the time. Apart from health issues, causes of sexual dysfunction reported in the *American Medical Journal* were job pressures, insufficient time, and lack of interest.

Many people may also have felt they lacked the basic qualifications for great sex. This could in part be why *Sex in America* found a "steady diminution of sexual activity" as people grew older:

There is that . . . mythology, that passionate sex is for the young and the beautiful and the unmarried. This exotic world of movies, television, and novels may be more of a disincentive than an incentive to sex with a partner. It is more an invitation to dreams than to action. Older people might have less partnered sex and spend less time at it because they think that frequent, time-consuming sex is no longer appropriate for them.

According to the survey, the declining sex life of "older people" did not begin at seventy or sixty or even fifty. Thirty—that was the ripe old age that marked the nation's decline into sexual decrepitude, according to *Sex in America*. The frequency of sexual dysfunction among young women reported a few years later further substantiated this finding.

As the decade went on, the evidence grew that constant exposure to sexual images did more than make people unhappily aware of their age and bodily shortcomings. Watching television, and presumably videos as well, made people passive, less inclined to engage in intellectual or physical activity. And if that were not enough to put a damper on a night of seduction, then an evening of explicitly sexy viewing could quench the flame altogether. Desensitization was a widely observed phenomenon of the 1990s, the outcome of too much second-hand excitement via the mass media and too much paralyzing anxiety from too-high sexual expectations.

One survey found that more Americans got pleasure from television than from sex. Other data, gathered at the end of 1995, showed that a majority of women preferred a good night's sleep. In Canada, approximately a third of both sexes said they would rather have chocolate. Commissioned by confectionery manufacturers, this survey was undoubtedly slanted. But it added to growing suspicion that advice books, videos, and sex aids were not necessarily the solution. In fact, they just might be part of the problem.

Swept Away by Confusion

Adding to the effects of information and entertainment overload was yet another source of individual anxiety. In a decade of gender politics, it was hard to know how to behave without giving offence.

The rules and language of political correctness that were intended to ensure repect for all, and to ease the relationship of men and women, sometimes complicated matters as much as they corrected inequities. It was bewildering enough that the term *actor* applied to even the sexiest female stars, now that *actress* had become incorrect usage. And how could a girl (that is, *person*—sex and age not relevant) who had just met a boy (ditto) make ladylike (substitute gender-neutral term "polite") inquiries about his (pronoun still permissible, but only for grammatical clarity) marital availability, when even the term "Bachelor of Arts" was giving way to the more acceptable "undergraduate degree"? It boggled even the most gender-neutral mind.

No longer knowing the right thing to say or do, a lot of people kept their feelings to themselves. If they flirted, would it be seen as sexual harassment or well-meant compliment? If they made a physical approach, was it attempted date rape or misinterpreted sexual signals? And when, if ever, was intercourse not a political act of aggression on one side, submission on the other?

These politicized controversies went beyond merely confusing and upsetting people. They threatened the intermittent truce between men and women that had originated in the eighties, often fueling whatever emotional and sexual strains individual couples might privately be facing. The psychologist Michael Miller called the intrusion of sexual politics into personal life "intimate terrorism"—a "widening cultural crisis" that was destroying relationships.

With every private act now potentially a power struggle, it had become "almost impossible," said Miller, "to think about love, sex, intimacy, or marriage without thinking about power":

The old sentimental image of Cupid has changed. He is . . . a fiercer god who all too often seems to exercise power with brutal or demonic intent.

Considering the continual outpouring of stories in the news about . . . rape, sexual harassment, or child abuse; and the alarming increase in domestic violence—everything appears to be conspiring to persuade us that our erotic impulses and intimate attachments create not happy couples and couplings but victims and oppressors.

And once we think this way, we have confused our private lives with public issues: "Modern intimacy, whatever else it might be, has become political."

A cartoon appeared in *Cosmopolitan* in December 1993 showing a woman and man, naked in bed together. As her lover sits up and gives her a dismayed look, the woman lies back, her own face etched with worry, and says to herself: "I think I faked the wrong kind of orgasm." It was a humorous acknowledgement of living and loving in a time when even the most personal of pleasures now ran the risk of being technically ill-informed, as well as politically incorrect and disempowering.

Sometimes Desperate Measures

It was a paradox of the decade that while desire might be diminished through desensitization, politicization, or both, some people sought it all the more desperately. This did not necessarily mean having more sex—people now regarded "sexual addiction" with less skepticism than they had in the previous decade. You could, they now believed, have too much sex (as well as too little). The nineties idea was to improve its quality and enjoyment—to do it right, by whatever means necessary.

For some, the right means was greater stimulation through experimentation. "Kink comes out of the closet," reported the *Ladies'*

Home Journal in 1996. Fewer people now had moral reservations about sexual practices once widely considered perverse. Some couples, for example, tried playful forms of "S and M" (sado-masochism) to spice up the physical side of their relationships. Props might include blindfolds, satin restraints, and perhaps a how-to manual.

Others ventured beyond their private chambers and patronized "swinging" clubs, where partner-swapping ranged from mere flirting to group sex. The patrons of one such Montreal establishment described their activity as a "lifestyle" that "eroticizes" long-term relationships. Still other swingers insisted that such sexual expression was not only an antidote to old-fashioned adultery but at its best was "almost like a cosmic experience." One woman who was seriously thinking of trying the swinging lifestyle echoed a wistful cultural theme now almost a century old. Despite her purportedly happy marriage, she wanted "something more."

Still others, whether in relationships or not, sought new sexual thrills through electronics, chemicals, or possibly both. By dialing a 900 number for telephone sex or connecting via modem to one of the Internet's virtual-sex sites, they got their kicks "without having to face up to actual faces," as one commentator put it. Where electronic communications failed, pharmaceuticals sometimes succeeded. With varying results, some people experimented by popping pleasure-intensifiers that ranged from vitamins to restricted-access drugs—all in the interest of "better sex through chemistry."

The pharmaceutical best-seller of the decade was the anti-impotence pill Viagra. Originally designed to relieve medical conditions, Viagra was soon in much wider demand. Suppliers could not keep up with all the requests from healthy men who wanted to try the pill as a performance-enhancer. By early in 1999 Viagra had become the biggest-selling drug of all time. Here at last, men hoped, was the "magic bullet" that would provide whatever was missing in their sex lives. Some women (mistakenly) thought so, too, and were willing to risk the pill's uncertain side effects, if only it would restore their lost desire.

One way or another—by adventuresome play, phone lines, or pills—some people must have found the physical gratification they sought, at least temporarily. But it remained questionable whether experimentation and intensified sensation could truly fill the sexual void in their lives with any lasting satisfaction. One respondent to the *Details* sex survey, a twenty-eight-year-old man, put an optimistic spin on the widespread feeling that profound erotic experience was always just beyond reach. When asked "What's the best sex you've ever had?" he replied, "I don't think I've had it yet."

Grasping at Passion

In the 1990s more and more people began to suspect that the "something" they sensed they were missing was *not* better sex. However uncertainly or misguidedly, they began to reach for something grander. Haltingly, tenuously, the old ideal of passion was taking new shape.

In popular culture it showed itself variously and intermittently, often in small but suggestive ways. Abandoning sexually explicit topics, the less sensational of the talk shows played matchmaker for the unattached, or staged "seminars" in romance for couples wanting to enhance their relationships. One of the decade's favorite movies was the 1993 *Sleepless in Seattle*, an old-fashioned romantic comedy whose main characters (played by Tom Hanks and Meg Ryan) share the 1990s sense of "missing something." Although he lives in Seattle, she in Baltimore, they eventually find each other and their true destiny. On a similar quest in real life, men and women advertised in personals columns all over North America. Repeatedly, they referred to "seeking" or "searching"—not just for a relationship but for one that would be "romantic," "loving," "honest," "special," and above all, "lasting."

A best-selling dating guide for women, *The Rules* (1995), echoed the same themes yet again. "We're talking marriage here," declared the authors, Ellen Fein and Sherrie Schneider, "real, lasting marriage, not loveless mergers." Nineties women, they argued, wanted "the whole package." Much talked about, the book was also widely criticized—for reviving the retrograde notion of playing hard to get, for perpetuating gender stereotypes, and for pitting men and women against each other. Undoubtedly, the critics had a case. But as one commentator pointed out, *The Rules* also contained "a hard core of common sense." In an age when openness often went to desperate extremes, it was an attempt to revive something of the mystique that had once sweetened—and spiced—the relationship of the sexes.

Another best-seller resonated more widely and deeply through the mood of the time. This was Robert James Waller's 1992 novel *The Bridges of Madison County*, followed by a movie version in 1995. Movie and book told the story of a brief, secret affair between a married woman and an itinerant photographer. In the way it struck a collective popular chord, it was the *Love Story* of the nineties, capturing, in the emotional and physical intensity of the protagonists' relationship, what so many felt was eluding them. And just as real people struggled to identify the voids in their lives, the two fictional lovers, and other characters who crossed their paths, reached for the right words to express the true meaning of the affair. It was a "dance" . . . "convergence" . . . "sheer power" . . . long-forgotten "old ways" unexpectedly rekindled in the indifferent present. All of that and more—it was "great passion."

By the later years of the decade, *The Bridges of Madison County* had mostly faded from popular memory. But in 1997, its half-articulated but powerful message found new expression in the movie *Titanic*. The doomed affair between Jack and Rose reflected back to us that old, lingering sense of something grand, something inexpressible, that stays just out of reach despite all our efforts to grasp it.

"There's got to be more." It was not only the silent conviction of romantic dreams but the freedom cry of many who walked away from their relationships. Except among those who were chronic seekers of sexual thrills, it was also a standard rationale for infidelity, itself a commonplace in the 1990s. Depending on the statistics used, 50 to 60 percent of Americans were unfaithful in relationships. The figure for Canada in the same year, 1998, was 70 percent.

Meanwhile, by some reckonings, the divorce rate in the United States was edging toward 60 percent in 1998. In Canada it reached 50 percent in 1999, up 15 percent in a decade. The most common reasons people gave for their failed marriages were too little freedom, lack of love, inadequate communication, and not enough sex. In other words, they were sure they were missing something— but it wasn't just sex. And whatever that *something* was, they didn't want to miss their chance to find it, when the opportunity arose.

Turning the Millennial Corner

If the decade of the nineties started out as a sometimes desperate search for better sex, it did not end that way. As many now realized, improving your sex life, if it was even possible, was not the key to happiness. Though the long revolution of the self could not be overturned, as the nineties unfolded people increasingly looked to invest in themselves and in their relationships something beyond sex or the minimal self of the eighties. Some turned to traditional religion, others to New Age spiritualism, while still others hesitantly charted their own independent paths toward something large and intangible with which to enrich their lives— "spirit," "a higher power," or simply "inner peace," as they variously called it. The trouble was, in a culture that still mainly promoted immediate gratification, it was hard to be sure just what would open the door to lasting fulfillment.

The uncertainties that men and women felt, as individuals and as couples, were compounded by the age itself. The approach of not only a new century but a new millennium made the immediate future loom both vaster and more unknowable than at any other time in the century. Some people looked for solace in the past, even trying to revive it—by adopting old-fashioned dating rules or by arguing for a universal return to traditional morality and family patterns. For others, firmly rooted in the present, this was a pointless exercise. New technologies and entertainments, as well as economic and social structures, had created an immense and unbridgeable gulf between contemporary life and most of the century that was now ending. There was no going back—you could only make the most of the imperfect present and await the largely unpredictable future.

But most of those who looked longingly back were imagining a past that had never really existed. And those who saw only the chasm of change were denying the connection of past, present, and future. While the nineties were distinctive in spirit and events, they also resonated with echoes from earlier days: the enthusiasm for sexual openness from the century's first years; the widespread faith in sex as the key to personal happiness; anxieties about physical attractiveness; and the fluid understanding of passion as advertising buzzword, synonym for sex, or something greater—something that to many seemed attainable. Similarly, the unfolding history of men and women would continue to reverberate with new forms of old beliefs and discontents, within individuals themselves and within their intimate relationships.

But on the eve of the new millennium it was—and would remain—possible to turn a corner and to take a new direction. No easy agenda, this would demand a deliberate effort, both personally and collectively, to embrace a future of renewed promise. It might begin by not merely looking back, but by reevaluating both past and present—mining them for what should be preserved, and leaving the rest behind. For it could just be that the nineties' feeling of missing something was not only a nebulous revival of an old ideal but a glimmering of future possibility.

Even so, the temptation would be to follow the less arduous route and to carry on as before, hoping for the best. Some people, after all, would still manage to find the happiness and quality of relationship—the passion—they sought. But with the future left to chance, many more would not be so lucky. In the new millennium, their search would go on. . . .

VII

BRAVE
NEW LOVE

2000 AND BEYOND

The twentieth century has passed into history, but the culture of sex is still with us, little changed since the 1990s. If anything, its hold is stronger than ever.

Yet a difference is beginning to be perceptible in the attitude of individuals. In the face of the dissatisfactions that are now endemic in contemporary relationships, people grasp all the more earnestly for what they are missing. The trouble is, the public culture of sex seems to have taken on a corresponding vigor of its own to militate more aggressively than ever against private desire, against people's most deeply felt dreams—against passion itself.

As the need for cultural change becomes more acute, the chances of its occurring quickly or easily appear to be growing even more remote. For now, then, the individual's best, and perhaps only defense is courage.

Embracing the Future

We stand on the peak of the consciousness of
previous ages, and their wisdom is available to us . . .
The only way out is ahead, and our choice is
whether we shall cringe from it or affirm it.
. . . We mold ourselves and our world simultaneously.
This is what it means to embrace the future.

— ROLLO MAY, *Love and Will*

This is an interlude. For the time it takes to read this we are poised between past and future. The events of last week or yesterday or ten minutes ago are part of the past, but we do not yet have the perspective to see them clearly as such. Nor can we look into the future with any certainty.

What we can do for now is to take stock of the century we have recently traveled and, from it, try to determine the next few steps that will take us most effectively into the future's uncharted territory. Alternatively, as we have often done, we can shut our eyes to the past and forge ahead without its insights. We have the power to mold ourselves and our future as we embrace it. In the search for passion, this might be a place where we merely pause, before carrying on as before. But it could be the point where, individually and collectively, we change direction, boldly affirming the possibilities of the future and heading more certainly toward what we most deeply desire.

The Contradictions of Sexual Freedom

Now part of history, the past century's revolution of self has left us its legacy: an array of choices and freedoms that extend more widely than ever before. Freedom, however, can lead to a host of personal anxieties, conflicts, and disappointments that are anything but freeing. Nowhere, perhaps, has this been more unhappily apparent than in the culture of sex. The solution, however, is not to reduce sexual freedom, but to find a way to experience it with greater quality as a culture, and more joy as individuals.

In our age of pluralism we harbor many dreams. And among them, the old ideal of passion has never died. Though overshadowed by cultural preoccupations with sexual technique, experimentation, and confession, it has survived in the private heart of individual aspiration.

Enclosing us all, still, is the culture of sex. As we look back on it without the myths that have often obscured it, we can now see a continuity that has threaded its way through a century of changes. Year by year from 1900, we have been cultivating openness about personal matters—sex in particular. Initially, openness fulfilled the high expectations we had of it, overturning ignorance and enhancing well-being. But as we moved further into explicitness and compulsive confession, the quality of public life began to erode, and at the same time we often failed to achieve our personal goals. In abandoning restraints on frank speech, casual manners, and graphic portrayals in entertainment, we did not create a closer society but settled instead for shallow approximations of intimacy, sociability, and community. In private, meanwhile, we lost desire, missed happiness, foundered in our commitments.

New Millennium, Same Old Sex

Now that we have crossed the threshold into the new millennium, there is little that is new in the culture of sex. The familiar statistics of body image problems, unhappy relationships, and desire disorder hold their own, while the how-to books continue to roll off the presses and the entertainment industry is still "sizzling with sex" (as one newspaper headline announced). In cyberspace, the newest frontier, virtual adultery and online sex addiction are also carryovers from the 1990s. Some people's addiction has now reached the acute stage and, according to one researcher, "just looking at the computer gets them aroused." Predictably, sex with a human partner has little or no appeal.

A poll by the home furnishing chain IKEA reported that 31 percent of the three hundred men and women who responded would rather clean their closets than have sex. What is significant about this poll is that almost nothing about it matters. The figure of 31 percent may, or may not, be representative of the larger population—either way, it doesn't matter. Many of the respondents likely answered with more humor than truth—which also doesn't matter. The survey is biased, since IKEA sells closet organizers, not sex—but this, too, doesn't matter. What does matter is the extent to which the culture of sex accommodates invasion of privacy and trivializes the very thing that sustains it.

Yet in spite of it all, as individuals we have managed to hold on to our dreams. But for how long, now that furniture stores conduct sex surveys and people form erotic attachments to circuitry encased in plastic? With little in culture to nurture them, our dreams must surely diminish. In the movie *Titanic*, Rose touches a deep chord in popular consciousness when she remembers that "*Titanic* was called the 'Ship of Dreams.'" In both the movie and real life the great tragedy was the unnecessary extinguishing of so many bright dreams.

Remaking Sex, Reclaiming Passion

To watch *Titanic* or any other movie is to experience other people's stories vicariously. At the same time, we remain active players in our own real-life dramas. In other words, however great its hold on us, we are never just bystanders in our own culture but its creators as well. Collectively, over many years we have made the culture of sex, if only by consuming its products and tacitly accepting its values. We thus have the power to change it.

Whether as individuals we seek our happiness through a permanent relationship modeled on the old ideal of passion, or through a perpetual series of transitory encounters, we all have the same agenda. We need to rescue the personal from careless exposure, standardization, and loss of pleasure. It comes down to removing what was once intimate from public life and putting it back into private space—the only space where body, feeling, and spirit can attain their fullest expression. We must reject the trivial, prurient, and exploitive in our culture, as we embrace the complicated, original, and profound—the wellsprings of passion.

Widespread change builds from small individual acts. Without returning to the inhibitions of the past, we can preserve the reticence necessary to keep our deepest feelings safe. We can, for instance, accumulate sexual knowledge in privacy—whether through books, tapes, or uninstructed experimentation—while refraining from airing it exhaustively in public or attending to those who do. Even in the tell-all, show-all culture of recent times, ignorance, the sex experts insist, is the root of our troubled relationships. Once widely a problem, ignorance has now become an overdone rationalization for the production of more and more sex studies and self-help materials, many of which do not inform so much as they contribute to oppressive standards of sexual performance and expression. Without denying the value of responsible sex education for those who want and need it, we can each exercise critical judgment as to what sort of sexual knowledge is truly necessary or beneficial for ourselves, and what is merely superfluous or blatantly exploitive.

Our greatest potential for bringing about cultural change is as consumers. By rejecting certain products and entertainments, we can help to promote a culture that nurtures private—and therefore uniquely satisfying—erotic and emotional expression. We can refuse to buy items whose advertising sets a uniform and, for most people, unattainable standard of sexual attractiveness. We can avoid books and magazine articles whose message to readers is that they are missing something that everyone else is getting. We can ignore the television, videos, and movies that seem to us to misuse sex. And we can turn off just one prurient talk show that delves intrusively into the purported dysfunction of private lives. We can resist anything and everything that suggests directly or otherwise that our own particular way of intimate expression is lacking in frequency, creativity, cosmetically reconstructed body parts, designer clothing, or exotic props.

Courage and the Will to Love

A crucial insight that has come down to us from the past century is that we are all participants in an ongoing interplay between public and private life. Culture has shaped us, as we have shaped it. Yet in the light of history we can also see the enduring power and magnitude of our creation, the culture of sex. For now, its grip may be too tenacious for us to throw it off and effect rapid change. If so, while we chip away at the colossus, the fulfillment that we seek will have to come primarily from ourselves as individuals. There will be little cultural support for such a quest.

But how, then, do we live with—and grow within—a deeply flawed culture that we cannot instantly and dramatically alter? The answer is that we need to draw upon our own inherent, too often unrecognized, capacity to seek and to experience sexual love in brave and freeing ways.

Of course, we could adopt the easier stance of arch realism and simply accept that ours is now a world in which preschoolers of both sexes suffer from negative body images (as recent studies show), and a larger than ever majority of adults live with sexual dysfunction and dissatisfaction. But in their hearts a great many people will never find such a world acceptable, and many also struggle daily with enormous unhappiness—about their relationships and about themselves as individuals. The plea for "something more" continues to be the haunting refrain of our times.

And more often than not, this inchoate longing far exceeds the bounds of sexual relationships. For in recent years the search for passion has been subsumed in a larger quest. Many people are now actively seeking to discover profound meaning in all areas of their lives, particularly in the realms of feeling and spirit. The mass popularity of psychological and spiritual advice books is one sign of this powerful drive for self-realization.

Thus, to achieve passion now—in the present cultural context—takes more than just keeping a watchful eye on the media and selectively rejecting certain images, attitudes, and scenarios. Such critical skills are only the beginning of what fulfilment demands. To grow further, the individual must strive to transcend culture—to separate the true self from the shallow self that too many people, unhappily, feel they should value. This is the culturally constructed self that derives its worth from physical beauty, perfect sex, and impossible love.

Rising above such unrealistic expectations and orchestrated dissatisfaction requires a profound understanding of one's own interaction with culture. What we each need is, in a word, courage— not the old physical virtue that once helped people to stay alive, but a radical new form of courage that involves mind, heart, and soul. For if the past century's history of personal dissatisfaction and disappointing relationships has taught us anything at all, it is this: To thrive in intimate life nowadays, we must first face and then turn our backs on those elements in culture that inhibit sexuality, negate passion, and poison relationships—because, most destructively of all, they wither the spirit.

This is the radical courage we each must call forth in order to find fulfillment, despite culture's many assaults on our psyches. Such courage is always quiet, private, and infinitely variable from one person to the next. It has nothing to do with polemics or the imposition of anyone's personal sexual morality on anyone else. It is what cannot be taught—it is self-knowledge—a deep inner certitude that is fully individual and greater than either intellect or ideology.

Most important, it is a form of courage that every one of us has the potential to summon. For it comes from what has driven the search for passion and has constantly endured in human nature: *the will to love*. When acted on with the courage that it engenders, our innate will to love not only empowers us to transcend culture but also fosters an individualism that is free of the narcissism so prevalent in contemporary life. And, in the end, this higher form of individualism is what will produce the cultural change that will enable greater numbers of us to conduct our lives—and our love relationships—with integrity, meaning, pleasure, and joy.

Little of this is entirely new. Decades ago, Rollo May and, later, Christopher Lasch identified the anxious defensiveness of the narcissistic self. This, as they both realized, is what stops the individual from abandoning the comfort zone of alienation and attaining true intimacy. But in recent years their insight has been all but forgotten amidst the daily bombardment of cultural messages that tie physical beauty and standardized sexuality to personal worth and happiness.

Worst of all, these spirit-cramping messages have blinded many people to the promise of fulfillment contained in this simple but essential truth: that what we desire in our private hearts resides in what we have always had—or had within reach. *In the human will to love, and in the courage to enact it with integrity, is where passion can be found.*

The Power of Imagination

Encompassing both courage and our natural will to love is an even greater force. *Imagination.*

We have reimagined the past, gathering what we could from the new vision. But if we are to achieve greater happiness, however we desire it—find passion, however we define it—we must also allow ourselves to imagine that we *can* shape the future to our greater satisfaction. And above all, we must be able to imagine and to act on it now.

"It is our imaginative participation in the coming day's possibilities," Rollo May said, "out of which comes the awareness of our capacity to form, to mold, to change ourselves and the day in relation to each other." True words in the middle of the twentieth century, they remain so today.

The interlude is almost over, the only way out ahead. We can resist change, deny the will to love, suppress courage—and make our way into a future that promises little better than the lengthening history of discontent we leave behind. Or we can take the other, still unmarked road and begin a new journey toward a future of fulfillment. If the search for passion was the history of the past century, then finding it could be the achievement of the next.

Passion Lost

NOTES

After first references in each chapter, I have used shortened titles in these notes.

Chapter 1: Reimagining the Past

Page

4   *the 1997 movie Titanic:* I have telescoped some scenes in my recounting; the characters Rose and Jack were played by Kate Winslet and Leonardo DiCaprio.

4   *Isidor Straus and his wife, Ida:* Philip Hind, Encyclopedia Titanica (1998),<http://www.rmplc.co.uk/eduweb/sites/phind/html/straus.html>; Walter Lord, *A Night to Remember* (1956; 1997); Lord, *The Night Lives On: New Thoughts, Theories, and Revelations about the Titanic* (1986); Charles Pellegrino, *Her Name, Titanic: The Untold Story of the Sinking and Finding of the Unsinkable Ship* (1988); Straus Family Historical Society (1996-8), <http://www. informationengineer.com/straus/straushp. htm>; I am also grateful for background information from Paul Heyer who has written on the enduring cultural significance of the *Titanic*, in Heyer, *Titanic Legacy: Disaster as Media Event and Myth* (1995).

5–6   *"Let us educate love . . . serene":* Jean Finot, *Problems of the Sexes* (1913), quoted in Marie Stopes, *Enduring Passion* (1928), 212.

6   *Foucault challenged . . . Victorian repression:* Michel Foucault, *The*

History of Sexuality, vol. 1., *An Introduction* (1976; trans. R. Hurley, 1978; reprint, 1980).

6 *Victorians created a culture of passion:* Patricia Anderson, *When Passion Reigned: Sex and the Victorians* (1995).

6 *"actually a way . . . gratification":* Peter Gay, *The Bourgeois Experience: Victoria to Freud*, vol. 1, *Education of the Senses* (1984), 107.

6 *people began to look critically at Victorian notions:* For further discussion, see Michael Mason, *The Making of Victorian Sexuality* (1994), 8–10.

7 *"Knowledge" became the catchword:* Marie Stopes, *Married Love* (1918; 1962), ix, xi.

7 *statistics:* Estimates of the divorce rate in the United States vary from 57 to 67 percent, reported on *Oprah Winfrey*, 8 and 24 February 2000 (although *Time Magazine*, 25 September 2000, 44, reported 49 percent); University of North Carolina study reported in *Journal of Family Medicine* (March 2000).

7 *Viagra bestselling drug: Vancouver Sun*, 2 May 1998, c3.

8 *study at Harvard:* Reported by Gina Ogden, *Oprah Winfrey*, 18 May 2000.

8 *"Sex for many . . . illusion":* Rollo May, *Love and Will* (1969), 14.

8 *consumerism:* See among others Roger Rosenblatt, ed., *Consuming Desires: Consumption, Culture, and the Pursuit of Happiness* (1999), 1–21, and Christopher Lasch, *The Culture of Narcissism: American Life in an Age of Diminishing Expectations* (1979), 136–8; on sex and consumerism, see Edwin Schur, *The Americanization of Sex* (1988), 84–95.

9 *commercial interests . . . how-to-do-it books:* Examples from advertising, fashion, and entertainment are given throughout the book; the frequency rates given in the text are from W. F. Robie, *Sex and Life* (1920), cited in Stopes, *Enduring Passion*, 139–40; Stopes herself was more flexible on the issue of frequency, allowing anything from twice a year to multiple times a day, as long as this was what both husband and wife wanted; William H. Masters and Virginia E. Johnson, *Human Sexual Response* (1966; 1986), are among others who have insisted that there is no norm, but whose clinical focus on response and technique has implied otherwise; other examples are cited at appropriate points below.

9 *"to transmute physiology . . . ":* May, *Love and Will*, 43.

10 *the movie Titanic:* I have reconstructed scenes in this section from

the original screenplay and my own viewing of the movie.

12 *"sociocultural patternings . . . orientation":* Schur, *Americanization of Sex,* 17.

12 *conservatives would like the clock turned back:* For further discussion, see Schur, *Americanization of Sex,* 15–21.

12–13 *Others, of more liberal persuasion:* A recent example of the typical argument is Naomi Wolf, *Promiscuities: The Secret Struggle for Womanhood* (1997), reviewed by Jean Bethke Elshtain, *Times Literary Supplement,* 6 June 1997, 12; Wolf calls for "better information that can shape a better sexual culture."

13 *"we need to turn the social clock forward":* Schur, *Americanization of Sex,* xiii–xiv.

13 *"ethic of commitment":* Schur, *Americanization of Sex,* 47–48; Barbara Dafoe Whitehead, *The Divorce Culture* (1997), 10.

13 *pluralism:* Ira L. Reiss, *An End to Shame: Shaping Our Next Sexual Revolution* (1990); see also Jeffrey Weeks, *Sexuality and Its Discontents: Meanings, Myths and Modern Sexualities* (1985), 258–60.

14 *redraw the boundaries between public and private life:* My observations on sexual openness, its impact on both public and private life, and the need to redefine the limits of both, owe much to Richard Sennett, *The Fall of Public Man* (1977); see also Julie C. Inness, *Privacy, Intimacy, and Isolation* (1992), viii, 9–10; Wendy Kaminer, *I'm Dysfunctional, You're Dysfunctional: The Recovery Movement and Other Self-Help Fashions* (1993), 29–33; Christopher Lasch, *The Culture of Narcissism,* 27–30; Thomas Nagel, "The Shredding of Public Privacy," *Times Literary Supplement,* 14 August 1998, 15.

14 *"History . . . future":* May, *Love and Will,* 325.

15 *"it reaches . . . this still night":* James Cameron, *Titanic* screenplay.

15 *musicians played ragtime and popular waltzes:* Lord, *The Night Lives On,* 138–39.

16 *so-called sexual revolution:* Others who have questioned the suddenness, uniqueness, or impact of the "revolution" include John D'Emilio and Estelle Freedman, *Intimate Matters: A History of Sexuality in America* (1988), 300, 325; George Frankl, *Failure of the Sexual Revolution* (1974); Linda Grant, *Sexing the Millennium: A Political History of the Sexual Revolution* (1993); Graham Heath, *The Illusory Freedom: The Intellectual Origins and Social Consequences of the Sexual 'Revolution'* (1978); Edward O. Laumann, John H. Gagnon, Robert T. Michael, and Stuart

Michaels, *The Social Organization of Sexuality: Sexual Practices in the United States* (1994), 542.

16 *shift from duty to individual needs:* My remarks in many ways reflect commentary in, among others, Lasch, *The Culture of Narcissism*; Paul Leinberger and Bruce Tucker, *The New Individualists: The Generation After The Organization Man* (1991). I differ, however, from sources that date contemporary individualism to the mid rather than early twentieth century: see, for example, Barbara Dafoe Whitehead, *The Divorce Culture* (1997), 4.

17 *Victorians . . . "prudery" or "hypocrisy" part of conventional wisdom:* For one of the latest instances, see Tom Hickman, *The Sexual Century: How Private Passion Became a Public Obsession* (2000), 7 and 10.

17 *"What did they do . . . grateful":* Charles Taylor, review of *One Nation, Two Cultures*, by Gertrude Himmelfarb, *Salon*, reprinted *Vancouver Sun*, 12 February 2000, E7; for additional commentary on the conservative critique of the sexual revolution and after, see Schur, *Americanization of Sex*, 15–21.

17 *"something more" . . . "meaning":* Extracted from author interviews, August 1996 to July 1997; respondents were between thirty-five and sixty years of age; the majority were single or divorced.

Chapter 2: Sex as the Key to Happiness

Page

21 *optimistic terms: New York Times*, 1 January 1900, 10, 12, 13, 14.

22 *"Knowledge is needed . . . bond":* Marie Stopes, *Married Love* (1918; 1962), xi.

23 *"Bow to the Wittiest . . .": Ladies' Home Journal*, June 1912, 80.

23 *"a crime to be fat": Vogue*, 1902, quoted in Joan Jacobs Brumberg, *Fasting Girls: The Emergence of Anorexia Nervosa as a Modern Disease* (1988), 243.

23 *"Too Fat": Leslie's Weekly*, 16 February 1905, 165; for another example, 167.

23 *feminine fashion and underclothing:* Brumberg, *Fasting Girls*, 239; Valerie Steele, *Fashion and Eroticism: Ideals of Feminine Beauty from the Victorian Era to the Jazz Age* (1985), chaps. 10, 11.

23 *the zipper:* Giles Foden, review of *Zipper: An Exploration in Novelty*, by Robert Friedel, *Times Literary Supplement*, 26 May 1995, 5–6.

24 *the corset survived:* For example, advertisements in *Saturday Night*, 24 December 1910, 32; *Ladies' Home Journal*, March 1912, 78; April 1912, 24, 34, 36, 37, 41, 66.

24 *brassiere "to save the figure . . .":* Quoted in Steele, *Fashion and Eroticism*, 228.

24 *Advertisements promoted various models:* For example, *Ladies' Home Journal*, March 1912, 74; March 1916, 69.

24 *"Dr. Charles' Flesh Food":* Advertised *Ladies' Home Journal*, 10 August 1905, 142.

25 *Roosevelt advocated the "strenuous life":* Kevin White, *The First Sexual Revolution: The Emergence of Male Heterosexuality in Modern America* (1993), 11.

25 *bearded gentleman had given way to youth:* Valerie Steele, "Appearance and Identity," in *Men and Women: Dressing the Part*, ed. Claudia Brush Kidwell and Valerie Steele (1989), 20.

25 *Yale University ideal:* Robert J. Higgs, "Yale and the Heroic Ideal, *Gotterdammerung* and Palingenesis, 1865-1914," in *Manliness and Morality; Middle-Class Masculinity in Britain and America, 1800-1940* (1987), 160–61.

25–26 *masculine ideal in clothing fashion:* Stuart and Elizabeth Ewen, *Channels of Desire: Mass Images and the Shaping of American Consciousness* (1982), 206; White, *The First Sexual Revolution*, 19–26.

26 *exercise magazine Physical Culture:* White, *The First Sexual Revolution*, 27–28.

26 *Coca-Cola:* For examples of advertisements, see Lawrence Dietz, *Soda Pop: The History, Advertising, Art and Memorabilia of Soft Drinks in America* (1973).

26 *1919 advertisement in the Saturday Evening Post:* White, *The First Sexual Revolution*, 22.

27 *separation of sex and reproduction:* Barbara Epstein, "Family, Sexual Morality, and Popular Movements in Turn-of-the-Century America," in *Powers of Desire: The Politics of Sexuality*, ed. Ann Snitow, Christine Stansell, and Sharon Thompson (1983), 117–30.

27 *"clear stone . . . gem":* Helen Apte, quoted in Margalit Fox, review of *Heart of a Wife: The Diary of a Southern Jewish Woman*, ed. Marcus D. Rosenbaum, *New York Times Book Review*, 10 January 1999, 25.

27 *avant garde:* Ellen Kay Trimberger, "Feminism, Men, and Modern Love: Greenwich Village, 1900-1925," in *Powers of Desire*, ed. Snitow, Stansell, and Thompson, 131–52.

28 *double standard:* Epstein, "Family, Sexual Morality, and Popular Movements," 120; Kathy Peiss and Christina Simmons, "Passion and Power: An Introduction," in *Passion and Power: Sexuality in History,* ed. Peiss and Simmons, with Robert A. Padgug (1989), 9.

28–29 *prostitution:* John D'Emilio and Estelle Freedman, *Intimate Matters: A History of Sexuality in America* (1988), 181–83; Timothy J. Gilfoyle, *City of Eros: New York City, Prostitution, and the Commercialization of Sex, 1790-1920* (1992), 257–69.

30 *sexes intermingle in new, informal ways:* D'Emilio and Freedman, *Intimate Matters,* 194–95.

30 *sexual harassment on the job:* Kathy Peiss, "'Charity Girls' and City Pleasures: Historical Notes on Working-Class Sexuality, 1880-1920," in *Passion and Power,* ed. Peiss and Simmons, 61–62.

30–31 *dating:* Peiss, "'Charity Girls' and City Pleasures," 58–61; White, *The First Sexual Revolution,* 80–105; D'Emilio and Freedman, *Intimate Matters,* 195–200.

31 *Chicago headline of 1919:* Quoted in D'Emilio and Freedman, *Intimate Matters,* 197.

31 *"The motion of the pelvic portions . . .":* Quoted in Peiss, "'Charity Girls' and City Pleasures," 59.

32 *1910 rate of premarital pregnancies:* D'Emilio and Freedman, *Intimate Matters,* 199.

32 *"vibrating on a chord . . .":* Quoted in Craig H. Roell, *The Piano in America, 1890-1940* (1989), 26.

32–33 *middle-class dating:* Peiss, "'Charity Girls' and City Pleasures," 59; White, *The First Sexual Revolution,* 14, 84.

33 *Snappy Stories:* White, *The First Sexual Revolution,* 61.

33–34 *Elinor Glyn:* Paul Ferris, *Sex and the British: A Twentieth-Century History* (1993), 20–21; Meredith Etherington-Smith and Jeremy Pilcher, *The It Girls* (1986; 1988), 99–108; Steele, *Fashion and Eroticism,* 206.

34 *"undulated round . . . like a serpent":* Quoted in Etherington-Smith and Pilcher, *The It Girls,* 103.

34 *draw in cheaper theaters was sex:* Peiss, "'Charity Girls' and City Pleasures," 59.

34 *painted images of skimpily clothed women:* For example, D'Emilio and Freedman, *Intimate Matters,* 199.

34–35 *Eve Tanguay, Sophie Tucker, Mae West:* Charles and Louise Samuels, *Once Upon a Stage: The Merry World of Vaudeville* (1974), 96–97, 102–4, 54–67.

35 *movie industry offered sex-related themes:* Examples given are from Kemp R. Niver, *D. W. Griffith, His Biograph Films in Perspective* (1974), 117–20, 121–25, 152–53; see also 21–22, 103–5, 154–57.

35 *Annette Kellerman:* Brumberg, *Fasting Girls,* 245.

35–36 *Theda Bara and Gloria Swanson:* James Card, *Seductive Cinema: The Art of Silent Film* (1994), 104, 217.

36 *"For the first time in the history . . . glamor of love making":* Quoted in D'Emilio and Freedman, *Intimate Matters,* 197.

36 *"sex o'clock" had struck:* Quoted in White, *The First Sexual Revolution,* 13.

37 *people craved accurate discussion:* D'Emilio and Freedman, *Intimate Matters,* 176–77; Angus McLaren, *A History of Contraception: From Antiquity to the Present* (1990), 202–24; for the British experience, see Lesley A. Hall, *Hidden Anxieties: Male Sexuality, 1900-1950* (1991); Steve Humphries, *A Secret World of Sex: Forbidden Fruit: The British Experience 1900-1950* (1988), 35–62; Roy Porter and Lesley Hall, *The Facts of Life: The Creation of Sexual Knowledge in Britain, 1650-1950* (1995), 246–70.

37 *Sexology:* Vern L. Bullough, "The Development of Sexology in the USA in the Early Twentieth Century," in *Sexual Knowledge, Sexual Science: The History of Attitudes to Sexuality,* ed. Roy Porter and Mikulas Teich (1994), 303–22; Bullough, *Science in the Bedroom: A History of Sex Research* (1994), 92–119; Henry L. Minton, "American Psychology and the Study of Human Sexuality," *Journal of Psychology and Human Sexuality* 1 (1988): 17–34.

37 *Sigmund Freud:* D'Emilio and Freedman, *Intimate Matters,* 223–24; Nathan G. Hale, *Freud and the Americans: The Beginnings of Psychoanalysis in the United States, 1876-1917* (1971); see also Peter Gay, *Freud: A Life for Our Time* (1988).

38 *Margaret Sanger:* Ellen Chesler, *Woman of Valor: Margaret Sanger and the Birth Control Movement in America* (1992); Walter Kendrick, *The Secret Museum: Pornography in Modern Culture* (1987), 152–57; McLaren, *History of Contraception,* 216–18; Margaret Sanger, *An Autobiography* (1938), 108–15.

39 *Sanger, Ellis, Wells:* Ruth Brandon, *The New Women and the Old Men: Love, Sex and the Woman Question* (1990), 222–25, 262–63.

39 *"To look the world in the face . . .":* Sanger, *Autobiography,* 110.

39 *Marie Stopes:* Ferris, *Sex and the British,* 79–86; Hall, *Hidden Anxieties,* 66–67, 72, 74, 84–88; McLaren, *History of Contraception,*

217–18; June Rose, *Marie Stopes and the Sexual Revolution* (1992).

40 *"the sensitive interrelation . . .":* Stopes, *Married Love,* 39.

40 *"repeal of reticence":* Agnes Repplier, *Atlantic,* 14 March 1914, quoted in White, *The First Sexual Revolution,* 13.

41 *"To the reticent . . .":* Stopes, *Married Love,* xiii.

Chapter 3: War and Revelation

Page

43 *war poets:* Adrian Caesar, *Taking It Like a Man: Suffering, Sexuality and the War Poets* (1993).

44 *Women in the Great War:* Gail Braybon, *Women Workers in the First World War* (1984); Jean Bethke Elshtain, *Women and War* (1987), 106–20; Yvonne M. Klein, ed. *Beyond the Home Front: Women's Autobiographical Writing of the Two World Wars* (1997).

45 *Britain's Social Purity and Hygiene Movement:* Steve Humphries, *A Secret World of Sex: Forbidden Fruit: The British Experience 1900-1950* (1988), 19–23.

45 *"Entirely resist . . . avoid any intimacy":* Quoted in Paul Ferris, *Sex and the British: A Twentieth Century History* (1993), 67.

45 *"They talk as if . . .":* Quoted in Cate Haste, *Rules of Desire: Sex in Britain, World War I to the Present* (1992), 33.

45 *Women Police Volunteers; Women's Patrols:* Ferris, *Sex and the British,* 57–62; Haste, *Rules of Desire,* 33–38.

46 *Patrols succeeded in irritating people:* Haste, *Rules of Desire,* 37; Max Pemberton quoted in Ferris, *Sex and the British,* 62.

46 *American purity movement:* Nathan G. Hale, *Freud and the Americans: The Beginnings of Psychoanalysis in the United States, 1876-1917* (1971), 254–58.

46 *aggressive propaganda campaign:* John D'Emilio and Estelle Freedman, *Intimate Matters: A History of Sexuality in America* (1988), 211–13; Kevin White, *The First Sexual Revolution: The Emergence of Male Heterosexuality in Modern America* (1993), 73–75.

47 *"Women Who Solicit Soldiers . . .":* Pamphlet, quoted in D'Emilio and Freedman, *Intimate Matters,* 212.

48 *Does any red-blooded man . . .":* American Social Hygiene Association, "Lecture to Troops," quoted in White, *The First Sexual Revolution,* 75.

48 *British premarital pregnancies and venereal disease:* Haste, *Rules of Desire,* 41, 49.

49 *Commonwealth troops hard hit:* Ferris, *Sex and the British,* 69–70.

49 *American fighting men fared better:* White, *The First Sexual Revolution,* 74.

49 *"it was unwise to think":* Patrick McGill of the London Irish, quoted in Modris Eksteins, *Rites of Spring: The Great War and the Birth of the Modern Age* (1989), 171.

49 *Freud explained it:* John Costello, *Virtue under Fire: How World War II Changed Our Social and Sexual Attitudes* (1985), 3, part of a brief discussion of World War I, 2–3.

50 *"In my heart there's cruel war . . .":* Sassoon, "Peace" (the "peace of death," that is), 2 April 1916, quoted in Caesar, *Taking It Like a Man,* 74.

50 *British women indulged:* Ferris, *Sex and the British,* 54–55, 64, 66; Haste, *Rules of Desire,* 40–41.

50 *wartime pop song:* Cited in Ian Whitcomb, *After the Ball: Pop Music from Rag to Rock* (1972), 64.

50 *French women gave freely:* Ferris, *Sex and the British,* 55; General F. P. Crozier quoted, 65.

51 *"romantic episode . . . Paradise":* Philip Gibbs, *Now It Can Be Told* (1920), quoted in Paul Fussell, *The Great War and Modern Memory* (1975), 283.

51 *Commonwealth soldiers vulnerable:* Ferris, *Sex and the British,* 69–70.

51 *French prostitution:* Ferris, *Sex and the British,* 71–72.

52 *Katherine Mayo was moved:* Mayo, "That Damn Y," 31, 207, 209.

52 *voices of American soldiers:* Mayo, "That Damn Y," 1, 56, 139.

52 *women insisted on getting into the thick:* Elshtain, *Women and War,* 112–13.

52 *women would "be in the way . . .":* Mayo, "That Damn Y," 59.

53 *Miss Frances Gulick:* Mayo, "That Damn Y," 116–19.

53 *"a fair common example . . .":* Mayo, "That Damn Y," 119.

53 *moments of comfort shared . . . scenes of wartime camaraderie:* Based on photographic material in *The Manchester Guardian History of the War,* vol. 9 (1919–20) and Mayo, "That Damn Y," artist and illustrator C. Leroy Baldridge: Baldridge, *"I Was There" with the Yanks on the Western Front, 1917-1919* (1919; 1972).

54–55 *"Kidding her in bon fransay . . .":* Baldridge, *"I Was There,"* n.p.

55 *We sat on the sofa:* Vera Brittain, *Testament of Youth: An Autobiographical Study of the Years 1900-1925* (1933; 1986), 131, quoted in Haste, *Rules of Desire*, 43.

56 *"Roland went to the front . . .":* Brittain, *Testament of Youth*, 135, 236.

56 *"France was the scene . . .":* Brittain, *Testament of Youth*, 372.

56 *1916 cigarette advertisement:* Author's collection; original source of publication unknown.

56–57 *"a real wedding . . .":* Mayo, *"That Damn Y"*, 101–2.

57 *"the air was thick . . .":* Mary Borden, *The Forbidden Zone* (1929), in Klein, ed. *Beyond the Home Front*, 71.

57 *"Short of actually going to bed . . . new depth":* Brittain, *Testament of Youth*, 165, 166.

58 *Strangers made love:* Ferris, *Sex and the British*, 74–75.

58 *"French kissing":* Ian Whitcomb, *After the Ball*, 68.

58 *people were disillusioned:* Klein, "Introduction," *Beyond the Home Front*, 8; Barbara Tuchman, *The Guns of August* (1962), 440.

58 *"growth of spirit . . . operate":* Mayo, *"That Damn Y"*, 410.

Chapter 4: A Clash of Moralities

Page

64 *Warner Fabian . . . "flaming youth":* Fabian, *Flaming Youth* (1923), cited in Paula S. Fass, *The Damned and the Beautiful: American Youth in the 1920s* (1977), 270.

64 *Russell . . . "morals of the community . . .":* Bertrand Russell, *Marriage and Morals* (1929), 4.

65 *Prohibition:* Keith Jeffery, review of *Prohibition: The 13 Years That Changed America*, by Edward Behr, *Times Literary Supplement*, 18 July 1997; Cheryl Krasnick Warsh, ed., *Drink in Canada: Historical Essays* (1993), especially essays by Ernest R. Forbes and Robert A. Campbell, 167, 173; Michael Woodiwiss, *Crime, Crusades, and Corruption: Prohibitions in the United States, 1900-1987* (1988), 6–7, 11.

66 *Zelda Fitzgerald:* Warren Sloat, *1929: America Before the Crash* (1979), 205–6, 343.

66 *"sensuous stimulation . . . God help your child":* Quoted in Paula S. Fass, *The Damned and the Beautiful: American Youth in the 1920s* (1977), 22.

67 *petting:* Fass, *The Damned and the Beautiful,* 262–68.

68 *boyish slenderness in vogue:* Joan Jacobs Brumberg, *Fasting Girls: The Emergence of Anorexia Nervosa as a Modern Disease* (1988), 239, 244–45; Brumberg, *The Body Project: An Intimate History of American Girls* (1997), 106–7; Lesley A. Hall, *Hidden Anxieties: Male Sexuality, 1900-1950* (1991), 137; Valerie Steele, *Fashion and Eroticism: Ideals of Feminine Beauty from the Victorian Era to the Jazz Age* (1985), 236–39.

69 *Mae West, "Don't tell me . . . yesterday's paper":* Quoted in Jon Tuska, *The Films of Mae West* (1973), 126–27.

69 *bras of the 1930s:* Brumberg, *The Body Project,* 109.

69–70 *men under pressure to achieve attractiveness:* Kevin White, *The First Sexual Revolution: The Emergence of Male Heterosexuality in Modern America* (1993), 18–24.

71 *"Sex appeal is . . . masculine . . .":* Quoted in White, *The First Sexual Revolution,* 19.

72 *Edmund Wilson:* Leon Edel, ed., Edmund Wilson, *The Twenties: From Notebooks and Diaries of the Period* (1975), passages quoted: 255, 319; for a more graphic example, see 412–13.

73 *Anaïs Nin:* Erica Jong, review of Nin, *Incest: From "A Journal of Love": The Unexpurgated Diary of Anaïs Nin, 1932-1934, Times Literary Supplement,* 23 June 1993, 3–4; Notice of Nin, *Fire: From "A Journal of Love": . . . 1934-1937, Times Literary Supplement,* 14 June 1996, 30.

73 *"The New Deal . . . the law":* Quoted in Walter Kendrick, *The Secret Museum: Pornography in Modern Culture* (1987), 182.

74 *vaudeville in decline:* Shirley Staples, *Male-Female Comedy Teams in American Vaudeville, 1865-1932* (1984), 189, 203–4.

74 *Theda Bara and successors:* James Card, *Seductive Cinema: The Art of Silent Film* (1994), 181–209.

75 *film censorship:* Leonard J. Leff and Jerold L. Simmons, *The Dame in the Kimono: Hollywood, Censorship, and the Production Code from the 1920s to the 1960s* (1990); Frank Walsh, *Sin and Censorship: The Catholic Church and the Motion Picture Industry* (1996).

76 *"Censorship made me":* Mae West, quoted in Martha McPhee, review of *Becoming Mae West,* by Emily Wortis Leider, *New York Times Book Review,* 27 July 1997, 11.

76 *Gone with the Wind:* Leff and Simmons, *Dame in the Kimono,* 79–108.

77　*Reich proclaimed revolution:* Wilhelm Reich, *The Sexual Revolution* (1935).

77　*later commentators:* Samuel S. Janus and Cynthia L. Janus, *The Janus Report on Sexual Behavior* (1993); Richard A. Posner, *Sex and Reason* (1992), 55; Ira L. Reiss, *An End to Shame: Shaping Our Next Sexual Revolution* (1990), 84–85.

77　*Parents complained . . . Dr. Mosher "shocked":* Robert S. Lynd and Helen Merrell Lynd, *Middletown: A Study in American Culture* (1929; 1956), 242; Reiss, *An End to Shame,* 84.

78　*"How life is . . . social taboos":* Lynd, *Middletown,* 265–67.

78　*"ownership of an automobile . . . offense in an automobile":* Lynd, *Middletown,* 253–58.

79　*women engaged in premarital intercourse:* Figures given are from Ferris, *Sex and the British,* 93; Nathan G. Hale, *Freud and the Americans: The Beginnings of Psychoanalysis in the United States, 1876-1917* (1971), 476.

79–80　*"the transitional condition . . . women":* Russell, *Marriage and Morals,* 78.

80　*birth control:* Angus McLaren, *A History of Contraception: From Antiquity to the Present* (1990), 226, 235.

80　*Freud and necessity of gratification:* Jonathan Ned Katz, *The Invention of Heterosexuality* (1995), 60.

80　*For centuries women . . .":* Margaret Sanger, *Happiness in Marriage* (1926; 1969), 139–40.

81　*"He must woo her . . . right":* Marie Stopes, *Married Love* (1918; 1962), 69; Stopes, *Enduring Passion* (1928), 11.

81　*"prepare his beloved . . . accomplish this":* Sanger, *Happiness in Marriage,* 125, 133.

81　*performance pressure on men:* White, *The First Sexual Revolution,* 76–79.

81　*"People have to learn . . . marriage problems":* Russell, *Marriage and Morals,* 16, 95; Sanger, *Happiness in Marriage,* 3, 6; Stopes, *Married Love,* xiii–xiv; Stopes, *Enduring Passion,* xi.

82　*other experts published advice books:* On early twentieth-century marriage manuals and the sexualization of love and marriage, see Steven Seidman, *Romantic Longings: Love in America, 1830-1980* (1991), 74–91.

82　*Mildred Spock:* Susan Bolotin, review of *Dr. Spock: An American Life,* by Thomas Maier, *New York Times Book Review,* 17 May 1998, 7.

82–83 *"When we consider . . . sex hunger":* Russell, *Marriage and Morals,* 6–7, 123.

83 *"With a woman whom we want . . .":* Wilson, *The Twenties,* 333.

84 *20 percent "may sometime be facing . . . divorce":* Willard Waller, *The Old Love and the New: Divorce and Readjustment* (1930), 338.

84 *change in attitude:* Lynd, *Middletown,* 111; *Fortune* survey cited in *American Sociological Review* 2 (1937): 665; Fass, *The Damned and the Beautiful,* 39, 78–80.

84 *"the modern tendency . . . elements of marriage:* Stopes, *Married Love,* 24.

84–85 *depression dealt North America a harsh blow:* John A. Garraty, *The Great Depression* (1986), 88, 182; Michiel Horn, ed., *The Dirty Thirties: Canadians in the Great Depression* (1972), 1–2.

85 *"sex deprivation . . . no end ahead":* Quoted in Pierre Berton, *The Great Depression, 1929-1939* (1990), 271.

86 *things had "toned down . . . lost its novelty":* Quoted in Fass, *The Damned and the Beautiful,* 270–71.

86 *"It's Only a Paper Moon":* Philip Furia, *The Poets of Tin Pan Alley: A History of America's Great Lyricists* (1990), 207.

86 *"sex adventure" magazines:* Lynd, *Middletown,* 241.

87 *overcrowding of public clinics:* Elizabeth Fee, "Venereal Disease: The Wages of Sin?" in *Passion and Power: Sexuality in History,* ed. Kathy Peiss and Christina Simmons, with Robert A. Padgug (1989), 181.

87 *1932 Royal Canadian Mounted Police Report:* Quoted in Horn, *The Dirty Thirties,* 269.

87 *"enduring happiness . . . essential":* Sanger, *Happiness in Marriage,* 27.

Chapter 5: In the Heat of Battle

Page

91 *D-Day:* Michael C. C. Adams, *The Best War Ever: America and World War II* (1994), 55; W. A. B. Douglas and Brereton Greenhous, *Out of the Shadows: Canada in the Second World War* (1977; 1995), 157; Henry Pelling, *Britain and the Second World War* (1970), 196.

91 *"lorries full of fighting men":* Irene Martin, in Colin Townsend and Eileen Townsend, eds., *War Wives: A Second World War Anthology,* (1989), 273.

92 *people listened to Bing Crosby, Frank Sinatra, Tommy Dorsey:* Leonora Pitt and Norma Troy, in Townsend, *War Wives*, 120, 230.

92 *pinup girls:* John Costello, *Virtue under Fire: How World War II Changed Our Social and Sexual Attitudes* (1985), 153–54.

93 *"Beauty is a duty . . .":* Pat Kirkham, "Beauty and Duty: Keeping Up the (Home) Front," in *War Culture; Social Change and Changing Experience in World War Two Britain,* ed. Pat Kirkham and David Thoms (1995), 16, 23.

93 *"war was gradually . . . killed and injured":* Quoted in Lauris Edmond, with Carolyn Milward, *Women in Wartime: New Zealand Women Tell Their Story* (1986), 253–54.

93 *"We got what we could . . .":* Letter to author, quoted in Costello, *Virtue under Fire,* 192.

94 *"The most wonderful days . . . memorable":* Costello, *Virtue under Fire,* 10.

94 *"A great experience . . . pretty exciting":* Quoted in Edmond, *Women in Wartime,* 33–34, 39.

94 *"There was more excitement . . . life":* "C. M.," in Townsend, *War Wives,* 84.

94 *"My standards of morality . . . a war on":* Quoted in Costello, *Virtue under Fire,* 7, 12–13, 258.

95 *"It's thrilling work . . . glamour":* Quoted in Costello, *Virtue under Fire,* 180.

95 *American and Canadian women worked:* V. R. Cardozier, *The Mobilization of the United States in World War II: How the Government, Military and Industry Prepared for War* (1995), 160–61; Ruth Roach Pierson, *Canadian Women and the Second World War* (1983), 10.

95 *"sex paradise":* Quoted in John D'Emilio and Estelle Freedman, *Intimate Matters: A History of Sexuality in America* (1988), 260.

95 *"in the shipyards . . .":* Quoted in Costello, *Virtue under Fire,* 188.

96 *British women with Canadian allies:* For a sampling of stories, see Barbara Barrett and Eileen Dicks, eds., *We Came from Over the Sea: British War Brides in Newfoundland* (1996).

97 Leonora Pitt, *"A brass band played . . ."* Townsend, *War Wives,* 116.

97 *GIs and British women:* Costello, *Virtue under Fire,* 230–32; Jenel Virden, *Good-Bye Piccadilly: British War Brides in America* (1996), 20–23.

97–98 *"They wooed the British girls . . . skirt a bit higher":* Leonora Pitt, in Townsend, *War Wives,* 116.

98 *out-of-wedlock birth rates:* Costello, *Virtue under Fire*, 203; Paul Ferris, *Sex and the British: A Twentieth-Century History* (1993), 144.

98 *increase in venereal infection:* Discussion of VD and measures to curb it among Allied troops is based on Costello, *Virtue under Fire*, 223, 226, 240–49; Cate Haste, *Rules of Desire: Sex in Britain, World War I to the Present* (1992), 112–15; Virden, *Good-Bye Piccadilly*, 24–27.

99 *"Hello, boyfriend . . . Pencillin?":* Costello, *Virtue under Fire*, 226, 243.

101 *"a pre-invasion VD-Day":* Costello, *Virtue under Fire*, 243.

101 *women in the armed forces:* Carol Burke, "'If You're Nervous in the Service . . .' : Training Songs of Female Soldiers in the '40s," in *Visions of War: World War II in Popular Literature and Culture*, ed. M. Paul Holsinger and Mary Anne Schofield (1992), 127–29; Cardozier, *The Mobilization of the United States in World War II*, 168–69; Costello, *Virtue under Fire*, 43–45, 48, 51, 55; Pelling, *Britain and the Second World War*, 187; Pierson, *Canadian Women and the Second World War*, 6–8.

102 *American survey . . . British military research:* Cited in Costello, *Virtue under Fire*, 65; Virden, *Good-Bye Piccadilly*, 25.

102 *"you stood by your bed . . .":* Leonora Pitt, in Townsend, *War Wives*, 116.

103 *"Some join the WACs . . . chores":* Quoted in Burke, "'If You're Nervous in the Service,'" 128.

103 *"organized martyrdom . . . over the mess":* Mary Lee Settle, *All the Brave Promises*, in Yvonne M. Klein, ed. *Beyond the Home Front: Women's Autobiographical Writing of the Two World Wars* (1997), 151–57.

104 *"I never walked . . . pretty funny":* Quoted in Costello, *Virtue under Fire*, 185–86.

104 *other circumstances of women's work:* William H. Chafe, "World War II as a Pivotal Experience for Women," in *Women and War: The Changing Status of American Women from the 1930s to the 1950s*, ed. Maria Diedrich and Dorothea Fischer Hornung (1990), 24–25.

105 *"very poor shadows . . .":* Diana Murray Hill, *Ladies May Now Leave Their Machines*, in Klein, *Beyond the Home Front*, 148.

105 *"the ordinary" was "still there":* Quoted in Edmond, *Women in Wartime*, 254.

105 *epidemic of weddings in the United States . . . British marriage rate also risen:* Costello, *Virtue under Fire*, 193–95.

106 *John Agar to Shirley Temple:* Shirley Temple Black, *Child Star: An Autobiography* (1988), 382.

106-7 *international war marriages:* Edmond, *Women in Wartime*, 46; Virden, *Good-Bye Piccadilly*, 1, 21, 32, 47.

107 *Isabel met Jack:* This couple is a composite, based on real people whose stories have been documented in Barrett and Dicks, *We Came from Over the Sea*, 4, 8, 22, 25, 33, 51; Costello, *Virtue under Fire*, 10–11, 194; Townsend, *War Wives*, 196.

108 *Leonora and Tom "arranged to be married":* Leonora Pitt, in Townsend, *War Wives*, 116–21.

109 *"I'm not bad . . . no sex involved":* Costello, *Virtue under Fire*, 12, 207.

109 *extramarital relationships led to strain:* For examples, see Costello, *Virtue under Fire*, 198–99.

110 *"Now I had to meet . . . hard decision":* C. M., in Townsend, *War Wives*, 84–85.

111 *"dreaded telegram . . . wanted to die":* Lilian Borthwick, in Townsend, *War Wives*, 291.

111 *Leonora Pitt's wartime love story:* Townsend, *War Wives*, 123.

111 *"Heartbroken . . . nice to know":* C. M., in Townsend, *War Wives*, 85–86.

112 *anti-war-bride sentiment:* Edmond, *Women in Wartime*, 45; Virden, *Good-Bye Piccadilly*, 116–19.

112 *most stayed:* Virden, *Good-Bye Piccadilly*, 105.

112 *rising tide of divorces:* Costello, *Virtue under Fire*, 262; Tom Hickman, *The Sexual Century: How Private Passion Became a Public Obsession* (2000), 82; Virden, *Good-Bye Piccadilly*, 27.

112 *traditional female jobs:* Pierson, *Canadian Women and the Second World War*, 23–24.

113 *Women pushed out of the workplace:* Chafe, "World War II as a Pivotal Experience for Women," 26–27; Pierson, *Canadian Women and the Second World War*, 26.

113 *did pave the way . . . laid the groundwork:* For further discussion of the war's impact on feminism, homosexuality, and related issues raised here, see Chafe, "World War II as a Pivotal Experience for Women," 21–33; Costello, *Virtue under Fire*, 69–72, 101–19, 242–43; Rose M. Kundanis, "Rosie the Riveter and the Eight-

Hour Orphan: The Image of Child Day Care During World War II," in Holsinger and Schofield, *Visions of War*, 138–46; Virden, *Good-Bye Piccadilly*, 25.

Chapter 6: The Flagrant Fifties

Page

117 *portrait of a decade:* Mary Louise Adams, "Youth, Corruptibility, and English-Canadian Postwar Campaigns against Indecency, 1948-1955," *Journal of the History of Sexuality* 6 (July 1995), 89–117; John D'Emilio, "The Homosexual Menace: The Politics of Sexuality in Cold War America," in *Passion and Power: Sexuality in History*, ed. Kathy Peiss and Christina Simmons, with Robert A. Padgug (1989), 226–40; Susan J. Douglas, *Where the Girls Are: Growing Up Female with the Mass Media* (1994), 21–42; Barbara Ehrenreich and Deirdre English, *For Her Own Good: 150 Years of the Experts' Advice to Women* (1978), 226–29; David Halberstam, *The Fifties* (1993); John N. Ingham, ed., *Sex 'n' Drugs 'n' Rock 'n' Roll: American Popular Culture Since 1945* (1988), 83–85; David Marc, *Comic Visions: Televison Comedy and American Culture* (1989), 49–81; J. Ronald Oakley, *God's Country: America in the Fifties* (1986); William L. O'Neill, *American High: The Years of Confidence, 1945-1960* (1986); William W. Savage, Jr., *Comic Books and America, 1945-1954* (1990); Warren Susman, "Did Success Spoil the United States? Dual Representations in Postwar America," in *Recasting America: Culture and Politics in the Age of Cold War*, ed. Lary May (1989), 19–33.

118 *The Bob Cummings Show:* Marc, *Comic Visions*, 78–79.

118 *Steve Allen booked Lenny Bruce:* Marc, *Comic Visions*, 71–72.

119 *I Love Lucy:* Halberstam, *The Fifties*, 199–200; Donna McCrohan, *Prime Time, Our Time: America's Life and Times Through the Prism of Television* (1990), 5, 53–55.

120 *Elvis Presley and Ed Sullivan:* Halberstam, *The Fifties*, 478–79.

121 *movies pushed the boundaries:* Leonard J. Leff and Jerold L. Simmons, *The Dame in the Kimono: Hollywood, Censorship, and the Production Code from the 1920s to the 1960s* (1990), 194–203, 206, 233.

121 *pulps survived in 1950s:* For examples of cover illustrations, see Steve Holland, *The Mushroom Jungle: A History of Postwar Paperback Publishing* (1993).

121 *romance paperbacks of the day:* For a typical cover illustration, see Catherine Osborne, "Cover Girls," *Quill & Quire,* July 1998, 46.

122 *literary publishing adopted showy artwork:* Julie Lasky, "Bookend," *New York Times Book Review,* 12 November 1995, 67.

122 *Peyton Place and Lolita:* Halberstam, *The Fifties,* 578–79; Leff and Simmons, *The Dame in the Kimono,* 217–19.

123 *beat generation:* Ingham, *Sex 'n' Drugs 'n' Rock 'n' Roll,* 140–41.

123 *Kerouac on Steve Allen:* Marc, *Comic Visions,* 68–69.

123 *Playboy:* Halberstam, *The Fifties,* 570–76; John Tebbel and Mary Ellen Zuckerman, *The Magazine in America, 1741-1990* (1991), 284–85.

124 *Conspicuous Consumption:* Except where otherwise indicated, this section is based on imagery in period magazines and in Thomas Hine, *Populuxe* (1986).

126 *"Status . . . Vancouver":* John R. Seeley and others, *Crestwood Heights* (1956), 3, 7.

126–27 *"conspicuous consumption" turned around:* Seeley, *Crestwood Heights,* 6–7.

127 *"Good Taste Is Never Extreme":* Quoted in Hine, *Populuxe,* 12.

127 *writer likened car design to Marilyn Monroe:* Hine, *Populuxe,* 101.

127 *Consumerism and adolescents:* Brumberg, *The Body Project: An Intimate History of American Girls* (1997), 113–18; Oakley, *God's Country,* 286; Grace Palladino, *Teenagers: An American History* (1996), xvi–xviii, 165; Seeley, *Crestwood Heights,* 103.

129 *decade emphasized women's physical assets:* Oakley, *God's Country,* 301–2.

130 *"considerable ambivalence . . . abuse":* Seeley, *Crestwood Heights,* 179, 181.

130 *depression:* Ehrenreich and English, *For Her Own Good,* 254–55.

130 *Dr. Spock had some recommendations:* Quoted in Ingham, *Sex 'n' Drugs 'n' Rock 'n' Roll,* 69.

130–131 *women in the workforce:* William H. Chafe, "World War II as a Pivotal Experience for Women," in *Women and War: The Changing Status of American Women from the 1930s to the 1950s,* ed. Maria Diedrich and Dorothea Fischer Hornung (1990), 28; Ehrenreich and English, *For Her Own Good,* 256–57; Oakley, *God's Country,* 298–99; Ruth Roach Pierson, *Canadian Women and the Second World War* (1983), 25.

132 *marital happiness depended on sexual fulfillment:* Ehrenreich and English, *For Her Own Good,* 218–20; Norman E. Himes, *Your*

Marriage (1940; 1955), 159; Fiona McCarthy, review of *Barbie's Queer Accessories*, by Erica Rand, *Times Literary Supplement*, 26 May 1995, 9; Steven Seidman, *Romantic Longings: Love in America, 1830-1980* (1991), 76–80, from which phrases quoted are taken.

132 *"all the data . . . of eroticism"*: J. Johnston Abraham, Introduction to Theodore Van de Velde, *Ideal Marriage* (1930; 1957), vii.

133 *Kinsey:* Discussion of Kinsey and his reports is based on Vern L. Bullough, *Science in the Bedroom: A History of Sex Research* (1994), 175–79; Halberstam, *The Fifties*, 278–80; Christopher Hitchens, review of *Alfred C. Kinsey: A Public/Private Life*, by James H. Jones, *Times Literary Supplement*, 5 December 1997, 7; Oakley, *God's Country*, 303–4; Richard Rhodes, review of *Alfred C. Kinsey: A Public/Private Life*, by James H. Jones, *New York Times Book Review*, 2 November 1997, 10–11.

133 *"wife-swapping":* Terry Gould, *The Lifestyle: A Look at the Erotic Rites of Swingers* (1999), 6, 30–31.

133–134 *his methods continuously debated:* Jones, cited in the previous note, has been among those to question the accuracy of Kinsey's findings. A more recent biography argues that there is no reason to believe that his results were seriously skewed: see Rachel P. Maines, review of *Sex the Measure of All Things: A Life of Alfred C. Kinsey*, by Jonathan Gathorne-Hardy, *New York Times Book Review*, 23 April 2000, 16.

135–136 *Max Eastman; Dori Schaffer:* Seidman, *Romantic Longings*, 97–100.

135 *sexual activity among teenagers:* Palladino, *Teenagers*, 166–69.

135–136 *stretching the limits of the norm:* Leon Edel, ed., Edmund Wilson, *The Fifties: From Notebooks and Diaries of the Period* (1986), 599; Halberstam, *The Fifties*, 585, on Grace Metalious; Seeley, *Crestwood Heights*, 177–78.

136 *I Love Lucy behind the scenes:* Halberstam, *The Fifties*, 200–201.

137 *Divorce had been rising:* Oakley, *God's Country*, 117.

137 *Critics called fifties hypocritical:* Susman, "Did Success Spoil the United States?" 33.

137 *"the supreme value . . .":* Seeley, *Crestwood Heights*, 383; see also 218.

138 *"We suffer . . . something we once had":* Marie Stopes, *Married Love* (1918; 1962), preface to 1956 edition, xviii; Wilson, "Sex," 207; the last commentary is quoted in Jeff Greenfield, *No Peace, No Place*, excerpted in Ingham, *Sex 'n' Drugs 'n' Rock 'n' Roll*, 114.

Chapter 7: A Partial Revolution

Page

141   *entertainment of the time:* Donna McCrohan, *Prime Time, Our Time: America's Life and Times through the Prism of Television* (1990), 123–29.

142   *changed the mood of the times:* Walt Crowley, *Rites of Passage: A Memoir of the Sixties in Seattle* (1995), xii; John N. Ingham, ed., *Sex 'n' Drugs 'n' Rock 'n' Roll: American Popular Culture Since 1945* (1988), 153.

144   *dances like the bird:* Charles Winick, *The New People: Desexualization in American Life* (1968), 17.

144   *Helen Gurley Brown's Sex and the Single Girl:* Discussed in Jane and Michael Stern, *Sixties People* (1990), 19–20.

145   *"the pill":* William L. O'Neill, *American High: The Years of Confidence, 1945-1960* (1986), 48–50.

145   *divorce rate:* Peter N. Carroll, *It Seemed Like Nothing Happened: The Tragedy and Promise of America in the 1970s* (1982), 32–33; Anne Steinmann and David J. Fox, *The Male Dilemma: How to Survive the Sexual Revolution* (1974), 8.

145   *Woodstock:* Roger Hutchinson, *High Sixties: The Summers of Riot and Love* (1992), 131–32.

146   *But Was It Revolution?:* For a sampling of debates about the revolutionary, or other, nature of the sixties and their aftermath, see Ellen Willis, review of *The Sixties,* by Arthur Marwick, *New York Times Book Review,* 8 November 1998, 16.

146   *Newsweek, 6 February 1967:* Quoted in John D'Emilio and Estelle Freedman, *Intimate Matters: A History of Sexuality in America* (1988), 307.

146   *"My eyes nearly popped . . .":* Oral reminiscence to author.

146   *icons and events of "revolution" not altogether new:* For additional commentary on the historical continuities that characterized the so-called sexual revolution, see D'Emilio and Freedman, *Intimate Matters,* 340–41; Ira L. Reiss, *An End to Shame: Shaping Our Next Sexual Revolution* (1990), 85–87; Paul Robinson, *The Modernization of Sex: Havelock Ellis, Alfred Kinsey, William Masters and Virginia Johnson* (1976), 189.

147   *"The period's famous 'sexual revolution' . . .":* Crowley, *Rites of Passage,* xii–xiii.

147   *"Contrary to conservative rhetoric . . .":* Crowley, *Rites of Passage,* xiii.

147   *Not everybody was doing it . . . :* On this and other historical themes in this book, I am grateful for informal input from my friend and colleague, Paulette Regan.

147   *"Those were the days" . . . "missed the sexual revolution":* Oral reminiscences to author.

148   *"Before this book . . . hallucinations":* Crowley, *Rites of Passage,* x.

149   *"the tainted war":* Lloyd B. Lewis, *The Tainted War: Culture and Identity* (1985).

149   *"the threat . . . going underground":* Loren Baritz, *Backfire: A History of How American Culture Led Us into Vietnam and Made Us Fight the Way We Did* (1985), 287.

149   *Students for a Democratic Society:* Ingham, *Sex 'n' Drugs 'n' Rock 'n' Roll,* 153.

150   *"They took a position . . .":* Crowley, *Rites of Passage,* 173.

151   *Miss America pageant of 1968:* D'Emilio and Freedman, *Intimate Matters,* 302.

151   *"problem that has no name":* Betty Friedan, *The Feminine Mystique* (1963; 1977), 11; and for quoted phrases following, see 5, 11, 17, 23, 326, 330.

152   *"She must learn to compete . . . to become complete":* Friedan, *The Feminine Mystique,* 361, 364.

153   *breakthroughs feminists applauded:* For the examples given and others, see Carroll, *It Seemed Like Nothing Happened,* 34–35; Suzanne Levine, Harriet Lyons, and others, eds., *The Decade of Women: A Ms. History of the Seventies in Words and Pictures,* introduced by Gloria Steinem (1980), 8–18.

153   *"stop giving lip service . . .":* Friedan, *The Feminine Mystique,* 360. *Rollo May:* Robert H. Abzug, "*Love and Will*: Rollo May and the Seventies Crisis of Intimacy," in *The Lost Decade: America in the Seventies,* ed. Elsebeth Hurup (1996), 79–88.

154   *"Just as the individual . . . apathy":* Rollo May, *Love and Will* (1969), 27–29, 185.

154   *"new puritanism . . . libido":* May, *Love and Will,* 45.

154   *no norms of sexual performance:* William H. Masters and Virginia E. Johnson, *Human Sexual Response* (1966; 1986), 300, 309.

154   *"So much sex . . . 'we are laid'":* May, *Love and Will,* 40, 47.

155–56   *"Having no hope of improving . . . repeated profession":* Christopher Lasch, *The Culture of Narcissism: American Life in an Age of Diminishing Expectations* (1979), 29, 326, 328.

156 *"They would deny . . . lives."* Edwin M. Schur, *The Americaniza-tion of Sex* (1988), 15.

155–156 *"the irrational . . . against all":* Lasch, *The Culture of Narcissism,* 21, 68.

157 *"failure . . . crumbling apart":* Tom Engelhardt, *Beyond Control: America in the Seventies* (1976), 1; George Frankl, *The Failure of the Sexual Revolution* (1974); Jim Hougan, *Decadence: Radical Nostalgia, Narcissism, and Decline in the Seventies* (1975), 7.

157 *"an ambiguous liberation . . . poverty or loneliness":* Barbara Ehren-reich and Deirdre English, *For Her Own Good: 150 Years of the Experts' Advice to Women* (1978), 286, 287–88.

158 *"a liberated sex style . . .":* Carroll, *It Seemed Like Nothing Hap-pened,* 25.

158 *"Nudity . . . my friends":* Linda Grant, *Sexing the Millennium: A Political History of the Sexual Revolution* (1993), 227.

158 Men *"are confused . . .":* Anne Steinmann and David J. Fox, *The Male Dilemma: How to Survive the Sexual Revolution* (1974), 4.

158 *"The battle of the sexes":* See, for example, Lasch, *The Culture of Narcissism,* 322; Steinmann and Fox, *The Male Dilemma,* 41, 121.

158 *"lying awake in the dark . . ."* Sally Kempton, "Cutting Loose," *Esquire Magazine,* July 1970, in Ingham, *Sex 'n' Drugs 'n' Rock 'n' Roll,* 341; see also Lasch, *The Culture of Narcissism,* 334–36.

158 *Men were fed up:* For related commentary, see Steinmann and Fox, *The Male Dilemma,* 9, 11.

159 *"response to the emergence . . .":* Lasch, *The Culture of Narcissism,* 323.

159 *viewer ratings:* McCrohan, *Prime Time, Our Time,* 205, 249.

160 *"People not only have to learn . . .":* May, *Love and Will,* 46.

160 *sobs of the audience:* Observed by the author and widely reported at the time.

Chapter 8: The High Costs of Loving

Page

163 *The 1980s:* Among other overviews of the decade, see Henry Southworth Allen, "The '80s," in Allen, *Going Too Far Enough: American Culture at Century's End* (1994); Kevin Doyle and Ann Johnson, eds., *The 1980s: Maclean's Chronicles the Decade* (1989); John Taylor, *Circus of Ambition: The Culture of Wealth and Power in the Eighties* (1989).

164 *"the idea was to be . . ."*: Allen, "The '80s," 149.

164 *"defensive core . . . surroundings"*: Christopher Lasch, *The Minimal Self: Psychic Survival in Troubled Times* (1984), 1, 18–19.

164 *minimal self had no gender:* Lasch, *The Minimal Self,* 20.

165 *"we the people . . . worried . . ."*: Allen, "The '80s," 144.

165 *passion had a "makeover":* Examples cited: advertisement for Emjoi hair removal system, *Cosmopolitan,* September 1989, 106; Nancy Anderson, *Work with Passion* (1986); Joseph Epstein, *Ambition, the Secret Passion* (1980).

166 *The "Buff" and the Beautiful:* Except where indicated otherwise, commentary in this section is based on a random sampling of *Cosmopolitan, Glamour, Time,* and *TV Guide,* 1983–89; and on Susan J. Douglas, *Where the Girls Are: Growing Up Female with the Mass Media* (1994), 245–68.

166 *"obsessions . . . thinness":* Allen, "The '80s," 151.

166 *"Shape up for super sex":* Mary Ann Crenshaw, *Shape Up for Super Sex* (1983), was among several such titles that appeared in the 1980s.

167 *"I'm worth it":* Quoted in Douglas, *Where the Girls Are,* 245.

168 *"media's relentlessly . . . most effective":* Douglas, *Where the Girls Are,* 268.

169 *turning forty a crisis:* Paul Leinberger and Bruce Tucker, *The New Individualists: The Generation After The Organization Man* (1991), 7; Michael P. Nichols, *Turning Forty in the Eighties: Personal Crisis, Time for Change* (1986); example of a mock funeral observed by author, c. 1985.

169 *genital herpes: Time,* 2 August 1982, 34–8; except where indicated otherwise, the remainder of the discussion of STDs and AIDS is based on Allen, "The '80s," 146; Richard Davenport Hines and Christopher Phipps, "Tainted Love," in *Sexual Knowledge, Sexual Science: The History of Attitudes to Sexuality,* ed. Roy Porter and Mikulas Teich (1994), 367–83; John Heidenry, *What Wild Ecstasy: The Rise and Fall of the Sexual Revolution* (1997), 274–76, 335–52; Jeffrey Weeks, *Sexuality and Its Discontents: Meanings, Myths and Modern Sexualities* (1985), 44–53; Weeks, "Values in an Age of Uncertainty," in Donna C. Stanton, ed., *Discourses of Sexuality: From Aristotle to AIDS* (1992), 389–411.

171 *"aura of terror":* Naomi Wolf, *The Beauty Myth* (1990), 168.

171 *"We can save each other . . ."*: Naomi Wolf, *Fire with Fire: The New*

Female Power and How It Will Change the 21st Century (1993), 131–32.

172 *rubber dental dams . . . case of genital warts:* Wendy Dennis, *Hot and Bothered: Men and Women, Sex and Love in the 90s* (1992), 31, which despite its subtitle contains considerable material from the 1980s.

172 *sex, lies, and videotape:* Described in Norman K. Denzin, *Images of Postmodern Society: Social Theory and Contemporary Cinema* (1991), 109–10.

172 *Blue Velvet:* Denzin, *Images of Postmodern Society*, 65–77.

173 *"wide gap . . . nothing to be afraid of":* Lillian B. Rubin, *Erotic Wars: What Happened to the Sexual Revolution?* (1990), 14.

173 *flood of how-to books:* Irene Kassorla, *Nice Girls Do—and Now You Can Too!* (1980); Michael Morgenstern, *How to Make Love to a Woman* (1981); Alexandra Penney, *How to Make Love to a Man* (1981; 1986); John Perry and others, *The G-Spot and Other Recent Discoveries about Human Sexuality* (1983).

174 *Hite and Sandra Kahn surveyed:* Shere Hite, *The Hite Report: A Nationwide Study of Female Sexuality*, and *The Hite Report on Male Sexuality* (both 1981); Sandra Kahn, *The Kahn Report on Sexual Preferences* (1981).

174 *Sexually Speaking:* Heidenry, *What Wild Ecstasy*, 300–301.

174 *sexual talk on television: Psychology Today*, September/October 1992, 12.

174 *"Oh God . . . Oh, oh—oh!":* Quoted in Denzin, *Images of Postmodern Society*, 107.

175 *people expected more from sex:* John D'Emilio and Estelle Freedman, *Intimate Matters: A History of Sexuality in America* (1988), 336–38; Lynne Segal, *Straight Sex: The Politics of Pleasure* (1994), 67.

175 *"benchmark for the decade": Playboy*, quoted in Heidenry, *What Wild Ecstasy*, 270.

175 *sex addiction:* Heidenry, *What Wild Ecstasy*, 320–21.

175 *Mary Calderone . . . "There is no such thing as too much sex":* Quoted in Heidenry, *What Wild Ecstasy*, 321.

176 *"We may well be angry . . . of marginal scholarly interest": Signs: Journal of Women in Culture and Society* 8 (Autumn 1982): 2.

176 *"What's this I hear about you leaving . . .": Cosmopolitan*, September 1989, 198.

176　*some wanted "equal rights . . ."*: Marianne Takacs, "Man Power," *Quest*, June/July/August, 1983, 71.

176　*"a much needed counterpoint . . ."*: Takacs, "Man Power," 75.

177　*"Brutality chic" . . . advertisement for Bocci shoes*: Valerie Cassel-ton, "Disturbing New Images," *Vancouver Sun*, 4 March 1985, c6.

177　*television exploited rape*: random sampling, *TV Guide*, 1983–89; see also Wolf, *The Beauty Myth*, 136–37.

177　*illustration accompanying Quest report*: *Quest*, June/July/August, 1983, 70–71; illustration by Julius Ciss.

177　*"Private Violence": Time*, 5 September 1983, 14–25.

177　*Andrea Dworkin*: Heidenry, *What Wild Ecstasy*, 112–13; Segal, *Straight Sex*, 112–13.

177　*blamed the victim*: See, for example, Sidney Katz, "Looking for Trouble," *Quest*, June/July/August 1980, 50.

178　*rape*: For an overview of debates about rape and related issues, see Adele M. Stan, ed., *Debating Sexual Correctness: Pornography, Sexual Harassment, Date Rape, and the Politics of Sexual Equality* (1995).

178　*"I feel more oppressed . . . women want?"*: Contemporary commentary noted by author.

178　*love and aggression in personal relationships*: For further discussion, see Michael Vincent Miller, *Intimate Terrorism: The Deterioration of Erotic Life* (1995).

178　*rate of divorce*: Samuel S. Janus and Cynthia L. Janus, *The Janus Report on Sexual Behavior* (1993), 191.

178　*"We, the people . . ."*: Allen, "The '80s," 150.

179　*Sex had become . . . demystified"*: George Leonard, *The End of Sex: Erotic Love after the Sexual Revolution* (1983), 12; Weeks, *Sexuality and Its Discontents*, 246; Edwin M. Schur, *The Americanization of Sex* (1988), xiii.

179　*did not necessarily promote satisfaction*: Schur, *The Americanization of Sex*, xiii, 4, 10.

179–80　*"recreational sex . . . thriving by it"*: Schur, *The Americanization of Sex*, 28–29.

180　*"single career women . . . house"*: Allen, "The '80s," 153.

181　*"ethic of commitment . . . stability"*: Schur, *The Americanization of Sex*, 47–48.

181　*people ill-equipped for commitment*: Schur, *The Americanization of Sex*, 47–48; see also Christopher Lasch, *The Minimal Self*, 18–19.

181 *opposing social and cultural forces:* Schur, *The Americanization of Sex,* 48, 69–85.

Chapter 9: The Barely Splendored Media

186 *advertising in magazines:* Commentary based on a sampling of *Cosmopolitan, Details, Flare, Glamour,* and *Vanity Fair,* August 1992 to May 1994.

186 *"Advertising . . . clothing":* John Leland and others, "The New Voyeurism," *Newsweek,* 2 November 1992, 101.

187 *"Mix up some sex . . .":* Dan Zevin, "The Pleasure Principle," *Us,* August 1992, 32.

187 *just one viewing day:* A representative composite, based on listings in *TV Guide,* 2–8 October 1993; Janice Kaplan, "Sex Wars: Sex on TV," *TV Guide,* 2–8 October 1993, 16–21; Leslie Van Buskirk, "Tuning In, Turning On: Soap Opera Sex," *Us,* August 1992, 64, 66.

187 *daytime television talk shows:* Unless otherwise indicated, commentary is based on a sampling, March 1991–January 1995.

188 *topics on a single day:* From *Shirley, Phil Donahue,* and *Maury Povich,* 13 January 1992. This and subsequent dates given with television shows indicate the telecast that I viewed.

188 *do-it-yourself sex videos:* "Sexy Home Videos," *Maury Povich,* 23 November 1993.

189 *hoping for information . . . sympathy:* Noted from sampling; and see also Vicki Abt and Mel Seesholtz, "The Shameless World of Phil, Sally and Oprah: Television Talk Shows and the Deconstructing of Society," *Journal of Popular Culture* 28.1 (1994): 182; Wendy Hundley (Dayton, Ohio), "The Morning After a Date with Geraldo," *Vancouver Sun,* 24 December 1994, E24.

190 *"I ask this question not to pry . . .":* Oprah Winfrey, quoted in Abt and Seesholtz, "The Shameless World of Phil, Sally and Oprah," 185.

190 *talk-show therapy:* Abt and Seesholtz, "The Shameless World of Phil, Sally and Oprah," 171–91; Wendy Kaminer, *I'm Dysfunctional, You're Dysfunctional: The Recovery Movement and Other Self-Help Fashions* (1993), 29–43.

190 *"ten stupid things" . . . "sizzlin' secrets":* Laura Schlessinger, *Ten Stupid Things That Women Do to Mess Up Their Lives* (1994),

Phil Donahue, 24 February 1994; Roger W. Libby, *Sex from Aah to Zipper: A Delightful Glossary of Love, Lust and Laughter* (1993), on *Shirley*, 20 January 1995; Cricket Richmond and Ginny Valletti, *Secrets of Sizzlin' Sex for Naughty but Nice Women Everywhere* (1994), *Gordon Eliot*, 2 Dec 1994.

191   *"STUD":* Observed by author while sitting in a traffic jam.

191   *American, Canadian, and British newspapers and magazines:* Among countless possible examples, *Details*, May 1996, 46–93; *Elle*, November 1996, 135–42; *London Sunday Mirror Magazine*, 17 October 1993, 28; *Self*, March 1996, 119–23, 179; *Vancouver Magazine*, November 1993, 36, 42; *Vancouver Sun*, 22 May 1993, C4.

191   *"erotic journeys" and "philosophies of sex":* Richard Rhodes, *Making Love: An Erotic Journey* (1992); Sallie Tisdale, *Talk Dirty to Me: An Intimate Philosophy of Sex* (1994).

191   *Hollywood stars tell all:* Pamela Anderson Lee to David A. Keeps, "Pam I Am," *Details*, May 1996, 112–19; Demi Moore to Leslie Bennetts, "Demi's State of Grace," *Vanity Fair*, December 1993, 178, 208; Julia Roberts to Kevin Sessums, "The Crown Julia," *Vanity Fair*, October 1993, 287, 292.

191   *Camille Paglia was forthcoming:* Camille Paglia to Chrissey Iley, "The Mouth That Roars," *London Sunday Times Magazine*, reprinted *Toronto Globe and Mail*, 22 January 1994, D5.

192   *experts also opened up:* John Gray, *Mars and Venus in the Bedroom: A Guide to Lasting Romance and Passion* (1995), 39; see also Sari Locker, *Mindblowing Sex in the Real World: Hot Tips for Doing It in the Age of Anxiety* (1995), 2–3.

192   *voluminous studies . . . more informal compilations . . . magazine-sponsored sex surveys:* For example, Samuel S. Janus and Cynthia L. Janus, *The Janus Report on Sexual Behavior: The First Broad-Scale Scientific National Survey since Kinsey* (1993); Robert T. Michael, John H. Gagnon, Edward O. Laumann, and Gina Kolata, *Sex in America: A Definitive Survey* (1994); Wendy Dennis, *Hot and Bothered: Men and Women, Sex and Love in the 90s* (1992); Jonathon Green, *It: Sex Since the Sixties* (1993); Anka Radakovich, "Love Rules," *Details*, May 1994, 112.

192   *Nancy Friday's latest collection . . . two earlier books:* Nancy Friday, *Women on Top: How Real Life Has Changed Women's Sexual Fantasies* (1991; 1993); *My Secret Garden: Women's Sexual Fantasies* (1973); *Forbidden Flowers: More Women's Sexual Fantasies* (1975).

192 *"women today . . . lexicon of human emotion":* Friday, *Women on Top*, 6.

192 *"never sleeps" . . . "repression":* Friday, *Women on Top*, 17.

192–93 *once people testified . . . "sham community":* Kaminer, *I'm Dysfunctional, You're Dysfunctional*, 30, 33; see also Richard Sennett, *The Fall of Public Man* (1976), 4.

193 *"Never have so many . . . cared so little":* Kaminer, *I'm Dysfunctional, You're Dysfunctional*, 33.

193 *"Monotonous . . . boring":* Victoria Branden, "Get That Grin off Your Face," *Books in Canada*, February 1994, 26.

193 *"over-exposed corpus":* TLA *Film & Video Guide, 1996-1997*, ed. David Bleiler (1996), 61.

194 *Sex "celebrated sadomasochism . . .":* Leland, "The New Voyeurism," 95.

194 *Mae West used the title Sex:* Discussed above, chap. 3.

194 *"I see myself . . . something happened":* Madonna, quoted in Leland, "The New Voyeurism," 95–96.

194 *people did yawn:* David Champagne, "Stabat Madonna," and Thomas Allen Harris, "Phallic Momma, Sell My Pussy, Make a Dollar," in *Madonnarama: Essays on Sex and Popular Culture* (1993), ed. Lisa Frank and Paul Smith, quoted in Lynn Crosbie, Review of *Madonnarama*, Toronto *Globe and Mail*, 31 July 1993, c6; see also Frank and Smith, Introduction to *Madonnarama*, 10–14; Linda Grant, *Sexing the Millennium: A Political History of the Sexual Revolution* (1993), 260–64; Camille Paglia, "Madonna in the Shallows: Madonna's *Sex*," and "Madonna as Gauguin," *Vamps and Tramps: New Essays* (1994), 367–69, 370.

194 *Oprah responded to criticism:* For example, Abt and Seesholtz, "The Shameless World of Phil, Sally and Oprah," 171–91.

194 *she began focusing . . . other hosts continued to favor sensationalism:* Based on extensive sampling of *Oprah Winfrey, Jenny Jones, Maury Povich*, and *Sally Jessy Raphael*, 1996–99.

195 *Ultimate Exposure:* Unless otherwise indicated, this section is based on CNN coverage, 17–18 August 1998, 11–12 and 21–22 September 1998, *Newsweek*, 2 February 1998, 31–45; *People*, 9 February 1998, 41.

196 *"Civilization is a delicate structure . . .":* Thomas Nagel, "The Shredding of Public Privacy," *Times Literary Supplement*, 14 August 1998, 15.

197 *"Life has become art . . .":* Quoted in Peter Biskind, review of

Life the Movie: How Entertainment Conquered Reality, by Neal Gabler, *New York Times Book Review*, 3 January 1999, 7.

Chapter 10: Doing It right—and Getting It Wrong

Page

199 *"passionate marriage . . . passion":* John Gray, *Mars and Venus in the Bedroom: A Guide to Lasting Romance and Passion* (1995); advertisement for Loving Better Videos, *New York Times Book Review*, 10 September 1995, 53; David Schnarch, *Passionate Marriage: Love, Sex, and Intimacy in Emotionally Committed Relationships* (1997; 1998).

201 *no sex with a fatty for Madonna:* Linda Grant, *Sexing the Millennium: A Political History of the Sexual Revolution* (1993), 268.

202–3 *cosmetic surgery . . . breast implants:* Helen S. Edelman, "Why Is Dolly Crying: An Analysis of Silicone Breast Implants in America as an Example of Medicalization, *Journal of Popular Culture* 28.3 (1994): 19–32; *Ms.*, special issue on breast implants, March/April 1996, 44–63; Naomi Wolf, *The Beauty Myth* (1990; 1991), 10, 232–54.

203 *40,000 submitted to breast implantation:* Angela Bonovoglia, "Implants on the Rise," *Ms.*, March/April 1996, 58.

204 *excessive exercise:* Mia Stainsby, "No Control," *Vancouver Weekend Sun*, 8 July 1995, A15–16.

204–5 *men "accounted for a big . . . "beefcake":* Maureen Dowd, "You're So Vain," *New York Times*, reprinted, *Vancouver Sun*, 5 January 1996, A16.

205 *"international hunks . . .":* *Leeza*, 26 October 1995.

206 *"homely, lolling . . .":* Don Gillmor, "Bed-time Reading for the Sexually Inclined," Review of recent books on sex, Toronto *Globe and Mail*, 23 April 1994, C9.

206 *average man made the most of what he had:* See, for example, Wendy Dennis, *Hot and Bothered: Men and Women, Sex and Love in the 90s* (1992), 177.

206 *"the fantasyland model . . .":* Bernie Zilbergeld, *Male Sexuality* (1978), quoted in Dennis, *Hot and Bothered*, 175.

206 *"Men Who Pump Up Their Sex Lives":* Maury Povich, 19 November 1993.

207 *simple numbers game:* Otto Krueger and Janet M. Thuesen, *16*

Ways to Love Your Lover (1994); Graham Masterton, *How to Make Love Six Nights a Week* (1991); "The 101 Best Places for a Quickie," "Fifty Fabulous Ideas for Driving Her Wild": Staci Keith, *Drive Your Woman Wild in Bed: A Lover's Guide to Sex and Romance* (1994), chaps. 23, 31.

207 *"steps," "tips," and lists:* Barbara Keesling, *Talk Sexy to the One You Love (and Drive Each Other Wild in Bed)* (1996); Keith, *Drive Your Woman Wild in Bed*; Sari Locker, *Mindblowing Sex in the Real World: Hot Tips for Doing It in the Age of Anxiety* (1995).

208 *"certain simple ideas . . . endless bliss":* Quoted in Bert Archer, "Help's in Your Headphones," review of self-help tapes, including *Real Moments for Lovers*, by Barbara De Angelis, *Quill & Quire*, April 1995, 32–33.

208 *"Discover the Secrets . . . dreamed possible!":* Advertisement for Love, Sex, Orgasm Videos, *New York Times Book Review*, 11 June 1995, 55; 13 August 1995, 29.

208 *advertisements for similar videos: Cosmopolitan*, December 1993, 231; *New York Times Book Review*, 15 May 1994, 23; 25 June 1995, 33; 16 July 1995, 25; 10 September 1995, 53; 2 June 1996, 32; 5 October 1997, 37; 4 January 1998, 25; *Psychology Today*, September/October 1992, 59; see also *New Woman*, January 1995, 118.

208 *assortment of additional sex aids:* See, for example, advertisements, *Cosmopolitan*, December 1993, 239; March 1996, 277, 281–83.

208 *"feverishly . . . device squad":* "Device Squad: Inventing Better Sex," *Details*, May 1994, 26–27.

209 *"Amazing Talking Condom":* Saturday Review, *Vancouver Weekend Sun*, 23 March 1996, D18.

209 *"Mindblowing sex . . .":* Locker, *Mindblowing Sex in the Real World*.

209 *acclaimed sex survey:* Edward O. Laumann, John H. Gagnon, Robert T. Michael, and Stuart Michaels, *The Social Organization of Sexuality: Sexual Practices in the United States* (1994); on its wide applicability, see the review by Paul Robinson, *New York Times Book Review*, 30 October 1994, 3, 22.

209 *abridged version:* Robert T. Michael, John H. Gagnon, Edward O. Laumann, and Gina Kolata, *Sex in America: A Definitive Survey* (1994).

209–10 *"although America . . . confound our expectations":* Michael, *Sex in America*, 114–15, and Table 8, 116–17, 246.

210   *not just a national trend:* Global figures, cited by *CTV Canada AM*, 22 September 1998; *Maclean's Magazine* survey, reported on *BCTV Evening News*, 18 December 1995; Angus Reid Poll, *CTV*, 4 March 1998.

210   *sexual dysfunction:* Jan Goodwin, "America Undercovers," *Ladies' Home Journal*, April 1996, 104; *Oprah Winfrey*, 15 January 1998; *American Journal of Medicine*, widely cited, including *Leeza*, 12 February 1999.

211   *modest rates characterized the 1990s:* For a conflicting finding, see Samuel S. Janus and Cynthia L. Janus, *The Janus Report on Sexual Behavior* (1993), 18; American sexual activity; possibly flawed, this report conflicts with other studies; for additional commentary, see Michael, *Sex in America*, 22, 24.

211   *source of anxiety:* See, for example, Sara Nelson, "Sex: How Much Is Enough?" *Glamour*, December 1993, 140; Marcelle Clements, "Is Sex Dead," *New Woman*, January 1995, 136; Anka Radakovich, "Love Rules," *Details*, May 1994, 111.

211   *celibacy:* Phil Johnson, "Army of Celibates Marches Single File into the Future," Toronto *Globe and Mail*, 6 April 1994, A22.

211   *concerns about performance:* Michael, *Sex in America*, 125–26.

211   *"There is . . . appropriate for them":* Michael, *Sex in America*, 121.

212   *Watching television . . . made people passive:* Robert William Kubey and Mihaly Csikszentmihalyi, *Television and the Quality of Life: How Viewing Shapes Everyday Experience* (1990), 172.

212   *Desensitization:* Vicki Abt and Mel Seesholtz, "The Shameless World of Phil, Sally and Oprah: Television Talk Shows and the Deconstructing of Society," *Journal of Popular Culture* 28.1 (1994): 172–73; Sylvere Lotringer, *Overexposed: Treating Sexual Perversion in America* (1990), 176–77; *NBC Nightly News Spot, KING 5*, 25 January 1995; Rick Roberts, on the prevalence of desensitization from media exposure to sex, *Leeza*, 12 February 1999; Dan Zevin, "The Pleasure Principle," *Us*, August 1992, 34.

212   *collectively high sexual expectations:* Radakovich, "Love Rules," 113.

212   *more got pleasure from television:* Kubey and Csikszentmihalyi, *Television and the Quality of Life*, xiii; the survey cited is not identified.

212   *women preferred a good night's sleep:* Harlequin Poll, reported, *BCTV Noon News*, 30 January 1996.

212   *both sexes would rather have chocolate:* Decima Research Survey, reported, *Vancouver Sun*, 26 September 1995, B1, B10.

213   *language of political correctness:* Commentary based on Canadian federal and provincial government guidelines, as reported, *Vancouver Sun*, 7 March 1995, B2.

213   *These politicized controversies:* For an introduction and overview, see Adele M. Stan, ed., *Debating Sexual Correctness: Pornography, Sexual Harassment, Date Rape, and the Politics of Sexual Equality* (1995).

213   *"intimate . . . crisis":* Michael Vincent Miller, *Intimate Terrorism: The Deterioration of Erotic Life* (1995), 15.

213–14   *"almost impossible . . . become political":* Miller, *Intimate Terrorism*, 12.

214   *"I think I faked . . .":* Cosmopolitan, December 1993, 236.

214   *sexual addiction:* Anthony Giddens, *The Transformations of Intimacy: Sexuality, Love and Eroticism in Modern Societies* (1992), 65–86.

214   *"Kink comes out . . .":* Goodwin, "America Undercovers," 98.

215   S/M *how-to manual:* R. M. Vaughan, review of *On the Safe Edge: A Manual for SM Play*, by Trevor Jacques and others, *Books in Canada*, February 1995, 43.

215   *"swinging" Montreal establishment:* Reported CTV *Canada AM*, 25 January 1999.

215   *other swingers . . . "something more":* Terry Gould, *The Lifestyle: A Look at the Erotic Rites of Swingers* (1999), 11, 100, 225.

215   *"without having to face . . .":* Donna Lypchuk, *Erotic Connections: Love and Lust on the Information Highway*, by Billy Wildhack, *Quill & Quire*, November 1995, 35.

215   *"better sex through chemistry":* John Morgenthaler and Dan Joy, *Better Sex through Chemistry* (n.d.), cited in Jordan Freid, "It's Better When You Swallow," *Details*, May 1996, 74.

215   *Viagra:* BCTV *Evening News*, 22 April, 1998; John Carlin, "The New Promise of Sexual Vigor," *Vancouver Sun*, 2 May 1998, C3; on Viagra and women, Randi Hutter Epstein, "The New Sexual Revolution," *Ladies' Home Journal*, September 1998, 188–91, 252–53.

216   *"What's the best . . . had it yet":* Radakovich, "Love Rules," 113.

216   *talk shows:* For example, *Oprah Winfrey*, 26 March 1996.

217   *"seeking" . . . "lasting":* From a random sampling of the personals column, "RSVP," *Vancouver Sun*, 1996–99.

217   *"We're talking marriage . . . whole package":* Ellen Fein and Sherrie Schneider, *The Rules: Time-Tested Secrets for capturing the heart of Mr. Right* (1996; 1996), 2–3.

217 *"a hard core of common sense":* Margaret Wente, "The Rules for Catching a Man," Toronto *Globe and Mail,* 16 November 1996, D9.

217 *"dance" . . . "great passion":* Robert James Waller, *The Bridges of Madison County* (1992), xii, 144, 153, 168.

218 *infidelity and divorce:* BCTV *Evening News,* 24 November 1998; CTV *Canada* AM, 22 September 1998 and 11 January 1999; George Feifer, *Divorce: An Oral Portrait* (1995); Aysan Sev'er, *Women and Divorce in Canada* (1992); Barbara Dafoe Whitehead, *The Divorce Culture* (1997); *Montel Williams,* 2 December 1998; *Oprah Winfrey,* 9 April 1998. Estimations of the U.S. divorce rate in the 1990s vary, and some sources suggest a slight decline to around 49 percent: see *Time Magazine,* 25 September 2000, 44.

219 *arguing for traditional family patterns:* See, among others, Danielle Crittenden, *What Our Mothers Didn't Tell Us: Why Happiness Eludes the Modern Woman* (1998).

Chapter 11: Embracing the Future

Page

224 *Freedom . . . anything but freeing:* Among others, the point has been variously made by Paul Leinberger and Bruce Tucker, *The New Individualists: The Generation after The Organization Man* (1991), 15; Rollo May, *Love and Will* (1969), 42; Roger Rosenblatt, ed., *Consuming Desires: Consumption, Culture, and the Pursuit of Happiness* (1999), 7.

225 *familiar statistics . . . no appeal:* For statistics, refer to notes to Chapter 1; "sizzling with sex," *Vancouver Sun,* 12 February 2000, E9, E11, E22; on virtual adultery, "Love on the Internet," *Love Chronicles,* aired 13 February 2000; online addiction reported New England Cable News <http://www.necn.com> 18 May 2000.

225 *poll by* IKEA: *Vancouver Sun,* 12 February 2000, I1.

226 *chord in popular consciousness:* The theme of dreams or dreaming is one of the most common in the many lavish and romantic websites dedicated to the movie *Titanic.* See, for example, "The Unsinkable Ship of Dreams," which comes complete with audio of—what else?—"Nearer, My God, to Thee" <http:// geocities .com/Hollywood/Studio/8958/unsinkable.html>.

227 *ignorance, sex experts insist, a problem:* Sue Johanson, *Sex Is Perfectly Natural, But Not Naturally Perfect* (1991; 1992), ix–xii; William H. Masters, interviewed CTV *Canada AM*, 23 August 1993; Robert T. Michael, John H. Gagnon, Edward O. Laumann, and Gina Kolata, *Sex in America: A Definitive Survey* (1994), 4–6; Ruth Westheimer, *Sex for Dummies* (1995), 3.

228 *preschoolers . . . majority of adults:* Study of five-year-olds, State College, Pennsylvania, reported CTV *Canada AM*, 10 January 2001; similar findings from another study were reported on CTV *Evening News*, 6 February 2001; elsewhere, in a survey of 9,000 women, 92 percent responded that their sex lives were "not what they should be": Oprah.com survey, reported on *Oprah Winfrey*, 7 February 2001; in another survey 42 percent of women and 31 percent of men were not sexually functional: reported *Oprah Winfrey*, 14 February 2001.

230–231 *"It is our imaginative participation . . .":* May, *Love and Will*, 224.

INDEX